ON BEING AMERICAN:

THE JURISPRUDENCE OF RUTH BADER GINSBURG

SUZANNE REYNOLDS AND SHANNON GILREATH, Editors

Cover design by Sara Wadford/ABA Design

Printed in the United States of America.

28 27 26 25 24 5 4 3 2 1

Library of Congress Cataloging-in-Publication Data

Names: Ginsburg, Ruth Bader, 1933-2020. | Reynolds, Suzanne, editor, compiler. | Gilreath, Shannon, 1977- editor, compiler.

Title: On being American : the jurisprudence of Ruth Bader Ginsburg / [edited/compiled by] Suzanne Reynolds and Shannon D. Gilreath.

Description: 1st edition. | Chicago : American Bar Association, 2024. | Includes index. | Summary: "In her work as an appellate judge, Justice Ginsburg translated this devotion into a jurisprudence focused on "We the People," substantively and procedurally. Substantively, Justice Ginsburg insisted that faithfully employed, the words of the Constitution supported an expansive understanding of who was included in "We the People," despite the framers' narrow understanding of the phrase when it appeared in the preamble to the Constitution. Expressed also as a jurisprudence of equality and opportunity, Justice Ginsburg believed that the phrase promised equal dignity for people despite their gender, gender identity, race, or disability. Procedurally, "We the People" shaped Justice Ginsburg's approach to the process of deciding cases, guiding every step of her judicial process-the way she read the Constitution and statutes, approached voting issues, and analyzed the demands of the separation of powers, for example. While the substantive contours of "We the People" have received the most attention, the full sweep of her jurisprudence appears also in the process she used in analyzing all issues. Justice Ginsburg's jurisprudence of "We the People" became the ordering principle of this book, explaining both the book's title and its topics. Instead of a general survey of Justice Ginsburg's work, the book tells the story of an advocate and a jurist committed to increasing in material ways the bundle of rights we all carry around with us as Americans. As Linda Greenhouse explained in the Foreword, the story begins with Justice Ginsburg's commitment to an America that enables people with diverse experiences to live together in civic harmony. Justice Ginsburg believed that because the American experience involved living in community, the religious expression of some of us had to yield when the expression oppressed others of us in ways endangering that harmony"-- Provided by publisher.

Identifiers: LCCN 2024028374 | ISBN 9781639055401 (paperback) | ISBN 9781639055418 (epub)

Subjects: LCSH: Judicial opinions--United States. | Ginsburg, Ruth Bader, 1933-2020. Judicial opinions. Selections. | Judicial process--United States. | Constitutional law--United States. | Election law--United States. | Reproductive rights--United States.

Classification: LCC KF213.G56 R49 2024 | DDC 347.73/2634--dc23/eng/20240627

LC record available at https://lccn.loc.gov/2024028374

We dedicate this book to our students—past, present, future—who will, like Ruth Ginsburg, change the world. With this volume, we remember her, but we anticipate you.

Contents

Foreword

Ruth Bader Ginsburg's American Vision

—Linda Greenhouse

At the White House Rose Garden ceremony on June 14, 1993, at which President Bill Clinton announced Ruth Bader Ginsburg's nomination to the U.S. Supreme Court, Ginsburg invoked the memory of her mother. "I pray that I may be all that she would have been," the future Justice Ginsburg said, "had she lived in an age when women could aspire and achieve and daughters are cherished as much as sons."

Ruth Bader Ginsburg's mother Celia Bader died in 1950 at the age of 48. There was nostalgia in her daughter's words, and love, but it was also possible to hear something more. Not by accident was Ruth Ginsburg's world no longer Celia Bader's. That the realities that limited her mother's opportunities and constricted her horizons had faded in the intervening decades was due in large measure to the courage and persistence of women who used the tools available to them to break down barriers and open doors. One of those tools was law. One of those women was Celia Bader's daughter.

Ruth Ginsburg had the imagination to envision a world different from the one she grew up in. Such an imagination—the ability to see beyond known borders—is a gift shared by all pioneers, an essential element driving profound change. Ginsburg's vision of sex equality encompassed a world in which men could be caregivers and women breadwinners. That vision fueled her project to use law to erase the barriers to any individual's choice of—to use a favorite Ginsburg word—a life course. This was the anti-stereotyping principle that is explored in this volume, the principle that the U.S. Supreme Court accepted gingerly at first in *Reed v. Reed*[1] in 1971 before fully embracing it a quarter of a century later in the Virginia Military Institute (VMI) case, Justice Ginsburg's most important majority opinion.[2]

The chapters that follow explore Ruth Bader Ginsburg's equality project in all its dimensions and implications including, as Suzanne Reynolds explains in the Introduction, how her jurisprudence related to her expansive vision of what it means to be an American. In defining Justice Ginsburg's legacy, the essays in this volume speak for themselves. So in this Foreword, I have chosen to focus on a different aspect of her legacy, one defined not by jurisprudential triumph but largely by defeat. The subject is religion.

If we don't often think of Justice Ginsburg in connection with the Court's religion jurisprudence, that is because her view of the essential balance between the First Amendment's two religion clauses was out of alignment with that of the Court's majority.[3] To her obvious dismay, an increasingly aggressive majority insisted on reading the Free Exercise Clause of the First Amendment so broadly as to eclipse competing interests and effect a near erasure of the amendment's Establishment Clause. "Religion *über alles*" was how, in private conversation, she sometimes described what she saw unfolding.

For two decades before her death in September 2020, Justice Ginsburg published or joined powerful dissenting opinions in nearly all the religion cases that advanced the majority's project. A decision in 2000, *Mitchell v. Helms*,[4] offered a hint of what was to come. The decision significantly expanded the types of equipment and other resources that the government could make available to private schools, including to religious schools. At the heart of Justice Souter's 49-page dissenting opinion, which Justice Ginsburg joined, was this reflection on the essentiality of the boundary that the Court was now inviting the government to cross:

---

[1] 404 U.S. 71 (1971).

[2] United States v. Virginia, 518 U.S. 515 (1996).

[3] In 2015, a collection of essays by well-known legal scholars, THE LEGACY OF RUTH BADER GINSBURG (Scott Dodson ed.), made no mention of religion.

[4] 530 U.S. 793 (2000).

> The establishment prohibition of government religious funding serves more than one end. It is meant to guarantee the right of individual conscience against compulsion, to protect the integrity of religion against the corrosion of secular support, and to preserve the unity of political society against the implied exclusion of the less favored and the antagonism of controversy over public support for religious causes.[5]

Because Justice Ginsburg's own dissenting opinions in later years often objected to religious accommodations that had the predictable effect of excluding women from access to benefits to which they were entitled, it was easy to assume that her strongly secularist position had its origin in her concern for women's welfare. But it is actually Justice Souter's dissent in *Mitchell* that more fully captures the basis for her concern about the Court's single-minded deference to religious claims: the threat such deference poses to "the unity of political society." Or to put it more precisely: the threat it posed to her vision of America.

Justice Ginsburg made her position clear in one of the few majority opinions she wrote on a religious subject. The question in *Cutter v. Wilkinson*[6] was whether a federal statute enacted in 2000, the Religious Land Use and Institutionalized Persons Act (RLUIPA), violated the Establishment Clause in requiring prison officials generally to accommodate the religious needs of prison inmates. Writing for a unanimous Court, Justice Ginsburg said the statute on its face was a permissible accommodation under the Establishment Clause. But she clearly saw around the next corner, the next case, warning that in "[p]roperly applying RLUIPA, courts must take adequate account of the burdens a requested accommodation may impose on nonbeneficiaries" and that "they must be satisfied that the Act's prescriptions are and will be administered neutrally among different faiths." An accommodation "must be measured so that it does not override other significant interests."[7]

In the *Hobby Lobby* case in 2014,[8] the majority failed to heed this warning in interpreting a related statute, the Religious Freedom Restoration

---

[5] *Id.* at 868 (Souter, J., dissenting).

[6] 544 U.S. 709 (2005).

[7] *Id.* at 720, 722.

[8] Burwell v. Hobby Lobby Stores, 573 U.S. 682 (2014).

Act (RFRA), to excuse the religiously observant owners of for-profit corporations from following federal law. The Affordable Care Act (ACA) required employers to include no-cost contraceptive coverage in their employee benefits plans. The owners of Hobby Lobby Stores, a national chain of craft stores with more than 1,000 employees, and the smaller Conestoga Wood Specialties objected that given their religiously based opposition to contraception and abortion, providing the coverage to their employees would make them complicit in sin. In her dissenting opinion, signed by the three other justices, Justice Ginsburg objected that "In the Court's view, RFRA demands accommodation of a for-profit corporation's religious beliefs no matter the impact that accommodation may have on third parties who do not share the corporation owners' religious faith—in these cases, thousands of women employed by Hobby Lobby and Conestoga or dependents of persons those corporations employ." Citing her own opinion in *Cutter v. Wilkinson* nine years earlier, she emphasized: "No tradition, and no prior decision under RFRA, allows a religion-based exemption when the accommodation would be harmful to others—here, the very persons the contraceptive coverage requirement was designed to protect."[9] Ruth Ginsburg's vision of America did not include corporate owners trampling the statutory rights of their employees for the sake of their own religious beliefs about how their employees should conduct their personal lives.

While the vote in *Hobby Lobby* was 5–4, the vote in most of the other important religion cases decided during her last years on the bench was more lopsided: 7–2, with only Justices Ginsburg and Sotomayor dissenting.[10] This was surprising enough to lead two scholars of the religion clauses, Micah Schwartzman and Nelson Tebbe, to suggest that the liberal bloc's two other members, Justices Breyer and Kagan, were engaging in strategic "appeasement," offering unreciprocated concessions in the vain hope of tempering inevitable outcomes.[11]

Whether the appeasement charge is well founded, it would never in any event have been Justice Ginsburg's approach to the subject of religion or

[9] *Id.* at 764 (Ginsburg, J., dissenting).

[10] Town of Greece v. Galloway, 572 U.S. 565 (2014) (upholding the practice of sectarian prayer at local government meetings, was also decided by a 5–4 vote, with Justice Ginsburg joining Justice Kagan's dissenting opinion).

[11] Micah Schwartzman & Nelson Tebbe, *Establishment Clause Appeasement*, 2019 Sup. Ct. Rev. 271 (2020).

any other. For example, she was the lone dissenter in *Fisher v. University of Texas at Austin* (Fisher I),[12] a decision that was a glaringly obvious compromise on the question of the role of race in university admissions. The university had modified its presumably race-neutral—and therefore presumably valid—"top ten-percent plan" by adding a limited but explicit consideration of race in order to assure a "critical mass" of racial minorities in an entering class. The Fifth Circuit had upheld the modified plan, but the Court, issuing an opinion of a mere 13 pages more than nine months after the oral argument, vacated the appeals court's decision and ordered further consideration of the question of "narrow tailoring."

Only Justice Ginsburg was willing to call out the hypocrisy inherent in the Court's professed concern that the university was deviating from what the majority deemed an appropriately race-neutral admissions system. "[O]nly an ostrich could regard the supposedly neutral alternatives as race unconscious," she wrote, reminding her colleagues that the 10-percent plan achieved a measure of racial diversity only because the high schools in Texas were so obviously segregated. "It is race consciousness, not blindness to race, that drives such plans."[13] There was no reason to insist that the Fifth Circuit take a "second look," she concluded, because the appeals court had already correctly concluded that the plan was consistent with Supreme Court precedent.

Her stance was similar in the *Masterpiece Cakeshop* case, in which the 7–2 majority ruled in favor of a baker who refused to bake a cake for the celebration of a same-sex marriage.[14] The baker, Jack Phillips, claimed that he was obliged as a Christian to avoid complicity in a sinful relationship. The Court ruled that statements appearing to disparage religious claims in general, made at a public hearing by two members of the state commission reviewing the case, meant that Phillips himself was the victim of anti-religious discrimination. The holding was an obvious dodge that enabled the Court to avoid the thorny free speech and free exercise questions that the case clearly presented. As she had in the Texas case, Justice Ginsburg, joined this time by Justice Sotomayor, called the majority out for its maneuver. "Whatever one may think of the statements in historical

[12] 570 U.S. 297 (2013).

[13] *Id.* at 335 (Ginsburg, J., dissenting).

[14] Masterpiece Cakeshop, Ltd. v. Colorado Civil Rights Commission, 138 S. Ct. 1719 (2018).

context, I see no reason why the comments of one or two Commissioners should be taken to overcome Phillips' refusal to sell a wedding cake," she wrote, noting that consideration of the case consumed several layers of review and numerous decision makers. "What prejudice infected the determinations of the adjudicators in the case before and after the Commission? The Court does not say."[15]

In her final years on the bench, Justice Ginsburg gave the majority no quarter in its accelerating religious favoritism. She was the only member of the Court to join Justice Sotomayor's dissent in the *Trinity Lutheran* case, in which the Court ruled that the state's exclusion of a church from eligibility for a playground-resurfacing grant amounted to anti-religious discrimination of a particularly "odious" kind.[16] The dissenting opinion was powerful, and the absence of Justices Breyer and Kagan was both puzzling and noteworthy, as Micah Schwartzman and Nelson Tebbe would later observe in their "appeasement" article.

"Today's decision discounts centuries of history and jeopardizes the government's ability to remain secular," Justice Sotomayor wrote. "History shows that the Religion Clauses separate the public treasury from religious coffers as one measure to secure the kind of freedom of conscience that benefits both religion and government."[17]

Predictably, and in short order, the Court built on *Trinity Lutheran,* migrating the no-discrimination principle established in that decision from a church playground to church school tuition. The Montana Supreme Court had invalidated a state program of tax credits for private school tuition, whether the school was secular or religious. The state court struck down the entire program for violating the "no aid" provision of the Montana Constitution, which barred public funds from supporting religious institutions. The Justices, this time by a vote of 5–4, overturned the decision on the ground that the no-aid provision, as interpreted by the state court, amounted to unconstitutional discrimination on the basis of religious "status."[18]

Justice Ginsburg's dissenting opinion, joined by Justice Kagan, stressed how far the majority had reached in order to arrive at its desired conclusion.

---

[15] *Id.* at 1751–52 (Ginsburg, J., dissenting).

[16] Trinity Lutheran Church of Columbia, Inc. v. Comer, 137 S. Ct. 2012, 2025 (2017).

[17] *Id.* at 2041 (Sotomayor, J., dissenting).

[18] Espinoza v. Montana Department of Revenue, 146 S. Ct. 2246 (2020).

Because the Montana court had invalidated the entire tax-credit program, there was no discrimination: "[S]ecular and sectarian schools alike are ineligible for benefits, so the decision cannot be said to entail differential treatment based on petitioners' religion."[19]

Her language in this instance was mild, and her dissent was in essence procedural: the Court was deciding a question that the case simply did not present. But there was no escaping the question presented by the "Bladensburg Peace Cross," a 40-foot Latin cross originally erected by private citizens as a World War I memorial and prominently placed along a well-traveled highway in a Maryland suburb of Washington, D.C. Now the cross was owned and maintained by a Maryland State agency. Did that arrangement violate the Establishment Clause? The majority said no, on the ground that "longstanding monuments, symbols, and practices" deserved a "presumption of constitutionality" despite their religious content.[20] Only Justice Sotomayor joined Justice Ginsburg in dissent.

"Decades ago, this Court recognized that the Establishment Clause of the First Amendment to the Constitution demands governmental neutrality among religious faiths, and between religion and nonreligion," Justice Ginsburg wrote. "Today the Court erodes that neutrality commitment, diminishing precedent designed to preserve individual liberty and civic harmony." She noted that "[t[he Latin cross is the foremost symbol of the Christian faith" and that "[b]y maintaining the Peace Cross on a public highway, the Commission elevates Christianity over other faiths, and religion over nonreligion."[21]

Civic harmony. A naïve ideal, perhaps, but it was core to Ruth Ginsburg's vision of what the Constitution was designed to achieve, just as the threat to civil society posed by unbridled religious supremacy was at the heart of her concern about the Court's course.

The harm inflicted on third parties by religious accommodation remained an abiding concern. In the Court's 2019 term, six years after the *Hobby Lobby* decision, the status of the ACA's contraception mandate remained, remarkably, unresolved. The latest challenge had initially been brought by an order of nuns, the Little Sisters of the Poor, who operated

[19] *Id.* at 2279 (Ginsburg, J., dissenting).

[20] American Legion v. American Humanist Association, 139 S. Ct. 2067, 2085 (2019).

[21] *Id.* at 2104 (Ginsburg, J., dissenting).

nursing homes for the elderly poor and who imposed no religious requirement on those they served or hired. They argued, as had Hobby Lobby's owners, that facilitating their employees' access to contraception in any way would make the nuns themselves complicit in sin. The Trump administration had responded by issuing a rule granting a broad range of employers exemptions from the mandate on religious or "moral" grounds. A federal appeals court had invalidated the rule. The Court's majority, deploring the fact that the nuns "have had to fight for the ability to continue in their noble work without violating their sincerely held religious beliefs," overturned the appeals court and upheld the rule.[22]

The Court heard argument in the *Little Sisters* case on May 6, 2020, at the height of the COVID-19 pandemic. The Court's building was closed, and the Justices participated by telephone from their homes—all except Justice Ginsburg, who dialed in from her hospital room at Johns Hopkins hospital, where she was being treated for an infection. She took an active part in the argument. Her engagement with the issue, undimmed in the years since *Hobby Lobby*, carried through to her dissenting opinion, joined only by Justice Sotomayor. "Today, for the first time, the Court casts totally aside countervailing rights and interests in its zeal to secure religious rights to the *n*th degree," she wrote.[23]

Justice Ginsburg was a careful writer, formal in her tone and extremely precise in her choice of words; it was never possible to confuse a Ginsburg opinion with one by any other Justice. "To the *n*th degree" is neither precise nor formal. It does not, in fact, sound like a phrase she would have retained in an edited draft. But she was running out of time. The Court issued the *Little Sisters* decision on July 8, 2020. Her dissent was her last published opinion. Ten weeks later, on September 18, 2020, Ruth Bader Ginsburg died.

Her voice, of course, lives on, in *United States Reports*, in the legions of young women she inspired, in the unlikely persona of "the notorious RBG" who spoke truth to power, and in the multifaceted legacy that this book explores.

---

[22] Little Sisters of the Poor Saints Peter & Paul Home v. Pennsylvania, 140 S. Ct. 2367, 2386 (2020).

[23] *Id.* at 2400 (Ginsburg, J., dissenting).

Acknowledgments

We thank the contributors to this volume for their reflections on Justice Ginsburg's legacy and how her project of intervening for equality through law might be sustained and strengthened in time. Special thanks are due to Linda Greenhouse for agreeing to write the Foreword to our book and for then delivering a chapter of much greater depth and insight than any writing to which the label "foreword" is usually attached. Thanks also to Professor Reva Siegel for many helpful conversations and suggestions.

Our appreciation is also due Wake Forest University law students Alex Calderon, Daniel Wilkes, Ally Chebuhar, and Russ Gore for their committed and excellent research assistance and to the staff of the Wake Forest University law library for additional support. Thanks also to the American Bar Association Press for its commitment to producing a new book on the enduring importance of Justice Ginsburg's jurisprudence, and to Justice Bob Edmunds for initially suggesting that we write it.

Finally, of course, we must thank Ruth Bader Ginsburg for her imagination to see what could and would be a more equal world, for her courage in *action* to change that world, and for inspiring us to pay it forward.

Introduction

"We the People" and the Jurisprudence of Ruth Bader Ginsburg

—Suzanne Reynolds

As I prepared for my second meeting with Justice Ginsburg, I began to understand something central to her character. She had agreed that I would interview her again, this time, as the main event of a conference on women in the judiciary. Since we had some open evenings for dinner, I asked her whom she would like on the guest lists. I fully expected that the list would involve my calling the offices of the governor, of various colleges and university presidents, and of assorted local celebrities. Indeed, the names she gave me were celebrated—if not to the general public, certainly to students of gender discrimination. Giving me the contact information from her personal address book, she asked that I find out if Stephen Wiesenfeld,[1] Sharon Frontiero,[2] and Yona Owens[3] were available. Because she had maintained close contact with the people she had represented over the years, she knew that these former clients lived in close enough vicinity to Asheville, NC, that

[1] Weinberger v. Wiesenfeld, 420 U.S. 636 (1975).

[2] Frontiero v. Richardson, 411 U.S. 677 (1973).

[3] Owens v. Brown, 455 F. Supp. 291 (D.D.C. 1978).

she felt comfortable in asking them if they would like to join us for dinner. And they did.

This experience helped me appreciate a trait perhaps surpassing the Justice's prodigious intellect—Ruth Bader Ginsburg's devotion to people who petition the judicial system for help. As I read the remembrances filling the digital space in the months following her death, I realized that everyone who spent time with Justice Ginsburg observed the same devotion. Her clerks, for example, recalled the impact of Ginsburg taking them to the D.C. jail and to Lorton Penitentiary, where the clerks saw "where paper defendants in appellate briefs served their all-too-real sentences."[4] One interviewer, contrasting the Justice's role as an advocate for clients with her role as an appellate judge, asked Justice Ginsburg how she transitioned from advocate to judge. Ginsburg responded, "I think I'm still an advocate."[5] Scholars assessing her many dissenting opinions concluded that she decided to dissent when "the Court ignored the factual realities of the litigants and the impact of the Court's decision on those litigants."[6]

In her work as an appellate judge, Justice Ginsburg translated this devotion into a jurisprudence focused on "We the People," substantively and procedurally. Substantively, Justice Ginsburg insisted that faithfully employed, the words of the Constitution supported an expansive understanding of who was included in "We the People," despite the Framers' narrow understanding of the phrase when it appeared in the Preamble to the Constitution. Expressed also as a jurisprudence of equality and opportunity,[7] Justice Ginsburg believed that the phrase promised equal dignity for people despite their gender, gender identity, race, or disability.

Procedurally, "We the People" shaped Justice Ginsburg's approach to the process of deciding cases, guiding every step of her judicial process—the way she read the U.S. Constitution and statutes, approached voting issues,

---

[4] Deborah Jones Merritt, *The Music of Ruth Bader Ginsburg*, 134 HARV. L. REV. 887, 888 (January, 2021).

[5] Caroline Kelly, *Ruth Bader Ginsburg: This Time in History Will Be Seen as 'an Aberration'*, CNN (Oct. 3, 2019, 10:18 PM), https://www.cnn.com/2019/10/03/politics/ruth-bader-ginsburg-justice-us-history-aberration/index.html.

[6] Christine M. Venter, *Dissenting from the Bench: The Rhetorical and Performative Oral Jurisprudence of Ruth Bader Ginsburg and Antonin Scalia*, 56 WAKE FOREST L. REV. 321, 337 (2021).

[7] For an article that explores this phrase in Justice Ginsburg's legacy, see *Symposium: Ruth Bader Ginsburg's Jurisprudence of Opportunity and Equality*, 104 COLUM. L. REV. 39 (2004).

and analyzed the demands of the separation of powers, for example. While the substantive contours of "We the People" have received the most attention, the full sweep of her jurisprudence appears also in the process she used in analyzing all issues.

Justice Ginsburg's jurisprudence of "We the People" became the ordering principle of this book, explaining both the book's title and its topics. Instead of a general survey of Justice Ginsburg's work, the book tells the story of an advocate and a jurist committed to increasing in material ways the bundle of rights we all carry around with us as Americans. As Linda Greenhouse explains in the Foreword, the story begins with Justice Ginsburg's commitment to an America that enables people with diverse experiences to live together in civic harmony. Justice Ginsburg believed that because the American experience involved living in community, the religious expression of some of us had to yield when the expression oppressed others of us in ways endangering that harmony.

With civic harmony as the bedrock, in the first chapter, Cary Franklin gives us Ginsburg's guiding principle for broadening the "who" and the "what" of American citizenship. The state must not regulate in a way that stereotypes some of its people but must instead allow them to pursue their chosen life courses. First as an advocate, and then as a jurist, Ginsburg argued that the right to live free from the shackles of stereotypes promoted equal protection of the laws in ways that other doctrines could not.

Unshackled from the stereotypes, these people, wrote Ginsburg, were "the originating source of all the powers of government.[8] In light of this philosophy, Justice Ginsburg believed in jealously guarding the franchise and in honoring the people's decision to expand it. As Alexander Tsesis demonstrates in chapter two on Justice Ginsburg's election jurisprudence, Justice Ginsburg insisted that the Court defer to Congress in its legislative efforts to protect the franchise. To that end, she urged the Court not to apply strict scrutiny to race-conscious districting principles that are designed to correct racial injustices in voting and to protect minority voters.[9] On other occasions, she wrote that the Court should uphold practices that had served the

---

[8] Ariz. State Legis. v. Ariz. Indep. Redistricting Commission, 576 U.S. 787, 813 (2015).

[9] Miller v. Johnson, 515 U.S. 900, 944 (Ginsburg, J., dissenting).

people well,[10] while respecting the people's decision to experiment with new methods to prevent gerrymandering that favored one party over another.[11]

Towards the end of her career as she dissented in abortion cases, Justice Ginsburg warned that the failure to adopt the anti-stereotyping principle posed the biggest threat in issues of reproductive choice. We do not know what Justice Ginsburg would have written in *Dobbs v. Jackson Women's Health Organization*.[12] We come as close as we can to a posthumous version of that opinion in the brief by Serena Mayeri, Melissa Murray, and Reva Siegel as amici curiae in *Dobbs*, included in this book in chapter three. This brief, filed barely a year after the death of Justice Ginsburg, rings with the clear tones of her life's work and pays homage to Justice Ginsburg's jurisprudence of what it means for women to be full members of "We the People."

Since her work as an advocate began in gender discrimination, how fitting that we consider what the Equal Rights Amendment (ERA) would have meant to Justice Ginsburg in a post-*Dobbs* world. As Julie Suk reminds us in chapter four, Ginsburg advocated for passage of the ERA throughout her life. At the same time, as a procedural purist, she believed that because of the time limits on ratification imposed by the enabling legislation, passage of the ERA might depend on beginning the ratification process all over again. Suk makes us certain, however, that Ginsburg would have believed that the ERA—now more than ever—demands our national attention.

In the concluding chapter, Shannon Gilreath helps us imagine how the story might continue if the Court embraced Justice Ginsburg's commitment to "We the People." For gay Americans, pursuing their life courses would require recognizing substantive rights that do not depend on similarity to heterosexual rights. For all issues properly analyzed under the Fourteenth Amendment, the Court would have to examine how inequality affects people burdened by discrimination, not in the abstract, but in the realities of their lives. Capturing Ginsburg's signature optimism, Gilreath assures us we can realize the change she imagined.

---

[10] Evenwel v. Abbott, 578 U.S. 54 (2016) (upholding legislative districts based on total population).

[11] *Arizona State Legislature*, 576 U.S. 787 (upholding the use of a nonpartisan commission to draw voting districts).

[12] 142 S.Ct. 2228, 213 L. Ed.2d 545 (2022).

To set the stage for the chapters that follow, this introduction looks both at the substantive content of "We the People" and at some of the ways the phrase shaped Justice Ginsburg's judicial process. While Justice Ginsburg brought her understanding of "We the People" to many subject areas,[13] this introduction hues closer to the topics of the authors of the following chapters, confining the illustrations to gender, race, and reproductive choice. For illustrations of how the phrase shaped Justice Ginsburg's judicial process, the introduction focuses on her approach to interpreting statutes and the Constitution. As we read in the chapters in this book and in the hundreds of opinions that form her judicial legacy, the jurisprudence of Ruth Bader Ginsburg reflects her conviction that the Constitution supports an expansive understanding of "We the People." This understanding served Justice Ginsburg as a substantive and procedural guide to issues before the Court and enabled her to define for us what it means to be an American.

I. The "Who" of "We the People"

A. Gender

Most famously, Justice Ginsburg insisted that "We the People" protected the full expression of personhood unhampered by state-sanctioned stereotypes on proper gender roles. Ginsburg developed this approach as a lawyer for the Women's Right Project (WRP) of the American Civil Liberties Union (ACLU), bringing cases on behalf of male and female plaintiffs who had suffered discrimination based on gendered stereotypes. As she later explained, "The message we were trying to get across was simply this: when you pigeonhole people on grounds of race, religion, whatever, you don't allow them to be free to be you and me (to borrow from the title of a wonderful song introduced in the 1970s by Marlo Thomas). People should not be held back by human-made laws from using whatever God-given talent they have. Girls as well as boys should be free to aspire and achieve."[14]

---

[13] See, for example, an analysis of Justice Ginsburg's contributions to disability rights in Samuel R. Bagenstos, *Justice Ginsburg and the Judicial Role in Expanding "We the People": The Disability Rights Cases*, 104 COLUM. L. REV. 49 (2004). Because of Justice Ginsburg's majority opinion, Bagenstos describes *Olmstead v. L.C.*, 527 U.S. 581 (1999), as the *Brown v. Bd. of Education* of disability law.

[14] *Annual John Paul Stevens Lecture: A Conversation with Associate Justice Ruth Bader Ginsburg*, 84 U. COLO. L. REV. 909, 922 (Fall 2013).

Ginsburg chose not to rely on more traditional approaches to discrimination because she believed that the anti-stereotyping principle held more promise for the ways women experienced it. Even before she became the director of the WRP, she had tested the anti-stereotyping principle in a case before the Tenth Circuit with a male plaintiff, Charles Moritz.[15] The IRS had denied tax deductions to Moritz, a lifelong bachelor, for expenses related to the care of his elderly mother—deductions that the IRS would have recognized if Moritz had been female. Urging the anti-stereotyping principle, Ginsburg argued that by enforcing traditional notions of the proper spheres for men and women, the state action violated the Fourteenth Amendment—and she won. She used this approach the same year for the brief to the Supreme Court in *Reed v. Reed*,[16] seeking to remedy the injustice Sally Reed suffered when denied the right to administer the estate of her deceased son. Arguing that the state was trying to steer Sally Reed into the home and out of the public sphere, Ginsburg convinced the Court of the constitutional concern raised by a statute that automatically favored the male family member seeking to administer the estate of the decedent. As she observed 25 years later as a member of that Court, it was "the first time [the Supreme] Court had ruled in favor of a woman who complained that her State had denied her the equal protection of its laws."[17]

In one significant way, the Ginsburg approach lived up to its promise.[18] When Justice Ginsburg wrote the majority opinion in *United States v. Virginia*,[19] which is perhaps her most significant, she pointed to the stereotypes on which Virginia relied to justify excluding women from admission to Virginia Military Institute (VMI). By the time of the VMI case, Supreme Court jurisprudence already reflected Justice Ginsburg's anti-stereotyping principle, holding that discrimination on the basis of sex required the state to offer an "exceedingly persuasive" justification for the different treatment of men and women where rank gender stereotyping deprived one sex of a benefit

[15] Moritz v. Commissioner, 469 F. 2d 466 (10th Cir. 1972).

[16] 404 U.S. 71 (1971).

[17] United States v. Virginia, 518 U.S. 515, 532 (1996).

[18] See also, for example, Chief Justice Rehnquist pointing to the evils of stereotyping in upholding provisions of the Family and Medical Leave Act. Nev. Dep't of Human Res. v. Hibbs, 538 U.S. 721 (2003).

[19] 518 U.S. 515 (1996).

the other enjoyed.[20] Virginia's justifications, unmasked by Justice Ginsburg, relied on overbroad generalizations and supposed innate differences that served only to "perpetuate historical patterns of discrimination."[21] Beliefs about the proper sphere for women once formed the basis to exclude women from higher education.[22] So too, Virginia's assumptions about how most women would handle the "adversative" environment of VMI did not justify excluding women who wanted exactly that kind of experience. Justice Ginsburg began her analysis in the VMI opinion by noting that for more than 100 years, women did not count among voters composing "We the People."[23] In closing, she observed:

> A prime part of the history of our Constitution, historian Richard Morris recounted, is the story of the extension of constitutional rights and protections to people once ignored or excluded. VMI's story continued as our comprehension of "We the People" expanded. There is no reason to believe that the admission of women capable of all the activities required of VMI cadets would destroy the Institute rather than enhance its capacity to serve the "more perfect Union."[24]

B. Race

In the setting of discrimination based on race, Justice Ginsburg's jurisprudence likewise drew on the experiences of "We the People" as she reached her conclusions, often in dissent.[25] In affirmative action cases, for example,

---

[20] See Miss. Univ. for Women v. Hogan, 458 U.S. 718 (1982).

[21] *United States v. Virginia*, 518 U.S. at 542.

[22] *Id.* at 536–37.

[23] *Id.* at 531.

[24] *Id.* at 557–58 [citations omitted].

[25] In fact, Ginsburg patterned her advocacy for gender equality on the lessons learned in the struggles combatting discrimination on the basis of race. Like Thurgood Marshall, Ginsburg favored an incremental approach. With carefully chosen plaintiffs, she focused on the concrete harm her clients had suffered from their gendered treatment, chipping away at instances of state-enforced gender stereotypes. In addition to Marshall, Pauli Murray also helped shape Ginsburg's litigation approach. Murray had played an important role in crafting the arguments on which Marshall had relied, and Ginsburg, in turn, relied heavily on Murray's work as she formulated her strategy for the WRP. Murray had so influenced Ginsburg's brief in *Reed v. Reed* that Ginsburg cited Murray as co-counsel. Brief for Appellant at 68, Reed v. Reed, 404 U.S. 71 (1971) (No. 70-4).

her jurisprudence demonstrated how acutely she appreciated the continuing impact of racial discrimination.

Because of her understanding of the way Black people continued to face discrimination, she tried—unsuccessfully—to protect the use of race-conscious distinctions. Aware of the lingering impacts of discrimination, she argued for a review of those distinctions less burdensome than strict scrutiny. Early in her tenure on the Court, a contractor challenged Congress's preference for minorities in bids for federal contracts. In *Adarand Constructors v. Pena*,[26] the Tenth Circuit had upheld the use of the preference in awarding a highway construction contract, but a majority of the Supreme Court reversed and remanded with instructions to the lower court to apply strict scrutiny to the manner of awarding the contract. While Justice Ginsburg tried to preserve a post-*Adarand* use of the preference program, she devoted most of her opinion to reminding the majority of the ways in which Black people continued to experience discrimination:

> [The lingering effects of discrimination], reflective of a system of racial caste only recently ended, are evident in our workplaces, markets, and neighborhoods. Job applicants with identical resumes, qualifications, and interview styles still experience different receptions, depending on their race. White and African-American consumers still encounter different deals. People of color looking for housing still face discriminatory treatment by landlords, real estate agents, and mortgage lenders. Minority entrepreneurs sometimes fail to gain contracts though they are the low bidders, and they are sometimes refused work even after winning contracts. Bias both conscious and unconscious, reflecting traditional and unexamined habits of thought, keeps up barriers that must come down if equal opportunity and nondiscrimination are ever genuinely to become this country's law and practice.[27]

She fought the same battle in trying to protect the use of affirmative action in college and university admissions programs. These programs should not succumb to a strict scrutiny review, she maintained, because of what Black and Brown people experienced in living their lives:

---

[26] 515 U.S. 200 (1995).

[27] *Id.* at 273–74 [footnotes omitted].

> Unemployment, poverty, and access to health care vary disproportionately by race. Neighborhoods and schools remain racially divided. African-American and Hispanic children are all too often educated in poverty-stricken and underperforming institutions. Adult African-Americans and Hispanics generally earn less than whites with equivalent levels of education. Equally credentialed job applicants receive different receptions depending on their race. Irrational prejudice is still encountered in real estate markets and consumer transactions.[28]

Because she looked at admissions from the perspective of the many Black students who continued to "encounter markedly inadequate and unequal educational opportunities,"[29] she cautioned against forecasting a sunset to affirmative action programs. Indeed, three years after her death, a new majority of Justices relied on that sunset to end the affirmative action programs at issue in the case before the Court.[30]

C. Reproductive Rights

Justice Ginsburg believed that full participation in "We the People" required, at a minimum, that the state not jeopardize the health of its citizens. Beyond this minimal obligation, the state should act in a way that recognizes the dignity and autonomy of personhood and allows people to exercise control over their own destinies. For these reasons, she maintained that the state had to act carefully in regulations involving pregnancy, mindful that age-old stereotypes kept women from full participation in the political and social life of the country and pushed them into the home, regardless of whether women had chosen that life course.

When she wrote in cases involving abortion, Justice Ginsburg reminded the Court of these basic premises, which a majority of the Court had acknowledged in *Roe v. Wade*[31] and continued to honor in *Planned*

---

[28] Gratz v. Bollinger, 539 U.S. 244, 299–300 (2003) (Ginsburg, J., dissenting) [footnotes omitted].

[29] Grutter v. Bollinger, 539 U.S. 306, 434–44 (2003) (Ginsburg, J., concurring).

[30] Students for Fair Admissions, Inc. v. President & Fellows of Harvard Coll., 143 S. Ct. 2141, 216 L. Ed.2d 857, 869 (2023).

[31] 410 U.S. 113 (1973).

Parenthood v. Casey[32] and *Stenberg v. Carhart*.[33] To Justice Ginsburg, a majority of the Court violated all these principles in *Gonzales v. Carhart*.[34] The majority found constitutional a statute regulating abortion that recognized no exception to protect a woman's health. In perhaps her most blistering dissent, Justice Ginsburg found the analysis and the result in *Carhart* "bewildering" and "irrational."[35] For Justice Ginsburg, the statute that the majority left standing, banning intact dilation and evacuation (D&E)[36] as a manner of abortion, violated the sacred tenet that the state not act in a way jeopardizing the health of its citizens.

While Justice Kennedy's majority opinion focused on the viewpoints of doctors and experts, Justice Ginsburg's dissent stands in stark contrast. Analyzing what it meant to be counted in "We the People," Justice Ginsburg reminded the Court that it had failed to put women making the abortion decision at the center of its analysis. Not only did the Court violate its obligation to preserve exceptions for the woman's health, but it had also stereotyped and patronized women seeking abortions, keeping from them accurate medical information to help them make their own informed choices. Instead, wrote Justice Ginsburg, "the Court [deprived] women of the right to make an autonomous choice even at the expense of their safety," and in that way, reflected "ancient notions about women's place in the family and under the Constitution—ideas that [had] long since been discredited."[37]

II. The "How" of "We the People"

Almost as dramatically as the substantive contours, Justice Ginsburg's judicial process underscored the centrality of "We the People" to her jurisprudence. Whether she was interpreting the words in the Constitution or in state or federal statutes, the impact of those words on the people of the republic guided her through the process. This approach flowed naturally from Justice Ginsburg's conviction that the constitutional order existed only through the

---

[32] 505 U.S. 833 (1992).

[33] 530 U.S. 914 (2000).

[34] 550 U.S. 124 (2007).

[35] *Id.* at 179, 191.

[36] The majority used the political name for the abortion procedure, partial-birth abortion, a phrase not recognized in the medical literature.

[37] *Id.* at 184–85.

will of the people, acting through the separate branches of government.[38] As she wrote in *Arizona State Legislature v. Arizona Independent Redistricting Commission*,[39] "the people themselves are the originating source of all the powers of government."

Because of the centrality of people to the constitutional order, Justice Ginsburg rejected both "original intent" and "textualism" as unhelpful—indeed, illegitimate—approaches to constitutional and statutory interpretation. Rather, she insisted that the people who empower its representatives to act are the people as currently constituted, and the interpretation of the Constitution and of legislation must respond to those people and to the real-world problems that the words of the relevant enactments were meant to address.

To address the real-world problems of real people, Justice Ginsburg insisted that textual analysis accurately consider the context in which the text operated, especially in the workplace. In *Ledbetter v. Goodyear Tire & Rubber Co.*,[40] a majority of the Court interpreted a provision of Title VII of the Civil Rights Act to require that an employee lost her claim for discrimination in her pay unless she pursued the claim within 180 days of each discriminatory payment. The majority insisted on this time limit whether the employee knew of the discrimination or not, and even if the pay discrepancy with her male counterparts built over time as the pay discrepancy increased. In her vigorous dissent, Justice Ginsburg insisted that the majority's "cramped" reading of Title VII violated the purpose of Title VII, the text of the provision as it interacted with other provisions in the Title, and the Court's precedents. She spent most of her dissent, however, schooling the majority on how the workplace works and what it was like to be a minority in that workplace trying to keep her job:

> Pay disparities often occur, as they did in Ledbetter's case, in small increments; cause to suspect that discrimination is at work develops only over time. Comparative pay information, moreover, is often hidden from the employee's view. Employers may keep under wraps the

[38] For more on this theme, see Daphna Renan, *Justice Ginsburg's Republican Jurisprudence*, 90 Geo. Wash. L. Rev. 1471 (2022).

[39] 576 U.S. 787, 813 (2015).

[40] 550 U.S. 618 (2007).

pay differentials maintained among supervisors, no less the reasons for those differentials. Small initial discrepancies may not be seen as meet for a federal case, particularly when the employee, trying to succeed in a nontraditional environment, is averse to making waves.

. . .

It is only when the disparity becomes apparent and sizable, *e.g.*, through future raises calculated as a percentage of current salaries, that an employee in Ledbetter's situation is likely to comprehend her plight and, therefore, to complain. Her initial readiness to give her employer the benefit of the doubt should not preclude her from later challenging the then current and continuing payment of a wage depressed on account of her sex.

. . .

The problem of concealed pay discrimination is particularly acute where the disparity arises not because the female employee is flatly denied a raise but because male counterparts are given larger raises. Having received a pay increase, the female employee is unlikely to discern at once that she has experienced an adverse employment decision. She may have little reason even to suspect discrimination until a pattern develops incrementally and she ultimately becomes aware of the disparity. Even if an employee suspects that the reason for a comparatively low raise is not performance but sex (or another protected ground), the amount involved may seem too small, or the employer's intent too ambiguous, to make the issue immediately actionable—or winnable.[41]

She drove home the point in several oral dissents from the bench. Reprimanding the Court for its wooden interpretation of Title VII in *Ledbetter*, she admonished from the bench that "Title VII was meant to govern real world employment practices and that world is what the Court ignores today."[42] Subsequently, when a plurality of the Court concluded that the Family and Medical Leave Act (FMLA) protected self-care leave only for

[41] *Id.* at 645, 650. In Justice Ginsburg's oral dissent from the bench, she called on Congress to remedy the absurd result the Court reached in *Ledbetter*, which it did. Lilly Ledbetter Fair Pay Act of 2009, Pub. Law 111-2. For more on the oral dissents of Justice Ginsburg, *see* Venter, *supra* n. 6.

[42] Oral Dissent of Justice Ginsburg at 7:44–7:51, Ledbetter v. Goodyear Tire & Rubber Co., 550 U.S. 618 (2007) (No. 05-1074), https://www.oyez.org/cases/2006/05-1074.

women, Justice Ginsburg explained from the bench that because of the realities of the workplace, the Act included men, too:

> The Act was designed to promote women's opportunities to live balanced lives at home having gainful employment. . . . The best way to protect women against losing their jobs because of pregnancy or childbirth, Congress determined, was not to order leaves for women only, for that would deter employers from hiring them.[43]

Dissenting later in the *University of Texas Southwest Medical Center v. Nassar*, which increased the burden of proving retaliation under Title VII, she pronounced from the bench that:

> . . . as anyone with employment experience can easily grasp, in-charge employees authorized to assign and control subordinate employees' daily work are aided in accomplishing the harassment by the superintending position in which their employer places them, and for that reason, the employer is properly held responsible for their misconduct.[44]

Focusing as she did on real-world problems, Justice Ginsburg's approach helped her pierce the sometimes-tortured policy arguments in contrary opinions with unpretentious metaphors that made her point. In *Shelby County v. Holder*,[45] for example, the majority relied on policy reasons to abandon the preclearance requirement of the Voting Rights Act, a requirement that all the justices acknowledged had helped control voting discrimination. All of the justices also acknowledged that voting discrimination continued. Nevertheless, the majority decided that since there was currently less voting discrimination, the Constitution required jettisoning the preclearance requirement.

---

[43] Oral Dissent of Justice Ginsburg at 0:25-1:03, Part Two, Coleman v. Ct. of Appeals, 566 U.S. 30 (2012) (No. 10-1016), https://www.oyez.org/cases/2011/10-1016.

[44] Oral Dissent of Justice Ginsburg at 3:52-4:18, Part Two, Univ. of Tex. Sw. Med. Ctr. v. Nassar, 570 U.S. 338 (2013) (No. 12-484), https://www.oyez.org/cases/2012/12-484.

[45] 570 U.S. 529 (2013). The majority insisted, also, that "current conditions" in voter restrictions based on race did not warrant the attention the preclearance requirement imposed. Since Shelby, photo ID laws, restrictions on mail voting, reductions on ballot returns, and searches of voter lists for non-citizens have proliferated, especially in states that had been subject to preclearance. Liz Avore, *10 Years Since Shelby County v. Holder: Where We Are and Where We're Heading* (June 27, 2023), https://votingrightslab.org/.

Shining a light on the illogic, Justice Ginsburg chided the majority, "Throwing out preclearance when it has worked and is continuing to work to stop discriminatory changes is like throwing away your umbrella in a rainstorm because you are not getting wet."[46]

As Justice Ginsburg's jurisprudence reminds us, if we steadfastly follow honorable principles, our path becomes clear. Certain that "We the People" belonged at the center of judicial analysis, Justice Ginsburg created a consistent jurisprudence of intellectual rigor and of great humanity.

[46] *Shelby*, 570 U.S. at 690.

1

The Arc of Anti-Stereotyping Doctrine

—Cary Franklin

More than a decade ago, I wrote an article called *The Anti-Stereotyping Principle in Constitutional Sex Discrimination Law*.[1] That article opened with a question: Why have most of the plaintiffs who have reached the Supreme Court in constitutional sex discrimination cases been men? Women in this country didn't obtain the right to vote until 1920, and they remain scarce in many of the nation's lawmaking bodies, in the boardroom, in the military, and in most high-paying sectors of the labor market. Gender-based violence and harassment is dismayingly common, and "discrimination against women when they are mothers or mothers-to-be"[2] remains one of the most significant drivers of inequality. So, what should we make of the fact that constitutional sex discrimination law in the United States has been built, in significant part, in cases brought by men claiming that *their rights* have been abridged on the basis of sex?

---

[1] Cary Franklin, *The Anti-Stereotyping Principle in Constitutional Sex Discrimination Law*, 85 N.Y.U. L. Rev. 83 (2010).

[2] Nevada Department of Human Resources v. Hibbs, 538 U.S. 721, 736 (2003) (internal quotation marks omitted).

The prevalence of male plaintiffs in constitutional sex discrimination cases is not an accident. These plaintiffs were the linchpin of Ruth Bader Ginsburg's strategy in the 1970s for persuading the Court to apply equal protection in the context of sex. Prior to 1970, only women had brought sex-based equal protection claims. But in 1970, Ginsburg, soon to be head of the American Civil Liberties Union's (ACLU's) Women's Rights Project (WRP), had a novel idea: She decided to challenge the constitutionality of sex-based state action in cases with male plaintiffs. By the time her decade-long litigation campaign ended, men far outnumbered women among the ranks of constitutional sex discrimination plaintiffs to reach the Supreme Court—a ratio that persists to this day.

Despite Ginsburg's monumental achievement, progressive commentators have often been critical of her use of male plaintiffs. Critics contend that these plaintiffs were "a strategic choice":[3] "Ginsburg was especially eager to argue cases brought by men [because] she thought judges might look more favorably on claims made by people of their own gender."[4] In this view, male plaintiffs allowed Ginsburg to address "what was primarily a women's issue"[5] by focusing on small but concrete harms to men. She ostensibly viewed male plaintiffs as "a useful tool,"[6] a way of demonstrating the harms of sex discrimination to Justices who couldn't recognize those harms when they were visited on women. Her campaign certainly bore fruit. More than a century after the ratification of the Fourteenth Amendment, the Court began to invalidate laws that discriminated on the basis of sex.

But, critics argue, Ginsburg's use of male plaintiffs came at a cost: Male plaintiffs embodied a conception of equality that was formalistic[7] and

---

[3] David Cole, *Strategies of Difference: Litigating for Women's Rights in a Man's World*, 2 LAW & INEQ. 33, 56 (1984).

[4] Judith Baer, *Advocate on the Court: Ruth Bader Ginsburg and the Limits of Formal Equality*, *in* REHNQUIST JUSTICE: UNDERSTANDING THE COURT DYNAMIC 216, 219 (Earl M. Maltz ed., 2003). For more examples of this claim, see Franklin, *supra* note 1, at 84 n.4.

[5] Cole, *supra* note 3, at 55.

[6] *Id.* at 39.

[7] *See, e.g.*, Mary E. Becker, *Prince Charming: Abstract Equality*, SUP. CT. REV. 201, 201 & n.1 (1987); Catharine A. MacKinnon, *Reflections on Sex Equality Under Law*, 100 YALE L.J. 1281, 1286–97 (1991) ("[T]he early feminist legal view was, implicitly, that if equality meant being the same as men . . . women would be the same as men. . . . The essentially assimilationist approach fundamental to this legal equality doctrine . . . was adopted in sex cases wholesale. . . .").

"empty at [its] core."[8] Critics contend that this formalistic conception of equality was useful for attacking sex classifications, but it was incapable of combatting the many forms of regulation that subordinate women without formally classifying on the basis of sex. Critics cite Ginsburg's use of male plaintiffs as evidence that she was satisfied with formal equality and failed to appreciate the inability of a "sex-blind" doctrine to disrupt persistent cycles of discrimination in a society whose ground rules were created by and for men.[9] If Ginsburg had targeted substantive inequalities between the sexes, critics charge, her campaign might have yielded an equal protection doctrine more attentive to women's subordination. Instead, she pressed claims by men that obscured "women's experience of second-class citizenship"[10] and suggested it was enough simply to strike formal classifications from the law. Thus, many commenters have concluded, "the problems that have arisen under the Supreme Court's . . . approach [to sex discrimination] are the direct result of men successfully arguing that they were discriminated against. . . ."[11]

The Anti-Stereotyping Principle challenged this account of the foundational constitutional sex discrimination cases. It argued that the dominant historical narrative, which identified formal equality as the philosophical ideal at the core of Ginsburg's campaign, obscured a richer set of claims regarding constitutional limits on sex-based state action. The article showed that Ginsburg used male plaintiffs to promote a transformative theory of equal protection founded on an anti-stereotyping principle. This anti-stereotyping principle prohibited state action that reflects or reinforces traditional conceptions of men's and women's roles. This principle was not anti-classificationist: It permitted the state to classify on the basis of sex in instances where doing so served to dissipate sex-role stereotypes. Nor was it simply anti-subordinationist: Because discrimination against women had

---

[8] Mary Becker, *Patriarchy and Inequality: Towards a Substantive Feminism*, U. CHI. LEGAL F. 21, 22 (1999).

[9] *See, e.g.*, CATHARINE A. MACKINNON, FEMINISM UNMODIFIED: DISCOURSES ON LIFE AND LAW 4 (1987) (arguing that "[p]articularly in its upper reaches, much of what has passed for feminism in law has been the attempt to get for men what little has been reserved for women"); Baer, *supra* note 4, at 231 ("[S]o far men have been the primary beneficiaries of the new sexual equality doctrine. Ruth Ginsburg has given no indication that this outcome troubles her.").

[10] MACKINNON, *supra* note 9, at 4.

[11] Mary Becker, *The Sixties Shift to Formal Equality and the Courts: An Argument for Pragmatism and Politics*, 40 WM. & MARY L. REV. 209, 252 (1998).

traditionally been viewed as a benefit to them, Ginsburg was concerned that an unrefined anti-subordination principle would provide courts with too little guidance about which forms of regulation violate equal protection. The anti-stereotyping principle was designed to provide such guidance. Its aim was to direct courts' attention to the particular institutions and social practices that perpetuate inequality in the context of sex.

The Anti-Stereotyping Principle recovered the philosophical and historical origins of this principle and analyzed its use by progressive social movements in the 1960s and 1970s. It showed that Ginsburg's male-plaintiff strategy was inspired not by "the thin abstract 'likes alike, unalikes unalike' of Aristotelian logic,"[12] but by the thicker and more contemporary anti-stereotyping logic of John Stuart Mill. Ginsburg witnessed this logic in action in Sweden in the 1960s, where it fueled an innovative campaign against sex-role enforcement. Anti-stereotyping theories were emerging in the United States in this period as well. The great civil rights and women's rights advocate Pauli Murray was developing anti-stereotyping ideas in her work, as were a wide range of radical feminist and lesbian, gay, bisexual, and transgender (LGBT) rights groups.

This chapter revisits some of this history and shows how Ginsburg translated these ideas into constitutional arguments. Her aim in representing male plaintiffs wasn't simply to remove some formal sex classifications from the law. She used male plaintiffs to develop a more expansive and more progressive claim that equal protection bars the state from acting in ways that reflect and reinforce traditional conceptions of how men and women should be. The power of this claim to subvert traditional gender hierarchies and destabilize widely-accepted forms of sex-based ordering was apparent from the start. Supporters and opponents of LGBT rights both insisted that barring the enforcement of traditional sex stereotypes would undermine state efforts to enforce heterosexuality and conventional gender identities. Advocates and activists in this period also recognized the implications of an anti-stereotyping principle for the state's regulation of pregnancy and reproductive rights. Before *Roe* was even decided, Ginsburg used the anti-stereotyping principle to argue against state action that deprived pregnant women of the right to decide for themselves if or when to become mothers.

[12] Catharine A. MacKinnon, *The Road Not Taken: Sex Equality in* Lawrence v. Texas, 65 OHIO ST. L.J. 1081, 1085 (2004).

Part of my aim in *The Anti-Stereotyping Principle* was to show how this principle became embedded in constitutional sex discrimination law in the male plaintiff cases of the 1970s. Scholars have critiqued those cases for enshrining in sex-based equal protection law an anti-classification principle as regressive as the anti-classification principle championed by white plaintiffs in race discrimination cases. This chapter argues, as *The Anti-Stereotyping Principle* did, that this criticism misreads those cases. Ginsburg's great achievement in the male plaintiff cases—aside from winning them—was persuading the Justices to adopt her anti-stereotyping framing. The Court in the 1970s incorporated anti-stereotyping reasoning into its opinions, even citing the Swedish and other anti-stereotyping advocates Ginsburg relied on in her briefs. Constitutional sex discrimination law has now barred the state from regulating in ways that reflect and reinforce traditional sex stereotypes for almost half a century.

This is not to say that the Court has always enforced this bar. *The Anti-Stereotyping Principle* examined several contexts in which the Court balked at the implications of anti-stereotying doctrine and opted to preserve the status quo instead of disrupting the state's enforcement of sex stereotypes. The article argued, however, that the Court's failure to block all forms of sex stereotyping did not stem from the inherent narrowness of the doctrine the Court created. The Justices of the Burger and Rehnquist Courts, almost all of whom came of age in the first half of the twentieth century, were unprepared to fully enforce anti-stereotyping doctrine. Advocates for and against LGBT rights in the 1970s recognized the far-reaching implications of anti-stereotyping doctrine for issues such as same-sex marriage and discrimination against gay and transgender people. But courts in that era were not prepared to apply anti-stereotyping doctrine in ways that would permit same-sex couples to marry or shield transgender people from discrimination. The same was true in the context of reproductive rights. It took a long time for courts to recognize that the regulation of pregnancy, and contraception and abortion, might reflect and reinforce traditional sex-role stereotypes.

The Anti-Stereotyping Principle examined the various limits and loopholes courts created to avoid enforcing anti-stereotyping doctrine when they found its implications too unsettling. But courts' application of this doctrine has changed over time. Social movement activism and evolving social values exposed the conventional prejudices underlying the limits and loopholes courts created in the 1970s to cabin the reach of anti-stereotyping doctrine, rendering them less tenable. The notion that the law bars the enforcement of traditional sex stereotypes about the jobs men and women should hold and the government benefits to which they are entitled, but not about who they should date or how they should express their gender identity seemed more plausible 50 years ago than it does today. It also seemed more plausible to shield abortion regulation from equal protection scrutiny on the theory that such regulation does not implicate sex-based equality concerns because pregnancy is "an objectively identifiable physical condition" that affects only some women.[13] *The Anti-Stereotyping Principle* showed how these limitations on the reach of anti-stereotyping doctrine eroded over time, as courts began to take the equal citizenship of women and LGBT people more seriously.

We are now in a very different place than we were in 2010. Some recent developments have furthered the trends described in *The Anti-Stereotyping Principle*. In 2015, the Court held that laws restricting marriage to different-sex couples violate the Fourteenth Amendment.[14] In 2020, the Court held that discrimination against gay and transgender people counts as sex discrimination under Title VII of the 1964 Civil Rights Act.[15] In 2022, Congress passed the Pregnant Workers Fairness Act (PWFA), a law designed to combat the powerful and various forms of traditional sex stereotyping and sex-role enforcement workers face when they become pregnant.[16] That same year, California amended its constitution to guarantee the right to abortion and other reproductive freedoms explicitly as a matter of equal protection.[17]

But there are also indications that the Court—rapidly transformed by President Trump's appointment of three new Justices, one of whom replaced Justice Ginsburg—is eager to reverse this trend, and maybe even to overrule or tacitly gut a half-century's worth of anti-stereotyping case law. The most

[13] Geduldig v. Aiello, 417 U.S. 484, 497 n.20 (1974).

[14] Obergefell v. Hodges, 576 U.S. 644 (2015).

[15] Bostock v. Clayton County., 140 S. Ct. 1731 (2020).

[16] *See* H.R. 2617–1626, 117th Cong. §§ 102–109 (2022). For more on how the PWFA puts constitutional sex discrimination law's anti-stereotyping doctrine into practice, see Reva B. Siegel, *The Pregnant Citizen, from Suffrage to the Present*, 19TH AMEND. ED. GEO. L.J. 167 (2020); *id.* at 218 (describing the PWFA as an "act[] of legislative constitutionalism" that "develop[s] the understandings of sex stereotyping that have been emerging since the dawn of the sex-discrimination cases").

[17] CAL. CONST. art. I, § 1.1.

conservative Justices on the Roberts Court always resisted applying sex-based legal protections in the contexts of reproductive and LGBT rights; they continued to embrace the doctrinal barriers their predecessors devised in the 1970s to thwart the application of anti-stereotyping doctrine in these contexts. These Justices, joined by some or all of the new Justices appointed by President Trump, may now command a majority on the Court. This means a majority may now support the refortification of old barriers limiting the reach of stereotyping doctrine. In fact, there are indications this majority may want to dispose of anti-stereotyping doctrine entirely, rewriting the history of sex-based equal protection law to suggest the law never barred anything more than a narrow set of formal classifications.

In the face of this emergent historical revisionism, it seems more critical than ever to examine the conceptual underpinnings of the foundational sex-based equal protection cases of the 1970s and to trace how the doctrine created in those cases has developed over time. Parts I and II of this chapter revisit those early cases and discuss both the surprisingly expansive doctrine they enshrined in law and the limits and loopholes courts in the 1970s created to avoid applying this doctrine in certain contexts. Part III examines how those limits and loopholes have eroded over the past half-century as the injustice and illogic of excluding pregnant people and LGBT people from sex-based antidiscrimination protections have become more apparent. Constitutional sex discrimination law has evolved in important ways over the past few decades, ways that are particularly relevant to some of the most pressing questions in constitutional law today. But, as Part IV shows, there's a new effort afoot among some judges to turn back the clock to the early 1970s, in part by pretending that the history and doctrinal development described in this chapter never happened. It is not clear if these efforts will succeed. But one way of combatting historical erasure is to keep telling the history that's being erased.

I. The Philosophical and Historical Underpinnings of the Anti-Stereotyping Principle

If one considers how the Burger Court reacted to Ginsburg's male plaintiffs, the notion that these plaintiffs were part of a conservative strategy to win constitutional protection against sex discrimination by eliciting sympathy and fellow feeling from male Justices is hard to sustain. The first time a male sex discrimination plaintiff appeared before the Court—as half of a married couple—the suggestion that he might be a victim of discrimination was treated as a joke.[18] In subsequent cases, when it became clear Ginsburg was serious about establishing the right of men to be free from sex discrimination, the laughter turned to confusion and disbelief, and, in some cases, to anger and disgust.[19] On one occasion, Ginsburg even ran into standing problems because the lawyers, judges, and law clerks involved in the case found it nearly impossible to believe that her client—who was challenging the constitutionality of a statute limiting "mother's benefits" to women—genuinely desired to stay home and care for his infant son.[20]

To understand why "[t]he fact that many of the cases Ruth Bader Ginsburg brought to the Court had male plaintiffs . . . did not make the Court's job any easier,"[21] it is useful to consider who these plaintiffs were. One of them, the first male plaintiff Ginsburg represented, was a lifelong bachelor and primary caregiver to his elderly and ailing mother.[22] Another was a stay-at-home father.[23] Several were married to women who contributed substantially to their support.[24] Most of them, in one way or another, rejected or failed to satisfy masculine gender norms circa 1975. If Ginsburg's aim had been to "capitalize[] on sex-based ingroup biases,"[25] selecting gender-bending men as plaintiffs would not have been a wise strategy.

---

[18] *See* Transcript of Oral Argument at 22, Frontiero v. Richardson, 411 U.S. 677 (1973) (No. 71-1694) *in* 76 LANDMARK BRIEFS AND ARGUMENTS OF THE SUPREME COURT OF THE UNITED STATES: CONSTITUTIONAL LAW (Philip B. Kurland, Gerhard Casper eds. 1975) ("THE COURT: . . . [D]iscrimination is against the man, is that it? MR. HUNTINGTON: I didn't mean to imply that—[laughter][.]").

[19] *See infra* text accompanying notes 97–110.

[20] *See infra* note 97.

[21] Linda Greenhouse, *Harry Blackmun, Independence and Path Dependence*, 56 HASTINGS L.J. 1235, 1242 (2004).

[22] Moritz v. Comm'r, 469 F.2d 466, 467 (10th Cir. 1972).

[23] Weinberger v. Wiesenfeld, 420 U.S. 636, 641 n.7 (1975).

[24] *See, e.g.*, *id.* at 639 (noting that plaintiff's wife's earnings were "substantially larger" than his and provided the "couple's principle source of support"); Frontiero v. Richardson, 411 U.S. 677, 680 & n.4 (1973) (noting that the male plaintiff/husband was a full-time college student with no earned income).

[25] Jennifer Yatskis Dukart, Comment, Geduldig *Reborn:* Hibbs *as a Success (?) of Justice Ruth Bader Ginsburg's Sex-Discrimination Strategy*, 93 CAL. L. REV. 541, 569 (2005).

Ginsburg was well aware of this. The groundbreaking sex discrimination casebook she published in 1974 opened with a note explaining that men and women both encounter discrimination when they deviate from "assigned roles," but that "the very assurance of [male] dominance marks out for even greater social disapproval men whose unconventional interests and abilities lead them to choose different lifestyles."[26] In 1975, in a series of lectures on "Gender and the Constitution," Ginsburg observed that even people who are "generally sympathetic to the elimination of impediments to equal opportunity for women find the notion of a central home and family role for men disquieting. The idea evokes a feeling of strangeness and the resistance that often attends the unfamiliar."[27] When the Justices ruled in favor of the plaintiff who sought "mother's benefits" to stay home with his infant son, a member of the ACLU's national board lauded Ginsburg for "a great job well done, particularly in light of the fact that there wasn't a male baby sitter among . . . them."[28] Nobody at the ACLU in the 1970s was under the impression that the male plaintiff cases were being argued before a "home crowd."[29]

If Ginsburg knew male sex discrimination plaintiffs would strike the Justices as odd, why did she choose to represent them? This chapter argues that male plaintiffs helped Ginsburg to convey to the Court a new theory of equal protection founded on an anti-stereotyping principle. To understand why Ginsburg was drawn to this principle and how she used it to challenge traditional forms of sex-based regulation, it's useful to examine where it came from.

A. The Philosophical Origins of the Anti-Stereotyping Principle

In a note attached to the first brief she wrote on behalf of a male plaintiff, Ginsburg explained that she had decided to test the constitutionality of sex-based state action in a case featuring a male caregiver because she

---

[26] Kenneth M. Davidson, Ruth Bader Ginsburg & Herma H. Kay, Text, Cases and Materials on Sex-Based Discrimination xii (1974).

[27] Ruth Bader Ginsburg, *Gender and the Constitution*, 44 U. Cin. L. Rev. 1, 34 (1975).

[28] Mailgram from George Slaff, Mayor, Beverly Hills, to Ruth Bader Ginsburg, Gen. Counsel, ACLU (Mar. 20, 1975) (on file with the Library of Congress, Manuscript Division, Ruth Bader Ginsburg Papers, Container 10, Folder: Weinberger v. Wiesenfeld Jan.–Mar. 1975).

[29] Ruth Bader Ginsburg, *Remarks for the Celebration of 75 Years of Women's Enrollment at Columbia Law School*, 102 Colum. L. Rev. 1441, 1443 (2002) (internal quotation marks omitted).

"believe[d], with Mill and the Swedes, that the principle must work both ways!"[30]

Ginsburg was of course referring to the British philosopher John Stuart Mill. Few works have been as influential in American feminist thought as Mill's 1869 essay, *The Subjection of Women*. The leaders of the women's suffrage movement were ardent proponents of Mill's work, and five decades after women in the United States won the right to vote, Mill's essay became one of the critical texts in the second wave of the women's movement.

The Subjection of Women appealed to feminists in the 1960s and 1970s for the same reason it appalled Mill's contemporaries. Mill contended in his groundbreaking essay that "certainly most, and probably all, of the existing differences of character and intellect between men and women were due to the very different attitudes of society toward members of the two sexes from their earliest infancy."[31] Mill's essay attacked this conventional wisdom with a simple question: If women are naturally inclined toward wife-and-motherhood, why is "the whole of the present constitution of society"[32] aimed at compelling them to adopt these roles?

The greater part of *The Subjection of Women* is devoted to showing that "[w]hat is now called the nature of women is an eminently artificial thing—the result of forced repression in some directions, unnatural stimulation in others."[33] Mill compared the development of "women's nature" to that of a tree, half of which was subjected to the artificial atmosphere of a hothouse: The shoots bathed in light and heat "sprout luxuriantly," while those "left outside in the wintry air, with ice purposely heaped all round them," wither and die of neglect.[34] When men see this malformed tree, Mill argued, they fail to "recognise their own work" and "indolently believe that the tree grows of itself in the way they have made it grow, and that it would die if one half of it were not kept in a vapour bath and the other half in the snow."[35]

---

[30] Letter from Ruth Bader Ginsburg to Jamison Doig, Professor Emeritus of Politics and International Affairs, Princeton Univ. (Apr. 6, 1971) (on file with the Library of Congress, Manuscript Division, Ruth Bader Ginsburg Papers, Container 5, Folder: Moritz v. Comm'r May 1971).

[31] SUSAN MOLLER OKIN, WOMEN IN WESTERN POLITICAL THOUGHT 216 (1979).

[32] JOHN STUART MILL, THE SUBJECTION OF WOMEN 32–33 (Prometheus Books 1986) (1869).

[33] *Id.* at 27.

[34] *Id.*

[35] *Id.*

This was radical, certainly, but perhaps the most radical aspect of Mill's writing on sex equality was that it debunked not only the myth of women's nature, but also the myth of men's nature. Mill argued that manliness, too, was a product of social and economic circumstances: In men, no less than in women, the tree grows in the way we have made it grow.

Mill's denaturalization of traditional sex roles profoundly influenced Ginsburg's thinking about equal protection. But his work wasn't the only factor underlying her decision to challenge sex discrimination using male plaintiffs. Mill recognized that sex discrimination shaped men's lives, but he did not envisage the bachelor caregivers, stay-at-home fathers, and male nurses who populated the ranks of constitutional sex discrimination plaintiffs in the Burger Court era.

Ginsburg frequently noted that her "eyes were first opened to the prospect [of a campaign for sex equality] in Scandinavia in the early 1960's, particularly in Sweden, where the contemporary women's movement started earlier than it did in the United States."[36] Ginsburg's interest in Sweden began in 1961, when she accepted a position researching Swedish law for Columbia Law School's Project on International Procedure.[37] In the course of her work, she learned Swedish, lived intermittently in Sweden, and became an expert on Swedish law.

This was a consequential moment to become immersed in Swedish law and culture, because in 1961, Sweden's approach to sex equality took "a new and unusual turn."[38] The catalyst for this turn was the publication of an article entitled *The Conditional Emancipation of Women* by a young journalist named Eva Moberg.[39] Moberg argued that "[b]oth men and women have *one* principal role, that of being people," and that women would never achieve equality as long as they were expected to pursue two roles while

---

[36] Ruth Bader Ginsburg, Transcript [1979], at 4 (on file with the Library of Congress, Manuscript Division, Ruth Bader Ginsburg Papers, Container 16, Folder: Writings File, Articles 1979); *see also* DAVIDSON, GINSBURG & KAY, *supra* note 26, at 927 (noting that Ginsburg "was awakened to the sex-role debate during visits to Sweden in the early 1960s").

[37] Herma Hill Kay, *Ruth Bader Ginsburg, Professor of Law*, 104 COLUM. L. REV. 2, 10–11 (2004).

[38] Alva Myrdal, *Foreword* to THE CHANGING ROLES OF MEN AND WOMEN 9 (Edmund Dahlström ed., Gunilla Anderman & Steven Anderman trans., Gerald Duckworth & Co. 1967) (1962).

[39] HILDA SCOTT, SWEDEN'S "RIGHT TO BE HUMAN": SEX-ROLE EQUALITY: THE GOAL AND THE REALITY 5 (1982).

men pursued only one.[40] To Ginsburg, who was living in Sweden at the time, it seemed that "[e]very cocktail party in the country . . . was consumed with talk of" Moberg's article,[41] and with the question, "why should a woman have two jobs and the man only have one?"[42] So, Ginsburg recalled: "I began to think of it."[43]

Ginsburg was not the only one who began to think of it. Known as *jämställdhet*, or gender equality, this theory quickly "became the leading ideology of the equality movement" in Sweden.[44] Advocates of *jämställdhet* argued "that imprisonment in the masculine role is at least as great a problem to men as conformity to a feminine ideal is to women" and "that a debate on liberation and equality must be about how men as well as women are forced to act out socially determined stereotypes."[45] This new understanding of equality prompted significant changes in Swedish law and policy, especially after Olof Palme, a prominent adherent of *jämställdhet*, became Prime Minister in 1969.

Palme and other Swedish sex equality advocates argued that a broad agenda of legal and social reforms would be necessary to combat sex-role stereotyping. In 1970, the Swedish Parliament implemented a new national school curriculum, which required schools to "work for equality between the sexes—in the family, on the labour market and within the community as a whole"—not simply by offering the same classes to girls and boys, but also "by counteracting traditional attitudes to sex roles and stimulating pupils to discuss and question the differences which exist between men and women in many fields in respect of influence, jobs and wages."[46]

---

[40] *Id.* (quoting Moberg).

[41] *See* David Von Drehle, *Conventional Roles Hid a Revolutionary Intellect: Discrimination Helped Spawn a Crusade*, WASH. POST, July 18, 1993, at A1.

[42] *Justice Ruth Bader Ginsburg: A "Lady" Who Led the Fight for Gender Equity*, DUKE L. MAG., Spring 2005, at 8 (alterations in original) (quoting Ginsburg), *available at* http://www.law.duke.edu/news/pdf/lawmagspr05.pdf.

[43] *Id.*

[44] Roger Klinth, *The Man and the Equal Family: A Study of the New Images of Masculinity in the Educational Radio and TV Programmes in Sweden, 1946–1971*, *in* STATE POLICY AND GENDER SYSTEM IN THE TWO GERMAN STATES AND SWEDEN, 1945–1989, at 169, 191 (Rolf Torstendahl ed., 1999).

[45] SCOTT, *supra* note 39, at 43.

[46] Läroplan för grundskolan [Curriculum for the Basic School] (Stockholm 1969), *quoted in* Ingrid Fredriksson, *Sex Roles and Education*, 19 INT'L REV. EDUC. 64, 70 (1973).

To combat discrimination against working women, Palme's government vastly increased the availability of daycare.[47] In 1974, it guaranteed the right to abortion,[48] and it introduced a parental leave system permitting fathers as well as mothers to take paid leave after the birth of a child, making Sweden the first country in the world to offer paid parental leave to men.[49] The government required recipients of certain government grants to hire roughly equal numbers of male and female employees, provided grants to employers who trained employees for sex-atypical jobs, and mandated that schoolchildren visit job sites in fields in which their sex was underrepresented.[50] Affirmative action programs designed to desegregate the workforce were opened to members of both sexes.[51] The government even began to consider how planning and zoning and public transportation networks could be redesigned to make it easier for everyone to combine work and family.[52]

Jämställdhet was premised on the belief that the subordination of women would continue as long as men were required to behave in traditionally masculine ways and that major social reform was required to liberate both sexes from prescriptive sex stereotyping. It was this anti-stereotyping philosophy that inspired Ginsburg to represent male plaintiffs. Because the "latter twentieth-century sex-equality movement [was] not peculiar to the United States,"[53] Ginsburg believed it made sense for American courts and advocates to consult legal traditions other than their own in thinking about what equal protection requires.[54] To this end, she included the text of a

---

[47] Jonas Hinnfors, *Swedish Parties and Family Policies, 1960–1980: Stability Through Change*, *in* State Policy, *supra* note 44, at 105.

[48] *See* Mary Ann Glendon, Abortion and Divorce in Western Law 22–23 (1987).

[49] Linda Haas, Equal Parenthood and Social Policy: A Study of Parental Leave in Sweden 14 (1992); Ruth Bader Ginsburg, *Introduction* to *The Status of Women*, 20 Am. J. Comp. L. 585, 590 n.25 (1972).

[50] Haas, *supra* note 49, at 27–28; Scott, *supra* note 39, at 25.

[51] Annika Baude, *Public Policy and Changing Family Patterns in Sweden, 1930–1977*, *in* Sex Roles and Social Policy: A Complex Social Science Equation 145, 149–52 (Jean Lipman-Blumen & Jessie Bernard eds., 1979).

[52] *See* Olof Palme, The Emancipation of Man, Address Before the Women's National Democratic Club (June 8, 1970), *in* Davidson, Ginsburg & Kay, *supra* note 26, at 944.

[53] Ginsburg, Transcript, *supra* note 36, at 4.

[54] *See, e.g.*, *A Conversation with Justice Ruth Bader Ginsburg*, 53 U. Kan. L. Rev. 957, 960 (2005) ("[W]hen our Constitution was composed, the brilliant men who wrote it looked abroad, to other systems, other thinkers. I don't think they meant to stop us from getting whatever enlightenment we can by looking beyond our borders."); Ruth Bader Ginsburg &

speech by Olof Palme, entitled "The Emancipation of Man," in her 1974 casebook,[55] and frequently cited it in law review articles and lectures.[56] She took key phrases and concepts in her briefs directly from this speech.[57] Her landmark brief in *Reed v. Reed* drew not only on "The Emancipation of Man," but also on the work of prominent Swedish sociologists and the 1968 *Report to the United Nations on the Status of Women in Sweden*, which she described as "a progress report indicating a pace more rapid than that of the United States."[58]

B. The "Revolt Against Sex-Role Structure" in the United States

Sweden may have embraced these ideas more rapidly than other countries, but anti-stereotyping philosophy was not limited to its borders. Social movements in the United States had begun to think in similar terms in the years prior to Ginsburg's campaign.

The civil rights movement in the United States had long argued that racial stereotyping curtailed the opportunities of racial minorities and helped to justify racial stratification.[59] In the 1960s, civil rights and women's rights advocate Pauli Murray began to apply these insights in the context of sex. Murray drew on the work of Swedish social scientist Gunnar Myrdal to expose the overlapping "myths built up to perpetuate the inferior status of women and of Negroes."[60] Both groups were widely thought to

---

Deborah Jones Merritt, *Affirmative Action: An International Human Rights Dialogue*, 21 Cardozo L. Rev. 253, 282 (1999) ("In my view, comparative analysis emphatically *is* relevant to the task of interpreting constitutions and enforcing human rights.").

[55] Davidson, Ginsburg & Kay, *supra* note 26, at 938.

[56] *See, e.g.*, Ginsburg, *supra* note 27, at 1; Ginsburg, *supra* note 49, at 589; Ruth Bader Ginsburg, *Treatment of Women by the Law: Awakening Consciousness in the Law Schools*, 5 Val. U. L. Rev. 480, 480 n.3 (1971).

[57] Palme's influence is particularly evident in Ginsburg's discussions of "double-edged discrimination." Palme's phrase "one-eyed sex-role-thinking" also appears often in the WRP's briefs. *See, e.g.*, Brief for Appellee at 45, Califano v. Goldfarb, 430 U.S. 199 (1977) (No. 75-699); Brief for Appellee at 18 n.11, Weinberger v. Wiesenfeld, 420 U.S. 636 (1975) (No. 73-1892); Brief for Appellants at 8, Kahn v. Shevin, 416 U.S. 351 (1974) (No. 73-78).

[58] Brief for Appellant at 15 n.11, 55 n.52, Reed v. Reed, 404 U.S. 71 (1971) (No. 70-4).

[59] Franklin, *supra* note 1, at 105–08.

[60] Pauli Murray & Mary O. Eastwood, *Jane Crow and the Law: Sex Discrimination and Title VII*, 34 Geo. Wash. L. Rev. 232, 234 (1965). Ginsburg too used Myrdal's work to show that

have "'inferior endowments in most of those respects which carry prestige, power, and advantages in society,'" but to be superior in the narrow set of roles to which they had been assigned.[61] Murray argued that these stereotyped judgments served to cement a social order that delimited opportunity on the basis of race and sex: "'As the Negro was awarded his 'place' in society, so there was a 'woman's place.'"[62]

As in Sweden, feminists who sought to liberate women from the enforcement of traditional sex stereotypes understood it would take more than formal equality. In 1970, the National Organization for Women (NOW; founded by Pauli Murray, Betty Friedan, and others) organized the Women's Strike for Equality, a mass demonstration staged in 40 cities across the United States.[63] The strike was intended to illustrate that "it was not possible to secure equality for women without fundamental changes in family life,"[64] and that such changes could not occur without policies designed to alleviate the pressure on women to conform to traditional roles. To this end, the strikers sought "to publicize three core movement claims: (1) free abortion on demand, (2) free 24-hour childcare centers, and (3) equal opportunity in jobs and education."[65] Reproductive rights and childcare were essential, the movement argued, because equal opportunity would remain elusive as long as women were expected to subordinate all other activities to the care of home and family.[66]

---

sex-based equal protection arguments drew on the claims of the civil rights movement and were founded on principles deeply rooted in American law. *See, e.g.*, Ginsburg, *supra* note 27, at 2–3.

[61] Murray, *supra* note 60 (quoting Gunnar Myrdal, An American Dilemma 1077 (2d ed. 1962)).

[62] *Id.*

[63] Robert C. Post & Reva B. Siegel, *Legislative Constitutionalism and Section Five Power: Policentric Interpretation of the Family and Medical Leave Act*, 112 Yale L.J. 1943, 1988–89 (2003).

[64] *Id.* at 1992.

[65] *Id.* at 1989 (internal quotation marks omitted).

[66] For this reason, NOW's 1967 Task Force on the Family urged the repeal of all laws restricting women's right to abortion, and argued that "[i]f women are to participate on an equitable basis with men in the world of work and of community service, child-care facilities must become as much a part of our community facilities as parks and libraries are." Nat'l Org. for Women, Task Force on the Family (1967), *reprinted in* Feminist Chronicles, 1953–1993, at 201, 201–02 (Toni Carabillo, et al., eds., 1993).

American feminists also argued that women would never have true choice of lifestyles if men were not afforded the same choice. NOW's founding Statement of Purpose rejected "current assumptions that a man must carry the sole burden of supporting himself, his wife, and family, and that . . . marriage, home and family are primarily woman's world and responsibility—hers, to dominate—his to support."[67] It advocated instead a "true partnership between the sexes" based on "an equitable sharing of the responsibilities of home and children."[68] Within a few years of its founding, NOW had convened the Task Force on the Masculine Mystique. The Task Force found that neither sex could escape the confines of the sex-role system without "a breakdown in job segregation by sex; workplace and state policies that supported men's sharing of child care equally with women; [and] changes in education and media to undermine sex role stereotyping."[69]

By the early 1970s, these ideas had begun to garner wider attention. There was "an enthusiastic . . . rebirth of interest" in "[s]ex roles and sex typing" among American social scientists in this period.[70] Sociologist Sandra Bem developed the influential Bem Sex-Role Inventory, which suggested that conformity to traditional sex roles might not be the desideratum of healthy psychological development for men or women.[71] In 1975, the journal *Sex Roles* was founded to meet the growing demand for original research on sex stereotyping and sex-role socialization.[72] By 1973 (the year the Court decided *Frontiero v. Richardson* in favor of a female Air Force officer and her financially dependent husband), even Dr. Spock—whose best-selling baby guide had long instructed parents to help their children conform to traditional sex roles—had begun to reconsider his stance. In an article in *Redbook*, he declared that caring for children was a job for men too, and

---

[67] NAT'L ORG. FOR WOMEN, STATEMENT OF PURPOSE (1966), reprinted in FEMINIST CHRONICLES, *supra* note 66, at 159, 162.

[68] *Id.* at 162–63.

[69] Michael A. Messner, *The Limits of "The Male Sex Role": An Analysis of the Men's Liberation and Men's Rights Movements' Discourse*, 12 GENDER & SOC. 255, 263 (1998).

[70] Jeffrey A. Kelly & Judith Worell, *New Formulations of Sex Roles and Androgyny: A Critical Review*, 45 J. CONSULTING & CLINICAL PSYCHOL. 1101, 1101 (1977).

[71] Sandra L. Bem, *The Measurement of Psychological Androgyny*, 42 CONSULTING & CLINICAL PSYCHOL. 155 (1974).

[72] For graphs depicting the astronomical growth in sex-role research in the 1970s, see Tim Carrigan, Bob Connell & John Lee, *Toward a New Sociology of Masculinity*, 14 THEORY & SOC'Y 551, 557–58 (1985).

that the new edition of his guide would underscore this idea by referring to parents using gender-neutral pronouns.[73]

Dr. Spock's embrace of gender-neutral pronouns points up an additional facet of the development of anti-stereotyping theory in the United States—its implications for sexual orientation and gender identity. In 1973, the same year Dr. Spock reported a change in his thinking, the American Psychiatric Association (APA) announced a far more significant, but not unrelated, change in its stance on healthy psychological development and adherence to traditional gender norms. The APA announced in 1973 that it would eliminate homosexuality from the list of mental illnesses in the Diagnostic and Statistical Manual of Mental Disorders.[74] As with many of the developments discussed above, this change occurred as a result of social movement activism, in this case by the gay and lesbian liberation groups that emerged in full force after the 1969 raid on the Stonewall Inn. These groups argued that deviation from traditional gender norms was not pathological—that, in fact, the pathology resided in the laws and social structures that enforced these norms. A primary aim of gay and lesbian liberation in this period was to show that sex with someone of the same sex bore a family resemblance to other sex-role transgressions—including the kind recently deemed acceptable by America's most famous pediatrician—and that true sex equality entailed freedom from sex stereotyping in *all* its guises.

"Gay liberation is a struggle against sexism," declared one of the first gay manifestos published in the wake of Stonewall.[75] "[S]exism," declared another, is "the founding oppression—the original inequality."[76] This diagnosis echoed throughout the writing of gay, lesbian, and bisexual activists

---

[73] Benjamin Spock, *How My Ideas About Women Have Changed*, REDBOOK, Nov. 1973, at 29, 34.

[74] *See* AM. PSYCHIATRIC ASS'N, HOMOSEXUALITY AND SEXUAL ORIENTATION DISTURBANCE: PROPOSED CHANGE TO DSM-II 2-3 (6th prtg. 1973).

[75] Allen Young, *Out of the Closet: A Gay Manifesto* (abr.), RAMPARTS, Nov. 1971, *reprinted as Out of the Closets, Into the Streets*, *in* OUT OF THE CLOSETS: VOICES OF GAY LIBERATION 6, 7 (KARLA JAY & ALLEN YOUNG EDS., 1972).

[76] Third World Gay Revolution & Gay Liberation Front, *Gay Revolution and Sex Roles*, CHICAGO GAY PRIDE, June 1971, *reprinted in* OUT OF THE CLOSETS, *supra* note 75, at 252, 258–59; *see also* John D'Emilio, *Foreword* to OUT OF THE CLOSETS, *supra* note 75, at xi, xix, xxi (noting that "gay liberationists . . . saw the battle against sexism as the very heart of their struggle" and that "[a]gain and again, in their articles, their manifestos, and their political fliers, these pioneering radicals turned to the same point: sexism").

who emerged in large numbers at the start of the 1970s.[77] Heterosexual and homosexual were salient categories, they argued, only because society differentiated so sharply between men and women: "[T]he imprisoning, artificial labels of gay, straight, and bi would be meaningless without the sex roles and 'correct gender identification' . . . that sexism imposes."[78] If homosexuality was defined as sexual desire for someone of the "wrong" sex, then laws regulating homosexuality were quite literally sexist, in the sense that they discriminated on the basis of sex. But the argument ran deeper than this. Gay and lesbian activists observed that a "'real man' and 'real woman' are not so by their chromosomes and genitals, but by their respective degrees of 'masculinity' and 'femininity,' and by how closely they follow the sex-role script in their relationships with individuals and society."[79] They noted that people who deviated from this script in any way (female construction workers, feminine men) were labeled "dyke," "faggot," and "queer." These labels were used to keep people in check, to deter them from "cross[ing] the terrible boundary" between male and female.[80]

Like American feminists in this period, supporters of gay and lesbian liberation extended their critique into the home, where traditional role divisions began to funnel boys and girls into separate spheres as soon as they were born. An influential 1971 essay entitled *Gay Revolution and Sex Roles* argued that "[t]he oppression of women and that of gay people are interdependent and spring from the same roots, but take different forms"[81]: Women are oppressed by how they fit into the traditional family structure; gay people are oppressed because they don't fit into this structure.

Part II shows how Ruth Bader Ginsburg drew on the anti-stereotyping arguments animating these movements in the early 1970s to challenge the

---

[77] Anti-stereotyping arguments were an important strand in LGBT liberation discourse in this period, but there were other strands as well. Gay liberation groups "saw themselves as one component of the decade's radicalism and regularly addressed the other issues that were mobilizing American youth," including racism, poverty, war, and global injustice. JOHN D'EMILIO, SEXUAL POLITICS, SEXUAL COMMUNITIES: THE MAKING OF A HOMOSEXUAL MINORITY IN THE UNITED STATES, 1940–1970, at 234 (2d ed. 1998).

[78] Third World Gay Revolution, *supra* note 75, at 258; *see also* RADICALESBIANS, THE WOMAN IDENTIFIED WOMAN (1970), *reprinted in* OUT OF THE CLOSETS, *supra* note 75, at 172, 173 (arguing that homosexuality is "a by-product of a particular way of setting up roles . . . on the basis of sex").

[79] Third World Gay Revolution, *supra* note 75, at 252.

[80] RADICALESBIANS, *supra* note 75, at 173.

[81] Third World Gay Liberation, *supra* note 75, at 254–55.

constitutionality of sex-based state action. Ginsburg cited gains made by movements for sex equality as evidence of a marked transformation in popular attitudes toward sex discrimination. But she did not cite these movements simply as evidence of social change. She used their arguments to develop a new theory of equal protection—one that addressed the particular mechanisms and forms of injury associated with sex-based state action.

II. The Development of Anti-Stereotyping Doctrine

When legal feminists in the 1960s and 1970s decided to challenge the constitutionality of sex-based state action, they faced two interlocking problems. First, up to this point, the Court's conception of discrimination had been forged primarily in the context of race. Pauli Murray drew important parallels between sex discrimination and race discrimination and showed how these forces interacted to doubly disempower Black women.[82] But in many instances, sex discrimination assumed a different shape than race discrimination: Women attended gender-integrated public schools, ate in gender-integrated restaurants, and lived in the same houses and neighborhoods as men. The fact that the subordination of women did not always or even primarily take the form of segregation presented sex equality advocates with a related problem: "Men holding elected and appointed offices generally considered themselves good husbands and fathers."[83] They believed their wives and daughters were well served by the status quo and viewed the law's "differential treatment of men and women not as malign, but as operating benignly in women's favor."[84]

Anti-stereotyping arguments were designed to combat this problem. Anti-stereotyping arguments enabled Ginsburg to foreground the state's enforcement of the male breadwinner–female caregiver model—a model that was not visible in the canonical race discrimination cases but had long entrenched women's secondary status. These arguments also provided an antidote to the "benign" discrimination problem. Ginsburg was wary of grounding her theory of equal protection solely in an anti-subordination

---

[82] *See, e.g.*, Pauli Murray, *Negro Women's Stake in the Equal Rights Amendment*, 6 HARV. C.R.-C.L. L. REV. 253, 255 (1971).

[83] Ginsburg, *supra* note 29, at 1442.

[84] *Id.*

principle. That principle, by itself, could not necessarily tell (historically paternalistic) courts which forms of regulation inflict gender-based harm, and Ginsburg was profoundly skeptical of the Justices' ability to "know[] [it] when [they] see it."[85] The anti-stereotyping principle helped to focus attention on the particular set of practices through which sex had been "made the groundwork of an inequality of legal right, and a forced dissimilarity of social functions."[86]

Social movements deploying anti-stereotyping arguments in the 1970s had numerous aims, but Ginsburg's project was a distinctly legal one: To crystallize a *mediating principle* that would give "meaning and content to an ideal embodied in the text" of the Equal Protection Clause.[87] The anti-stereotyping principle provided a "guide for decision"[88] that courts and other legal actors could understand and implement. It allowed Ginsburg to focus the Court's attention on a particular set of laws and social practices that had contributed in deep and sustained ways to the oppression of women. It was also sufficiently capacious to cover other forms of sex-role enforcement, as courts' understanding of which laws and social practices enforce sex stereotypes evolved over time. This was a signal advantage of the anti-stereotyping principle, but it was also a liability. Opponents of the women's movement used the potentially far-reaching implications of the anti-stereotyping principle in controversial domains such as abortion and same-sex marriage to attack the entire antidiscrimination project in the context of sex.

This Part will show how Ginsburg persuaded the Court to adopt the anti-stereotyping principle and why it remained cabined within such narrow doctrinal parameters in the 1970s.

A. "The Traditional Division Within the Home"

Ginsburg's first male plaintiff was Charles Moritz, a sexagenarian book editor and life-long bachelor who lived with and cared for his ailing mother in Denver. Moritz's troubles began when he took a deduction on his 1968

[85] Ginsburg, *supra* note 27, at 15 (paraphrasing Justice Stewart's famous observation about obscenity in *Jacobellis v. Ohio*, 378 U.S. 184, 197 (1964) (Stewart, J., concurring)).

[86] John Stuart Mill, Principles of Political Economy, in 3 Collected Works of John Stuart Mill 765 (Univ. of Toronto Press 1965) (1848).

[87] Owen M. Fiss, *Groups and the Equal Protection Clause*, 5 Phil. & Pub. Aff. 107, 107 (1976).

[88] *Id.* at 108.

federal income tax return for expenses related to his mother's care. Although he was otherwise qualified for the deduction, which was intended to help family caregivers, the IRS determined Moritz was ineligible because of his sex. When Ginsburg learned of Moritz's predicament, she volunteered to represent him pro bono, judging his case "as neat a craft as one could find to test sex-based discrimination against the Constitution."[89]

The government's refusal to extend to bachelors the family caregiving incentives it granted to single women perfectly illustrated the point sex equality advocates were making in this period: Laws and customs that steer men out of the domestic sphere reinforce restrictions on women's participation in the public sphere, and the maintenance of such role divisions perpetuates long-standing inequalities between the sexes. The fact that the government was responsible for the role enforcement in this case enabled Ginsburg to transform popular anti-stereotyping arguments into sex-based equal protection arguments. She began, in *Moritz*, to construct a theory of equal protection that would bar the state from acting in ways that perpetuate traditional sex and family roles.

Ginsburg argued in her brief in *Moritz* that Congress's assumption that bachelors lack caregiving responsibilities, and the financial penalty it imposed on those who did shoulder such responsibilities, provided a striking illustration of the way in which the government entrenched traditional roles in the family—using carrots and sticks to steer men and women into the male breadwinner–female caregiver paradigm. Although Ginsburg's client was a man, her brief focused as much on women as on men. Her goal was to demonstrate how "sex-role pigeonholing"[90] preserved traditional role divisions in the family and forced women to assume caregiving roles. In fact, when Ginsburg learned of *Reed v. Reed*, a contemporaneous sex discrimination case featuring a female plaintiff protesting sex-role-enforcing state action, she devised a plan to present both cases to the Supreme Court at the same time. By pairing the cases, Ginsburg hoped to show the Court that equality for women would remain a distant goal as long as men were

[89] Letter from Ruth Bader Ginsburg, Professor of Law, Rutgers Univ. Sch. of Law, to Melvin L. Wulf, Legal Dir., ACLU (Nov. 17, 1970) (on file with the Library of Congress, Manuscript Division, Ruth Bader Ginsburg Papers, Container 5, Folder: Moritz v. Comm'r 1967–1970).

[90] Ruth Bader Ginsburg, *Women's Right to Full Participation in Shaping Society's Course: An Evolving Constitutional Precept*, in TOWARD THE SECOND DECADE: THE IMPACT OF THE WOMEN'S MOVEMENT ON AMERICAN INSTITUTIONS 176 (Betty Justice & Renate Pore eds., 1981).

deterred from pursuing traditionally female activities, and that equal protection barred the state from prescribing sex roles for either sex.

Ginsburg incorporated much of the material from her *Moritz* brief into her brief in *Reed*, which became known as the "grandmother brief." Her goal in the "grandmother brief" was to show how vast numbers of laws and policies contributed to a broader pattern of sex-role enforcement that associated men with the marketplace and women with the home. In sections entitled "Male as head of household" and "Women and the role of motherhood," she asserted that "[t]he traditional division within the home—father decides, mother nurtures—is reinforced by diverse provisions of state law."[91] She tried to show the Court that vast swathes of regulation long considered natural and benign helped to prop up a sex-role system that trapped both sexes in conventional roles and sharply curtailed women's freedom and equality.

In the end, Ginsburg's plan to present the cases to the Court simultaneously was thwarted. The Tenth Circuit sat on *Moritz* until after the Court decided *Reed*. Both cases resulted in historic victories for the plaintiffs. But the fact that the Court wrote only a very terse opinion in *Reed*, and didn't hear *Moritz*, left it unclear how fully the Justices had embraced Ginsburg's anti-stereotyping arguments.

B. The "Most Spectacular of the Court's Gender Discrimination Decisions"

Ginsburg always contended that *Weinberger v. Wiesenfeld*[92] was the "most critical"[93] of the foundational sex discrimination cases. Stephen Wiesenfeld came to Ginsburg's attention in 1972 when he wrote a letter to his local newspaper protesting sex discrimination in the Social Security system.[94] Wiesenfeld explained that he and his wife had "assumed reverse roles": She

---

[91] Brief for Appellant, *supra* note 58, at 32–35.

[92] 420 U.S. 636 (1975).

[93] Ruth Bader Ginsburg, *Interpretations of the Equal Protection Clause*, 9 HARV. J.L. & PUB. POL'Y 41, 43 (1986); *see also*, *e.g.*, Ruth Bader Ginsburg, *Remarks on Women Becoming Part of the Constitution*, 6 LAW & INEQ 17, 22 (1988) (referring to *Wiesenfeld* as "one of the key cases in the evolution of the Supreme Court's current approach").

[94] *See* Stephen Wiesenfeld, Letter to the Editor, *Social Security Inequality*, THE HOME NEWS (NEW BRUNSWICK), Nov. 27, 1972 (on file with the Library of Congress, Manuscript Division, Ruth Bader Ginsburg Papers, Container 10, Folder: Weinberger v. Wiesenfeld 1972–1973).

was the primary breadwinner, he was dependent on her earnings.[95] When his wife died giving birth to their first child, Wiesenfeld applied for "mother's benefits," a form of assistance designed to enable widows to stay home with their children after the death of the family breadwinner.[96] His application was denied on the basis of sex.

One of the chief obstacles Ginsburg confronted in this case was the incredulity and discomfort her client's desire for "mother's benefits" aroused in the government's lawyers. Her opposing counsel at trial argued that Wiesenfeld lacked standing to sue because it defied credibility to suggest that a man would choose to stay home with a baby instead of going to work.[97] At the Supreme Court, Solicitor General Robert Bork raised similar questions about the genuineness of Wiesenfeld's desire to act as a "mother." Bork implied that with "three university degrees,"[98] Wiesenfeld was perfectly capable of supporting himself and would not forego career opportunities to stay home with a baby. Bork mistakenly informed the Court that Wiesenfeld had been dependent on his wife because he was enrolled in school—an error Ginsburg was quick to cite as evidence of "the tenacity of one-eyed sex-role thinking."[99] Ginsburg argued that the government's repeated insinuations that her client's time was too valuable to be spent taking care of a baby indicated that it viewed childcare as a fine activity for women but a degrading one for men. She argued that such judgments, particularly when enforced by the state, operated to keep both sexes in their place and thus deprived them of equal protection.

---

[95] *Id.*

[96] *Id.*

[97] *See* Transcript of Oral Argument at 28–32, 60, Wiesenfeld v. Sec'y of Health, Educ. & Welfare, 367 F. Supp. 981 (D.N.J. 1973) (No. 268-73) (on file with the Library of Congress, Manuscript Division, Ruth Bader Ginsburg Papers, Container 10, Folder: Weinberger v. Wiesenfeld 1973) ("[T]hey say that men, of course, will work. Mr. Wiesenfeld will, of course, continue working, says the defendant, although we will debate that."); *see also* Memorandum from Richard Blumenthal, Law Clerk, to Justice Harry A. Blackmun 8 (Dec. 23, 1974) (on file with the Library of Congress, Manuscript Division, Harry A. Blackmun Papers, Box 203, Folder 6, Weinberger v. Wiesenfeld) (advising the Justice that "[a] question should be raised at oral argument as to whether appellee is continuing to receive these benefits, or whether he has [returned to work]").

[98] Brief for Appellant at 4, Weinberger v. Wiesenfeld, 420 U.S. 636 (1975) (No. 73-1892).

[99] Brief for Appellee at 18 n.11, Wiesenfeld, 420 U.S. 636 (1975) (No. 73-1892). The expression "one-eyed sex-role thinking" was Olof Palme's. *See supra* note 57.

By 1975, Ginsburg had been presenting anti-stereotyping arguments to the Court for nearly five years. Her efforts were rewarded in *Wiesenfeld*, which held that the restriction of "mother's benefits" to women violated the constitutional rights of *both* sexes.[100] The Court explained in its opinion that discrimination "that results in the efforts of female workers . . . producing less protection for their families than is produced by the efforts of men"[101] is not a boon to women: The government restricted "mother's benefits" to women not to compensate them for discrimination in the labor market, as the Solicitor General contended, but "because it believed that they should not be required to work"[102]—and that men should be. The Court held that the Fourteenth Amendment prohibited laws motivated by this kind of stereotyping. Such stereotyping denigrated the efforts of working women and it denigrated the domestic contributions of men like Stephen Wiesenfeld, who "was dependent upon his wife for his support"[103] and had made the gender-nonconforming choice to stay home with his son. The Court ruled that the state had no legitimate interest in trying to force the plaintiff to assume a breadwinning role.[104] In fact, the Court asserted that, in the absence of sex-role enforcement, even men "in the typical family" might choose to stay home with their children and the Fourteenth Amendment barred the state from deciding that these men "would, or should be required to, continue to work."[105]

The idea that men might assume the role of mothers, and that the Constitution protected their right to do so, was mind-boggling to some of the Justices. When Justice Brennan, who wrote for the Court in *Wiesenfeld*, circulated his opinion, Justice Blackmun annotated the passages about stay-at-home fathers with question marks and exclamation points (Brennan's suggestion that Stephen Wiesenfeld "may well have" stayed home with his son even if his wife had lived elicited a "WOW!").[106] Despite his surprise,

---

[100] 420 U.S. 636 (1975).

[101] *Id.* at 645.

[102] *Id.* at 650.

[103] *Id.* at 645.

[104] *Id.* at 651–52.

[105] *Id.*

[106] William J. Brennan, Second Draft of Opinion of the Court, Weinberger v. Wiesenfeld (circulated Mar. 1975) (on file with the Library of Congress, Manuscript Division, Harry A. Blackmun Papers, Box 203, Folder 6, Weinberger v. Wiesenfeld).

however, Blackmun signed on. Justices Powell, Burger, and Rehnquist had stronger reservations. Justice Powell wrote a concurring opinion, joined by the Chief Justice, arguing that the Court should have treated *Wiesenfeld* as a simple equal pay case: The statute was unconstitutional because it deprived working women of benefits that accrued to working men.[107] Powell argued that there was no need for the Court to condone the plaintiff's departure from masculine gender norms.[108] The statute permitted recipients to earn a small amount of money, so extending "mother's benefits" to men did not necessarily imply that it was acceptable for them to "forgo work and remain at home to care for children."[109] Behind the scenes, Powell admitted that he found the thought of men receiving "mother's benefits" repulsive. He fretted to his law clerk that the Court's decision would induce "a high level of indolence" and swell "the ever increasing welfare rolls" as men quit their jobs to stay home with their kids.[110]

Despite Powell's reservations, the idea that laws that reflect or reinforce traditional sex stereotypes violate equal protection soon became doctrine. In *Stanton v. Stanton*, the Court invalidated a Utah statute that terminated parental obligations to girls at 18 but required parents to support boys until they turned 21.[111] The state claimed that the law simply reflected the fact that girls leave school and marry at a younger age than boys. But the Court held that the law reinforced sex stereotypes: "[I]f the female is not to be supported so long as the male, she hardly can be expected to attend school as long as he does, and bringing her education to an end earlier coincides with the role-typing society has long imposed."[112] Four years later, in *Orr v.*

---

[107] *Wiesenfeld*, 420 U.S. at 654–55 (Powell, J., concurring). Justice Rehnquist advocated a similarly formalistic approach. *Id.* at 655 (Rehnquist, J., concurring in the result).

[108] *Id.* at 654 (Powell, J., concurring) ("It is immaterial whether the surviving parent elects to assume primary child care responsibility rather than work, or whether other arrangements are made for child care.").

[109] *Id.*

[110] Memorandum from Julia "Penny" Clark, Law Clerk, to Justice Lewis F. Powell, Jr. 3 (Jan. 17, 1975) (on file with the Washington and Lee University School of Law, Lewis F. Powell, Jr. Papers, Supreme Court Case Files, Powell Archives, 73-1892 Weinberger v. Wiesenfeld), *quoted in* SERENA MAYERI, REASONING FROM RACE: FEMINISM, LAW, AND THE CIVIL RIGHTS REVOLUTION 123 n.99 (2011).

[111] 421 U.S. 7 (1975).

[112] *Id.* at 14–15.

Orr,[113] the Court struck down Alabama's rule that husbands but not wives could be required to pay alimony on the ground that such rules "effectively announc[ed] the State's preference for an allocation of family responsibilities under which the wife plays a dependent role."[114] The Court held that equal protection precludes the state from seeking to "reinforce[] . . . that model among [its] citizens."[115] Similarly, in 1982, the Court held that Mississippi's exclusion of men from a state nursing school violated the Fourteenth Amendment because it "lends credibility to the old view that women, not men, should become nurses, and makes the assumption that nursing is a field for women a self-fulfilling prophecy."[116] Ginsburg did not bring any of these cases. Over time, and as a result of her campaign, anti-stereotyping had become ingrained in the Court's own understanding of equal protection.[117]

C. Limits and Loopholes in the Court's Application of Anti-Stereotyping Doctrine

The Court's adoption of anti-stereotyping doctrine did not result in the immediate eradication of all sex-role-enforcing state action. As with all constitutional doctrines, the Court's application of anti-stereotyping doctrine was influenced by social norms and ideologies. These influences were particularly apparent in the Burger Court's failure to extend anti-stereotyping doctrine into the realms of reproductive and LGBT rights. Legal feminists and other progressives were frustrated in the 1980s by the limits of constitutional sex discrimination law. As this section shows, however, those limits were not inherent in the doctrine the Court adopted. Anti-stereotyping doctrine directly implicated reproductive and LGBT rights.

---

[113] 440 U.S. 268 (1979).

[114] *Id.* at 279.

[115] *Id.*

[116] Miss. Univ. for Women v. Hogan, 458 U.S. 718, 730 (1982).

[117] Intermediate scrutiny doctrine, which emerged in tandem with the anti-stereotyping principle, dictates that sex-based state action is constitutional only when it "serve[s] important governmental objectives" and is "substantially related to achievement of those objectives." Craig v. Boren, 429 U.S. 190, 197 (1976). The anti-stereotyping principle pervades both stages of this inquiry, shaping what constitutes an important governmental interest and what means qualify as sufficiently narrowly tailored to serve this interest. Since this test was introduced in 1976, the Court has never upheld a sex classification after determining that it reflects or reinforces sex stereotypes.

In fact, Ginsburg had planned in one of her very first cases to demonstrate how the curtailment of reproductive rights violates equal protection. Not long after *Reed*, she began work on a case that perfectly illustrated "the sex equality dimension of laws and regulations regarding pregnancy and childbirth."[118] The case, *Struck v. Secretary of Defense*,[119] concerned an Air Force regulation mandating the immediate discharge of any female officer upon a determination that she was pregnant or had given birth to a live child. Ginsburg's client, Susan Struck, was an Air Force captain who became pregnant while serving in Vietnam. The Air Force encouraged Struck to have an abortion and thereby preserve her job, but she preferred, for religious reasons, to continue her pregnancy and to place the child for adoption after it was born.[120] Although Struck used only accumulated leave time to cover the period in which she gave birth, and was ready to return to work shortly thereafter, the Air Force ordered her discharge.[121]

Ginsburg argued that this mandatory discharge policy was "more a manifestation of cultural sex role conditioning than a response to medical fact and necessity."[122] If Struck had broken a limb or developed a drug addiction, the Air Force would have granted her convalescent leave and rehabilitative services, and allowed her to use accumulated leave time to extend her recovery period before returning to active duty. Among medical conditions, pregnancy alone triggered mandatory discharge, even though the physical disability it entailed was briefer and less serious than numerous other disabilities that routinely afflicted Americans serving in Vietnam. It was not pregnancy, but pregnancy discrimination and policies limiting reproductive choice that truly disabled Captain Struck.

Ginsburg argued that the Air Force's treatment of pregnancy stemmed from its "thinly veil[ed]"[123] preference for the male breadwinner–female caregiver model. The same set of regulations that mandated the discharge of pregnant women and new mothers granted men a generous array of additional benefits to encourage them to remain in the service when they became

[118] Ginsburg, *supra* note 29, at 1447.

[119] 409 U.S. 1071 (1972).

[120] Brief for the Petitioner at 56, Struck v. Sec'y of Def., 409 U.S. 1071 (1972) (No. 72-178).

[121] *Id.* at 4–5.

[122] *Id.* at 35 n.28 (quoting Heath v. Westerville Bd. of Educ., 345 F. Supp. 501, 505–06 n.1 (S.D. Ohio 1972) (internal quotation marks omitted)).

[123] *Id.* at 55.

fathers.[124] Ginsburg observed that the mandatory discharge policy punished poor women—especially poor single women—by depriving them of essential prenatal care and threatening them with destitution.[125] The policy also adversely affected wealthier women, as it "reinforce[d] societal pressure to relinquish career aspirations for a hearth-centered existence."[126]

The Court never heard these arguments. At the eleventh hour, the Air Force granted Struck a waiver and the case disappeared from the Court's docket.[127] This turn of events would prove highly consequential, because it meant that the Court would confront the constitutionality of abortion regulation in *Roe v. Wade*, in 1973, prior to its adoption of anti-stereotyping doctrine and in a case that did not frame reproductive rights as a matter of sex equality. The Court held in *Roe* that the Fourteenth Amendment guaranteed the right to abortion. But it grounded its holding in the Due Process Clause and did not consider how abortion regulation might reflect or reinforce traditional sex stereotypes.

The disappearance of *Struck* meant that the Court also heard *Geduldig v. Aiello*[128] prior to the development of anti-stereotyping doctrine. *Geduldig* involved a Fourteenth Amendment challenge to a provision exempting normal pregnancy disability from coverage under California's otherwise comprehensive disability insurance system. Six Justices concluded that California's denial of coverage to pregnant women did not warrant special scrutiny because pregnancy was a "real" difference. Because men and women were differently situated with respect to pregnancy, the state's regulation of pregnancy did not trigger sex-based equal protection concerns.

Reva Siegel has dubbed this kind of thinking "reasoning from the body."[129] She and others have long observed that the Court in *Geduldig* "reason[ed] about reproductive regulation in physiological paradigms, as a form of state action that concerns physical facts of sex rather than social questions of gender," causing it to miss the ways in which regulations

---

[124] *Id.* at 55, 67.

[125] *Id.* at 36–37.

[126] *Id.* at 37.

[127] Struck v. Sec'y of Def., 409 U.S. 1071, 1071 (1972).

[128] 417 U.S. 484 (1974).

[129] Reva Siegel, *Reasoning from the Body: A Historical Perspective on Abortion Regulation and Questions of Equal Protection*, 44 Stan. L. Rev. 261, 261 (1992).

respecting "'real' physical difference between the sexes . . . can nevertheless be sexually discriminatory."[130]

It is impossible to know whether the Justices in *Roe* and *Geduldig* would have recognized the powerful sex stereotyping that often attends the regulation of pregnancy if they had heard *Struck*. Perhaps. Or perhaps not: Five of the six Justices in the majority in *Geduldig* were born before women obtained the right to vote (the sixth, Justice Rehnquist, was born just after, in 1924). All of them came of age in an era in which the exclusion of pregnant women and mothers from the public sphere was viewed as entirely natural, an outgrowth of biological difference and a benign reflection of the fact that women's primary calling is to have children and care for their families.

This same attachment to traditional stereotypes about men's and women's roles also contributed to the failure of courts in the 1970s to apply anti-stereotyping doctrine in the context of LGBT rights. Indeed, the strong continuity between women's rights and LGBT rights claims was often used as a cudgel against the women's movement in the 1970s. Phyllis Schlafly, a leading conservative lawyer and activist, frequently emphasized the pro-LGBT implications of feminist claims in order to galvanize opposition to the Equal Rights Amendment (ERA). Chief among Schlafly's arguments against the ERA was that it would destroy the traditional American family, in significant part by outlawing discrimination against homosexuals and granting same-sex couples the right to marry. After all, Schlafly asserted, "[i]t is precisely 'on account of sex' that a state now denies a marriage license to a man and a man, or to a woman and a woman."[131] If the ERA were to pass, she argued, a "homosexual who wants to be a teacher could argue persuasively that to deny him a school job would be discrimination 'on account of sex.'"[132] Schlafly insisted that most Americans would not welcome this prospect. They valued traditional sex roles and believed the law should not protect people who deviated from them.

Schlafly—and contemporaneous LGBT rights advocates—were right that doctrine barring the state from enforcing traditional sex stereotypes cast doubt on the constitutionality of laws that discriminated against people

---

[130] *Id.* at 264–65.

[131] Phyllis Schlafly, The Power of the Positive Woman (1977).

[132] *Id.* at 90.

who failed to conform to traditional gendered expectations with respect to their sexual partners or gender identity. But LGBT people were still regarded by many Americans in the 1970s as social pariahs. Even women's rights advocates in this period generally avoided acknowledging the powerful implications of their arguments for LGBT rights, partly out of fear that the implications of anti-stereotyping doctrine for laws enforcing heterosexuality and cis-genderedness would inhibit the development of women's rights. Judges, however, proved quite capable of developing doctrinal barriers and loopholes that shielded sex-based regulation of gender identity and sexual object choice from the general prohibition on sex stereotyping. (There was no great genius behind these loopholes. For decades, courts basically just asserted that the enforcement of traditional sex stereotypes regarding gender identity and the sex of one's romantic partners were exempt from general prohibitions on sex stereotyping because these regulations were aimed at LGBT people.)

Part III examines how these early limits on the reach of anti-stereotyping doctrine in the contexts of reproductive and LGBT rights eroded as Americans increasingly came to understand the injustice and the illogic of excluding LGBT people and pregnant people from the protection of constitutional sex discrimination law.

III. The Evolution of Anti-Stereotyping Doctrine

Half a century has passed since the Court's adoption of anti-stereotyping doctrine. One of the central features of the law's development over this period has been the erosion of barriers courts erected in the 1970s to shield certain customary and well-accepted forms of regulation from the law's reach.

In 1974, in *Geduldig*, the Court appeared to place the regulation of pregnancy beyond the reach of sex-based equal protection law. But in 1996, in *United States v. Virginia*[133]—in an opinion written by Justice Ginsburg—the Court reasoned very differently about the regulation of pregnancy. The Court observed in *Virginia* that "[p]hysical differences between men and

133 518 U.S. 515 (1996).

women . . . are enduring."[134] But, the Court explained, "we have come to appreciate" that "'[i]nherent differences' between men and women" are "cause for celebration . . . not for denigration of the members of either sex or for artificial constraints on an individual's opportunity."[135] Historically, the Court had granted lawmakers broad leeway to discriminate on the basis of "real differences," such as pregnancy. But in *Virginia*, the Court held that:

> [even in cases involving such differences,] sex classifications may be used to compensate women for particular economic disabilities [they have] suffered, to promot[e] equal employment opportunity, [and] to advance full development of the talent and capacities of our Nation's people. But such classifications may not be used, as they once were, to create or perpetuate the legal, social, and economic inferiority of women.[136]

This holding signaled an important shift in the Court's reasoning about "real differences." In the past, "real differences"—most notably, pregnancy—served as a check on the reach of anti-stereotyping doctrine. But in *Virginia*, anti-stereotyping doctrine serves as a check on the state's regulation of "real differences." *Virginia* makes clear that anti-stereotyping doctrine governs all instances of sex-based state action, whether or not "real differences" are involved. In fact, *Virginia* suggests that equal protection law should be particularly alert to the possibility of sex stereotyping in contexts involving "real differences" because such contexts have often been the cite of particularly powerful forms of sex-role enforcement.

The Court echoed and expanded on these insights in 2003, in *Nevada Department of Human Resources v. Hibbs*.[137] *Hibbs* concerned the constitutionality of a provision of the Family and Medical Leave Act (FMLA) guaranteeing eligible employees 12 weeks of family caregiving leave. Williams Hibbs (another male caregiver) requested leave to care for his ailing wife. His employer responded by challenging the constitutionality of the leave guarantee, arguing that Congress lacked the power to enact this

---

[134] *Id.* at 533.

[135] *Id.*

[136] *Id.* at 533–34 (first and second alterations in original) (internal citations and quotation marks omitted).

[137] Nev. Dep't of Human Res. v. Hibbs, 538 U.S. 721 (2003).

guarantee under Section 5 of the Fourteenth Amendment because an affirmative grant of leave was unnecessary to enforce Section 1's equal protection guarantee. Hibbs's employer argued that if Congress was concerned about sex discrimination in the allocation of family leave, it could enact a law barring such discrimination, and that affirmatively guaranteeing leave went beyond what was necessary to prevent the differential treatment of male and female employees.

The Court rejected this argument. Chief Justice Rehnquist, writing for the Court in *Hibbs*, explained that sex discrimination was rampant in many states' parental leave policies in particular, and that such discrimination was "not attributable to any differential physical needs of men and women, but rather to the pervasive sex-role stereotype that caring for family members is women's work."[138] The Court held that sex-role stereotyping was so powerful in the context of family caregiving that Congress very reasonably concluded that a simple anti-discrimination law would be insufficient to solve the problem. Something more was needed to disrupt the steering of men and women into different sex and family roles, especially when they became parents.

The most notable aspect of *Hibbs*, from the perspective of this chapter, is the Court's treatment of pregnancy under the Equal Protection Clause. Fifty years ago, in *Geduldig*, the Court failed to recognize how laws regulating pregnancy might violate equal protection. In *Hibbs*, the Court had no difficulty recognizing that laws regulating pregnancy can, and often do, violate equal protection. The Court explained in *Hibbs* that Congress enacted the FMLA's leave provision after concluding that sex discrimination in the workplace is often tied "'to the pervasive presumption that women are mothers first, and workers second,'" and that this "'ideology about women's roles has in turn justified discrimination against women when they are mothers or mothers-to-be.'"[139] The Court endorsed Congress's judgment that guaranteeing family leave to all employees is an appropriate means of combatting the tsunami of unconstitutional sex-role stereotyping visited on women when they become pregnant.

---

[138] *Id.* at 731.

[139] *Id.* at 736 (quoting The Parental and Medical Leave Act of 1986: Joint Hearing on H.R. 4300 before the Subcomm. on Labor-Management Relations and the Subcomm. on Labor Standards of the H. Comm. on Education and Labor, 99th Cong., 2d Sess., 100 (1986).

In reasoning this way about pregnancy, and the troubling persistence of sex discrimination against "mothers-to-be," the Court in *Hibbs* treats *Geduldig* as defunct. In fact, the only citation to *Geduldig* in *Hibbs* comes in Justice Scalia's dissenting opinion.[140] The Court in *Hibbs* cites *Virginia* as the decision that establishes the modern framework for deciding constitutional sex discrimination cases[141]—a framework within which the *Hibbs* Court matter-of-factly treats discrimination against pregnant workers as sex discrimination. *Virginia* made clear and *Hibbs* reinforces that equality protections extend to contexts involving "real differences," and that the regulation of pregnancy is no longer exempt from scrutiny to determine if it enforces traditional sex stereotypes.

The Anti-Stereotyping Principle examined the implications of this doctrinal evolution for laws regulating abortion. When I wrote that article, in 2010, abortion cases remained almost entirely path-dependent on *Roe* in the sense that they were argued and decided within a substantive due process framework. (Which is not to say abortion decisions weren't influenced by the development of sex-based equal protection law: *Planned Parenthood of Southeastern Pa. v. Casey*[142] borrowed heavily from equal protection law.[143] But *Casey* occurred prior to *Virginia* and *Hibbs*, and it was framed as a substantive due process decision.) By 2010, however, anti-abortion activists had begun to take sharper aim at abortion rights and to campaign more aggressively for the appointment of judges committed to overturning *Roe*. One of the central aims of *The Anti-Stereotyping Principle* was to trace the evolution of sex-based equal protection law since *Casey* to call attention to the development of this alternative ground for the abortion right. Now that *Dobbs*[144] has rejected *Roe*'s substantive due process framework, these developments in equal protection law have become critically important to determining the constitutionality of abortion regulation. Equal protection law, post-*Virginia* and *Hibbs*, does not bar the state from regulating abortion. But it requires the state

[140] *Id.* at 751.

[141] *Id.* at 728–730, 736.

[142] 505 U.S. 833 (1992).

[143] For more on *Casey*'s incorporation of sex-based equal protection law, see Cary Franklin & Reva Siegel, *Equality Emerges As a Ground for Abortion Rights After* Dobbs, *in* ROE V. DOBBS: THE PAST, PRESENT, AND FUTURE OF A CONSTITUTIONAL RIGHT (Geoffrey R. Stone & Lee Bollinger eds., forthcoming 2023).

[144] Dobbs v. Jackson Women's Health Org., 142 S. Ct. 2228 (2022).

to do so in a way that avoids perpetuating women's subordination or reinforcing traditional sex-role stereotypes. Regulation that reflects or reinforces the long-standing assumption "that women can simply be forced to accept the 'natural' status and incidents of motherhood"[145] fails to meet this test.[146]

The evolution of sex-based equal protection law has important implications in other contexts as well. I wrote in *The Anti-Stereotyping Principle* about the (relatively new, at that time) expansion of sex-based anti-stereotyping doctrine into LGBT rights jurisprudence. By 2010, courts had begun to hold that discrimination on the basis of sexual orientation and gender identity reflects and reinforces traditional sex stereotypes about how men and women should be and thus violates legal prohibitions on sex discrimination. Ten years later, the Court held in its landmark decision in *Bostock v. Clayton County*, that discrimination on the basis of sexual orientation and gender identity is sex discrimination under Title VII of the 1964 Civil Rights Act. *Bostock* built on numerous decisions by federal district and appellate courts (and by the Equal Employment Opportunity Commission) that reached the same conclusion.[147] For instance, in one of the cases later consolidated in *Bostock*, the Sixth Circuit explained that, whatever courts may have held in the past, when LGBT people were treated as second-class citizens, it now found no reason "to exclude Title VII coverage for non sex-stereotypical behavior simply because the person is a transsexual," and that "[u]nder any circumstances, [s]ex stereotyping based on a person's gender non-conforming behavior is impermissible discrimination."[148]

Courts have also recognized discrimination against LGBT people as sex discrimination in constitutional cases. In the past few years, states have passed an unprecedented barrage of laws aimed at transgender people. Many of the constitutional challenges brought against these laws have succeeded because "many courts . . . have held that various forms of discrimination against transgender people constitute sex-based discrimination for purposes

---

[145] *Casey*, 505 U.S. at 928 (Blackmun, J., concurring in part, dissenting in part).

[146] For a more comprehensive account of the application of equal protection law to abortion regulation, see *supra* note 143.

[147] For discussion of decisions predating *Bostock*, see Cary Franklin, *Living Textualism*, SUP. CT. REV 119, 137–140 (2020).

[148] E.E.O.C. v. R.G. &. G.R. Harris Funeral Homes, Inc., 884 F.3d 560, 572, 578 (6th Cir. 2018), *aff'd sub nom.* Bostock v. Clayton Cnty., 140 S. Ct. 1731 (2020) (internal quotation marks omitted) (second alteration in original).

of the Equal Protection Clause because such policies punish transgender persons for gender non-conformity, thereby relying on sex stereotypes."[149]

As in the context of abortion, the Court's rejection of physiological naturalism and adoption of an approach to equal protection focused instead on social relations has enabled this evolution in LGBT law. As Serena Mayeri, Melissa Murray, and Reva Siegel have observed, the test for sex discrimination *Virginia* articulates "breaks with the physiological naturalism of cases like *Geduldig*. Rather than 'reason[ing] from the body' (and asserting that 'only women can become pregnant' or that 'pregnancy is an objectively identifiable physical condition with unique characteristics') as *Geduldig* did, *Virginia* reasons from social relations."[150] The Court explains in *Virginia* that whatever "'inherent differences'" may exist between the sexes (and it's worth noting that the Court puts that phrase in quotation marks), the adjudication of sex discrimination cases does not turn on chromosomes or body parts; it turns on how regulators are using sex. *Virginia* explains that sex-based state action may be used "to compensate women for particular economic disabilities [they have] suffered, to promot[e] equal employment opportunity, [and] to advance full development of the talent and capacities of our Nation's people."[151] Regulators are not required to ignore "inherent differences" when seeking to achieve these aims. But, *Virginia* explains, regulation based on such differences may not be used "for denigration of the members of either sex or for artificial constraints on an individual's opportunity."[152]

The Court's rejection of the physiological naturalism of the 1970s has made it harder for opponents of LGBT rights to justify discrimination against LGBT people by invoking "real differences" between the sexes. Prior to *Obergefell*, opponents of LGBT rights frequently invoked "real differences" to defend the exclusion of same-sex couples from marriage.[153] Today, "real

---

[149] Grimm v. Gloucester Cnty. Sch. Bd., 972 F.3d 586, 608 (4th Cir. 2020); *id.* at 608–09 (citing numerous federal appellate and district courts that have issued similar rulings).

[150] Reva B. Siegel, Serena Mayeri & Melissa Murray, *Equal Protection in* Dobbs *and Beyond: How States Protect Life Inside and Outside of the Abortion Context*, 43 Colum. J. Gender & L. 67, 77 (2022) (internal citations omitted).

[151] United States v. Virginia, 518 U.S. 515, 533 (1996) (internal citations and quotation marks omitted) (alterations in original).

[152] *Id.*

[153] Franklin, *supra* note 1, at 168 n.448; Kenji Yoshino, *The Best Argument Against Same-Sex Marriage, and Why It Fails*, Slate (Dec. 13, 2010), https://slate.com/news-and-politics/2010/12/robert-p-george-s-argument-against-gay-marriage-fails.html.

differences" are being invoked to justify all manner of trans-exclusionary laws and policies. *Virginia*'s analysis of state action that seeks to regulate "real differences" is directly relevant to determining the constitutionality of these laws. As the Fourth Circuit observed in *Grimm v. Gloucester County School Board*, "the Supreme Court has recognized 'inherent differences' between the biological sexes that might provide appropriate justification for distinctions, see *Virginia* (citing, as examples of appropriate sex-based distinctions, 'compensat[ing] women for particular economic disabilities' and 'promot[ing] equal employment opportunity')."[154] But regulations prohibiting transgender people from using restrooms that correspond with their gender identity—like many other trans-exclusionary laws—do neither of these things. As the Fourth Circuit held, they "punish individuals for failing to adhere to gender stereotypes" and, in so doing, violate "a central tenet of equal protection in sex discrimination cases."[155]

IV. Reflections on Anti-Stereotyping Post-*Dobbs*

In one sense, this chapter tells a very particular story. It tells the story of how male plaintiffs in the 1970s helped to enshrine in law an anti-stereotyping principle, the implementation of which has evolved over time as Americans have grown increasingly skeptical of laws and policies that enforce traditional sex stereotypes, even in contexts where the grip of those stereotypes has been especially tenacious. It took decades before the Court was willing to extend the anti-stereotyping doctrine it developed in the 1970s to contexts such as pregnancy and LGBT rights.

But in another sense, the story in this chapter is part of a much larger story about how constitutional interpretation evolves over time as social movement activism and social change cause judges to reconsider old doctrines designed to shield seemingly benign forms of regulation from legal scrutiny. The Fourteenth Amendment was enacted in 1868, but it took nearly a century for the Court to hold that equal protection bars racial segregation in schools and more than a century to hold that it prohibits bans on interracial marriage. In the interim, the Court embraced doctrinal limitations akin

---

[154] *Grimm*, 972 F.3d at 607–08 (internal citations omitted).

[155] *Id.* at 609 (internal citations and quotation marks omitted).

to the ones described in this chapter. It characterized education and marriage as "social rights" and declared that these were not the sorts of rights the Fourteenth Amendment protects. It deployed "separate but equal" ideology to explain why certain traditional social arrangements—for example, in segregated schools and in railcars—fell outside the reach of race-based equal protection law. The "real differences" doctrine and the anti-LGBT loopholes courts developed several decades later to limit the reach of sex equality law served the same purpose and functioned in much the same way as these earlier limits on the law's reach.

Like the earlier limitations courts imposed in race cases, the limitations described in this chapter have eroded over time as American understanding of equality has expanded. As in the context of race, this isn't simply or even primarily a story about the Court. Change in all of these contexts involved all three branches of government, state and local governments, social institutions, social movements, and the American people. *The Anti-Stereotyping Principle* describes in greater detail the social and legal changes that preceded decisions extending sex-based antidiscrimination protections into the contexts of reproductive and LGBT rights. I'll mention just a few here. In 1978, a few years after the Court's decision in *Geduldig*, Congress responded with the Pregnancy Discrimination Act (PDA), which defined pregnancy discrimination as sex discrimination for purposes of Title VII.[156] In 1993, Congress enacted the FMLA, a law motivated by the recognition that sex discrimination is often at its fiercest in the regulation of pregnancy and motherhood. More recently, this recognition has fueled the enactment of Pregnant Worker Fairness Acts. One could tell the same story about the many loci of change in the context of LGBT rights. That story would include, among many other developments, Congress's repeal of Don't Ask, Don't Tell in 2010,[157] President Obama's announcement in 2011 that the Department of Justice would no longer defend the Defense of Marriage Act,[158] and the rulings by multiple government agencies and federal courts in the years prior to *Bostock* that discrimination on the basis of sexual orientation and gender identity is sex discrimination.

[156] 42 U.S.C. § 2000e(k).

[157] Don't Ask, Don't Tell Repeal Act of 2010, Pub. L. No. 111-321, 124 Stat. 3515 (2010).

[158] *See* Letter from Att'y Gen. Eric H. Holder, Jr., to John A. Boehner, Speaker, U.S. House of Representatives (Feb. 23, 2011), at http://www.justice.gov/opa/pr/2011/February/11-ag-223.html.

The fact that the changes discussed in this chapter were a half-century in the making, and that they involved a democratically engaged Court slowly dismantling the limitations it had erected to cabin the reach of sex-based antidiscrimination law, is one of the reasons it's so shocking to witness how Justice Alito treats this history in *Dobbs*. *Dobbs* involved a substantive due process challenge to the constitutionality of a Mississippi abortion restriction, and the Court used this opportunity to ask not only if substantive due process barred this particular restriction, but if substantive due process protects the abortion right at all, for example, if *Roe* was correctly decided. *Dobbs* was not an equal protection case; the parties in *Dobbs* did not assert an equal protection claim on which the Court could rule.[159] Justice Alito nonetheless took it upon himself to reach out, in dicta, and opine on the applicability of equal protection in the context of abortion. He asserted that sex-based equal protection challenges to abortion restrictions are "squarely foreclosed by our precedents" because these restrictions regulate "a medical procedure that only one sex can undergo."[160] Because abortion restrictions regulate "real differences," they do not involve any sex-based disparate treatment and thus fall outside the scope of constitutional sex discrimination law.

How does Justice Alito square this analysis with the very different approach to "real differences" the Court adopts in *Virginia* and *Hibbs*? He doesn't even try. He simply excludes those decisions—and decades of pregnancy-related developments in sex-based antidiscrimination law—from his analysis and rests his assertions about the regulation of pregnancy on *Geduldig*, as if the defunct reasoning in that 50-year-old case accurately captured the current state of the law. But *Geduldig* was sidelined decades ago. Prior to Justice Alito's dicta in *Dobbs*, no majority opinion of the Court had invoked *Geduldig* to interpret the Equal Protection Clause since Congress's repudiation of its reasoning in 1978 in the PDA.[161] And it's not as if the Court simply ignored the relationship between pregnancy and equal protection in the intervening decades. The Court explicitly stated in *Virginia* that it "ha[d] come to appreciate" that the regulation of "inherent differences," such as pregnancy, may violate sex-based equal protection law. In *Hibbs*, the

[159] Judge Carlton Reeves, who decided *Dobbs* in the district court, noted that the plaintiffs had amended their complaint to drop their equal protection challenge to Mississippi's statute. Jackson Women's Health Org. v. Currier, 349 F. Supp. 3d 536, 539 (S.D. Miss. 2018)).

[160] Dobbs v. Jackson Women's Health Org., 142 S. Ct. 2228, 2245 (2022).

[161] Siegel, Mayeri & Murray, *supra* note 149, at 76.

Court repeatedly endorsed Congress's understanding that the regulation of "mothers to be" not only can run, but often runs, afoul of equal protection.

It's possible that Justice Alito's invocation of *Geduldig* in dicta in *Dobbs* is an aberration, and that *Geduldig* will ultimately remain on the scrapheap of discarded precedents. I wouldn't bet on it, however. I suspect Justice Alito trotted out *Geduldig* in *Dobbs* because he at least, and possibly the other Justices who joined his opinion, intend to try to rewrite the history of sex-based antidiscrimination law in a way that silently erases the legal developments described in this chapter. *Dobbs* itself provides grounds for this suspicion. Justice Alito's dicta in *Dobbs* puts forth a revisionist account of sex-based equal protection law, suggesting that pregnancy's status as a "real difference" short-circuits any inquiry into whether its regulation reflects or reinforces sex stereotypes—and that such regulation could qualify as sex discrimination only if it "'effect[s] an invidious discrimination against members of one sex or the other.'"[162] Alito asserts that restrictions on abortion do not qualify as discriminatory under this test because "the 'goal of preventing abortion' does not constitute 'invidiously discriminatory animus' against women."[163]

Other conservative judges have already begun to run with this revisionist account of the law. Just recently, the Sixth Circuit broke with other federal courts and upheld two state bans on gender-affirming medical treatments for transgender minors.[164] Chief Judge Jeffrey Sutton, a major figure in the Federalist Society and a prominent conservative "feeder judge," repeatedly cites *Dobbs* and *Geduldig* in his majority opinion for the proposition that heightened review under sex-based equal protection law "does not apply in the context of medical procedures unique to one sex or the other."[165] (He very tellingly observes that the Supreme Court has articulated this approach to "real differences" twice: "[o]ne year ago [in *Dobbs*], and nearly fifty years ago [in *Geduldig*]."[166] Like Justice Alito, he omits any mention of legal developments that occurred in the intervening half-century.)

---

[162] *Dobbs*, 142 S. Ct. at 2246 (quoting Geduldig v. Aiello, 417 U.S. 484, 496 n.20 (1974)).

[163] *Id.* (quoting Bray v. Alexandria Women's Health Clinic, 506 U.S. 263, 273–274 (1993), a statutory case about the purposes of private actors protesting at an abortion clinic that had nothing do with what qualifies as sex-based state action under equal protection).

[164] *See* L.W. *ex rel.* Williams v. Skrmetti, No. 23-5600, 2023 WL 6321688 (6th Cir. Sept. 28, 2023).

[165] *Id.* at 16.

[166] *Id.* at 14.

Chief Judge Sutton posits that laws banning transgender girls from taking estrogen and transgender boys from taking testosterone are akin to laws regulating pregnant women; all of these laws regulate medical procedures unique to one sex and thus raise no equal protection concerns, unless plaintiffs can show the law was motivated by an invidious desire to hurt members of one sex or the other.[167] He concludes that bans on gender-affirming care are not motivated by animus against either sex and thus raise no sex-based equal protection concerns.[168]

It's as if we're back in the early 1970s, before the development of contemporary sex-based equal protection law and before the Court's recognition that laws regulating "real differences" can and often do unconstitutionally enforce traditional sex stereotypes. I suspect that when Justice Ginsburg knew she was dying and expressed her "most fervent wish . . . that [she] . . . not be replaced until a new president is installed,"[169] this was the outcome she most feared: that her work and the work of generations of Americans—advocates, judges, legislators, scholars, people from all walks of life—who helped to build more capacious and just understandings of equal protection in the context of sex might be torn down in an instant by a new handful of Justices inclined to ignore the history and legal developments of the past 50 years.

When I first told the story of Ginsburg's male plaintiffs in 2010, my aim was to demonstrate the continuity between more recent decisions extending sex-based equality protections into the contexts of reproductive and LGBT rights and older decisions extending such protections to male caregivers who defied traditional sex-role expectations. *The Anti-Stereotyping Principle* aimed to show how the founding principles of constitutional sex discrimination law had been, and were still being, extended into new contexts as courts (even quite conservative courts, such as the Rehnquist Court) came to recognize that forms of regulation once considered natural and benign actually perpetuated

---

[167] *Id.*

[168] Chief Judge Sutton is not the only prominent conservative federal judge currently attempting to revive *Geduldig* to block transgender rights claims. *See also, e.g.*, Adams *ex rel.* Kasper v. Sch. Bd. of St. Johns Cnty., 57 F.4th 791, 808–10 (11th Cir. 2022) (Lagoa, J.); Adams *ex rel.* Kasper v. Sch. Bd. of St. Johns Cnty., 3 F.4th 1299, 1331–34 (11th Cir.) (Pryor, J., dissenting), *rev'd en banc*, 57 F.4th 791 (11th Cir. 2022).

[169] Nina Totenberg, *Justice Ruth Bader Ginsburg, Champion of Gender Equality, Dies at 87*, NPR (Sept. 18, 2020), at https://www.npr.org/2020/09/18/100306972/justice-ruth-bader-ginsburg-champion-of-gender-equality-dies-at-87.

inequality. But the Court has now shifted very rapidly and very far to the right. It appears to be embarking on a new project—withdrawing protections that have been extended into the contexts of reproductive and LGBT rights and potentially subverting the anti-stereotyping framework that has guided sex-based antidiscrimination law for nearly 50 years.

The Justices' modus operandi for achieving these ends seems to be historical erasure. In this, they have plenty of company. Numerous governments and other institutions in the United States have recently taken steps to restrict the teaching of slavery, to ban the teaching of Critical Race Studies and LGBT history, to remove books on race, gender, and sexuality from public libraries, to eliminate Gender Studies courses, and to prohibit classroom discussion of "systemic racism, sexism, oppression, and privilege" and the role of these forces in "maintain[ing] social, political, and economic inequalities."[170]

This is not a salutory trend from the standpoint of civil rights and democracy. But underlying these attempted acts of historical erasure is an insight worth noting. It's harder to turn back the clock on civil rights and resurrect retrograde social arrangements if people know about the terrible histories of discrimination various groups have endured in this country, about the work that has gone into combatting such discrimination, and about the laws and legal doctrines we've created to prohibit this discrimination. This insight motivates recent attempts to erase history. But it also motivates this chapter. The doctrine that grew out of Ginsburg's male plaintiff cases and evolved over the past 50 years provides constitutional grounds for resisting the kind of retrenchment that occurred in *Dobbs* and for protecting and reconstructing reproductive rights and LGBT rights. So this chapter isn't a eulogy, and it's not a lament for what we've lost (for the unfathomable loss of Ruth Bader Ginsburg). This chapter is about the constitutional doctrine she helped to create and how this doctrine can continue to combat sex discrimination in the future, in all its forms—if we can keep it.

---

[170] The quotations are from Fla. Stat. §1007.25(3)(c) (2023). For more on these efforts, see, e.g., Am. Libr. Ass'n, The State of America's Libraries 2023, https://www.ala.org/news/sites/ala.org.news/files/content/state-of-americas-libraries-report-2023-web-version.pdf; 2023 CRT Forward: Tracking the Attack on Critical Race Studies, UCLA Sch. of Law Critical Race Studies Program (Apr. 6, 2023), https://crtforward.law.ucla.edu/wp-content/uploads/2023/04/UCLA-Law_CRT-Report_Final.pdf; Movement Advancement Project, Equality Maps: LGBTQ Curricular Laws, at www.mapresearch.org/equality-maps/curricular_laws (last visited Oct. 5, 2023).

2

Justice Ginsburg's Election Jurisprudence

—Alexander Tsesis

Over the course of two and a half decades as Associate Justice, Ruth Bader Ginsburg's opinions in the field of election law evinced a sustained commitment to constitutional self-governance and political representation. Her voting rights opinions, dealing with matters as diverse as ballot initiatives and redistricting, often stressed the need for judges to defer to state and federal lawmakers who sought to expand and safeguard the franchise.

Whether writing for the majority or dissenting, Justice Ginsburg grounded her opinions in the constitutional principle of federalism. Writing for the majority in *Evenwel v. Abbott*, Justice Ginsburg found that the Fourteenth Amendment's guarantee of equal representation did not require a state to draw legislative voting districts on the basis of eligible voters.[1] State legislatures could instead draw legislative districts based on a state's total population, rather than based solely on voting-eligible population.

---

[1] 578 U.S. 54, 71 (2016) (relying on founding and Reconstruction-era histories to hold that "[c]onsistent with constitutional history, this Court's past decisions reinforce the conclusion that States and localities may comply with the one-person, one-vote principle by designing districts with equal total populations" rather than "the voter-eligible population of districts").

Ginsburg's opinion found the roots of the total-population districting scheme in the history of American representative democracy, longstanding practices, and judicial opinions.[2] Her opinion drew on earlier Supreme Court holdings, including landmark opinions from the liberal Warren Court era, *Wesberry v. Sanders*[3] and *Reynolds v. Sims*.[4] Those cases made clear that the principle of one person, one vote rendered the creation of voting districts based on total population constitutionally legitimate in state and federal elections.[5] In those precedents, the Court had "always assumed the permissibility of drawing districts to equalize total population."[6] Her opinion furthered the ideals of the Warren Court that state and federal representatives address the needs of each person living in their districts irrespective of whether they were eligible to vote and regardless of their place of domicile.[7]

Writing for the majority in *Arizona State Legislature v. Arizona Independent Redistricting Commission*,[8] Justice Ginsburg further demonstrated her democratic sensibilities. Her opinion recognized that under the Elections Clause, Article I, Section 4, the people retain the power to maintain democratic institutions against legislative efforts to gerrymander districts favorable to one political party over another.[9] The Arizona State legislature brought a challenge arguing that a ballot initiative violated the Elections Clause of the U.S. Constitution. The initiative put authority to draw voting districts into the hands of a nonpartisan commission composed of ordinary voters.[10] Writing in dissent, Chief Justice Roberts argued that the Arizona Independent Redistricting Commission violated that Clause by adopting a

---

[2] *Id.* at 73–75.

[3] 376 U.S. 1, 7–8 (1964) (holding that Article I, § 2, required that House of Representative members be elected "by the People of the several States" in order that "one man's vote in a congressional election . . . be worth as much as another").

[4] 377 U.S. 533 (1964) (holding that the one-person, one-vote principle applied under the Equal Protection Clause of the Fourteenth Amendment to both houses of a state's legislature).

[5] Evenwel, 578 U.S. at 68.

[6] Evenwel, 578 U.S. at 72. The majority refused to consider whether "States may draw districts to equalize voter-eligible population rather than total population." *Id.* at 75.

[7] *See* Gray v. Sanders, 372 U.S. 368, 381 (1963); Baker v. Carr, 369 U.S. 186, 194 (1962); Gaffney v. Cummings, 412 U.S. 735, 746, 748 (1973).

[8] 576 U.S. 787 (2015) (hereinafter *AIRC*).

[9] *Id.* at 819.

[10] *Id.* at 792.

statewide referendum, Proposition 106, and thereby deprived the Arizona legislature of authority to draw congressional and state legislative districts.[11]

Ginsburg rejected a textualist reading of the Elections Clause;[12] instead, she found that the people speaking through a ballot initiative could authorize a commission that would draw districts to keep political parties from diluting the vote in the parties' favor. She framed her reasoning in a rubric that reflected the relevance of history and tradition to adjudication of a legal challenge brought by lawmakers to prevent enforcement of a popular referendum meant to expand the people's participation in democracy. "Our Declaration of Independence, ¶ 2," she wrote in a particularly remarkable passage about American historical aspiration, "[drew] from [John] Locke in stating: 'Governments are instituted among Men, deriving their just powers from the consent of the governed.' And our fundamental instrument of government derives its authority from 'We the People.' U.S. Const., Preamble."[13] Her opinion also quoted Hamilton at the New York ratifying convention on the adoption of the federal Constitution, "[T]he true principle of a republic is, that the people should choose whom they please to govern them."[14]

Justice Ginsburg found the Declaration of Independence relevant to constitutional culture[15] and the nation's roots in representative democracy to have contemporary meaning. Most importantly, Justice Ginsburg's majority opinion demonstrated that the "history and purpose" of the Elections Clause was rooted in the "animating principle of our Constitution that the people themselves are the originating source of all the powers of government."[16] That perspective, as Professor Vikram Amar points out, makes clear that the people can be intrinsic to state lawmaking by initiating

---

[11] *Id.* at 824–2 (Roberts, C.J., dissenting).

[12] Daphna Renan, *Justice Ginsburg's Republican Jurisprudence*, 90 Geo. Wash. L. Rev. 1471, 1483 (2022).

[13] *AIRC*, 576 U.S. at 820.

[14] *Id. See New York Ratifying Convention First Speech of June 21* (Hamilton), https://founders.archives.gov/documents/Hamilton/01-05-02-0012-0011. *See also* Mark Graber, *The Declaration of Independence and Contemporary Constitutional Pedagogy*, 89 S. Cal. L. Rev. 509, 526 (2016).

[15] Ginsburg failed to flesh out, however, how the Declaration of Independence can be anything more than an ad hoc interpretive device for lower court judges.

[16] *AIRC*, 576 U.S. at 813.

referenda that enable them to engage in direct democracy.[17] The will of the people through their representatives remained for Justice Ginsburg as the anchor of American democracy.

Apart from *Evenwel* and *Arizona Independent Redistricting Commission*, Justice Ginsburg's other significant contributions in the area of election law appear in dissents. In many of them, she demonstrated sustained concern for racial equality and supported Congress's authority to prevent state racial discrimination. With her dissents, she pressed the majority to further refine and clarify their arguments. Moreover, Ginsburg found from experience that every term a few dissenting opinions in draft form actually swayed enough colleagues to become the majority opinions.[18]

When Justice Ginsburg concluded that the Court was thwarting the people's legislative representatives from enforcing laws designed to expand the federal or state franchises, her dissents could be caustic. For example, she thought that we should not be complacent about the successes achieved in ending racial voting injustice, but should maintain strong laws that prevented backsliding, a position she defended in her dissent in *Shelby County v. Holder*.[19]

Arguably her greatest contribution in the field of protecting the suffrage appeared in her *Shelby County* dissent. The *Shelby* majority effectively nullified the preclearance requirements of Section 5 of the Voting Rights Act of 1965 (VRA), holding that Section 4 of the VRA was antiquated, politicized, and violative of states' equal sovereignty.[20] Congress had passed the law to enforce the Fifteenth Amendment's prohibitions against racialized

---

[17] Vikram David Amar, *What the Supreme Court's Arizona Redistricting Ruling Means for Presidential (not Just Congressional) Election Reform*, VERDICT (July 8, 2016), https://verdict.justia.com/2015/07/08/what-the-supreme-courts-arizona-redistricting-ruling-means-for-presidential-not-just-congressional-election-reform.

[18] Ginsburg, for example, found that the dissent of Justice Scalia in United States v. Virginia, 518 U.S. 515 (1996), helped her refine her equal protection argument in the opinion she authored for the majority in the same case.

[19] 570 U.S. 529 (2013).

[20] *Id.* at 556 ("There is no valid reason to insulate the coverage formula from review merely because it was previously enacted 40 years ago. If Congress had started from scratch in 2006, it plainly could not have enacted the present coverage formula. It would have been irrational for Congress to distinguish between States in such a fundamental way based on 40-year-old data, when today's statistics tell an entirely different story. And it would have been irrational to base coverage on the use of voting tests 40 years ago, when such tests have been illegal since that time. But that is exactly what Congress has done.").

restraints on voting.[21] Section 5 of the statute required that before covered states and political subdivisions made changes to voting procedures, they obtain preclearance from the Department of Justice or a judicial panel of the District of Columbia District Court.[22] For decades, the Act had been an essential instrument for addressing widespread racial discrimination in voting. Covered states and localities bore the onus of proving that the proposed modifications would not regressively diminish the ability of minority voters to register and participate in elections.[23] States with long histories of voting discrimination remained obligated to obtain federal approval unless they qualified for the VRA's bailout provision. Bailouts could be granted with proof that the petitioning government entity had, for ten preceding years, not used forbidden tests or other discriminatory devices purposefully to restrict voting.[24]

By holding unconstitutional Section 4(b)'s coverage formula, the Supreme Court rendered Section 5's preclearance provision inoperative in the absence of new congressional action to update statistical studies Congress had relied on to demonstrate the existence of continued discrimination through restrictive voting laws. Justices Stephen Breyer, Sonia Sotomayor, and Elena Kagan joined Justice Ginsburg in dissent.

Justice Ginsburg criticized the majority for refusing to defer to Congress on a matter over which the Fifteenth Amendment granted legislators broad enforcement latitude. She described the VRA as "one of the most consequential, efficacious, and amply justified exercises of federal legislative power in our Nation's history."[25] Additionally she castigated the majority, explaining that "[t]hrowing out preclearance when it has worked and is continuing to work to stop discriminatory changes is like throwing away your umbrella in a

---

[21] *Id.* at 535, *citing to* South Carolina v. Katzenbach, 383 U.S. 301, 309 (1966) (stating that Congress found the VRA was to "address entrenched racial discrimination in voting, 'an insidious and pervasive evil which had been perpetuated in certain parts of our country through unremitting and ingenious defiance of the Constitution.'" Nw. Austin Mun. Util. Dist. No. One v. Holder, 557 U.S. 193, 217 (2009) (Thomas, J., concurring) (mentioning Fifteenth Amendment source of Congressional authority).

[22] Voting Rights Act of 1965 § 5 (codified at 42 U.S.C. § 1973c (2006)).

[23] Beer v. United States, 425 U.S. 130, 141 (1976) ("[T]he purpose of § 5 has always been to insure that no voting-procedure changes would be made that would lead to a retrogression in the position of racial minorities with respect to their effective exercise of the electoral franchise.").

[24] 42 U.S.C. § 1973b(b) (2006); *Shelby County*, 570 U.S. at 557.

[25] *Shelby County*, 570 U.S. at 562 (Ginsburg, J., dissenting).

rainstorm because you are not getting wet."[26] While the majority understood that the VRA's preclearance requirement had facilitated meaningful progress, it found congressional reenactments lacked adequately extensive empirical evidence of a continued need for its enforcement.[27] From Ginsburg's perspective, on the other hand, the Act continued to be relevant because it prevented states from using second-generation criteria to suppress minority voters.[28]

The majority, nevertheless, enjoined the federal government from continuing to enforce a mandatory preclearance provision of the VRA. Under prior federal law, the United States had the burden of proving racial discrimination on a county-by-county basis. Under the VRA, on the other hand, preclearance required states to provide the Attorney General with sufficient information to prove that the alteration was done with a nondiscriminatory purpose and effect.[29] Mandatory preclearance not only served to prevent states from regressing, but also incentivized state and local governments to negotiate solutions with the federal government rather than risk litigation. In effect, as she would say in a later dissent, *Shelby County* had rendered "the Act's § 4 coverage formula obsolete."[30] She argued that the majority had "effectively nullified § 5's preclearance requirement."[31] Preclearance had been particularly effective. It had allowed the nation to achieve much more than might have been possible solely through case-by-case litigation.

Justice Ginsburg's dissent powerfully challenged the majority's premises. She warned that "without the continuation of the Voting Rights Act of 1965 protections, racial and language minority citizens will be deprived of the opportunity to exercise their right to vote, or will have their votes diluted, undermining the significant gains made by minorities in the last 40 years."[32] In ominous words, she cautioned the Court that "history repeats itself."[33]

---

[26] *Id.* at 590 (Ginsburg, J., dissenting).

[27] Ellen D. Katz, *Dismissing Deterrence*, 127 Harv. L. Rev. F. 248, 249 (2014) (asserting that *Shelby County* required "extensive evidence of widespread and ongoing unconstitutional conduct to support congressional remedial action").

[28] *Shelby County*, 570 U.S. at 560 (Ginsburg, J., dissenting).

[29] Branch v. Smith, 538 U.S. 254, 263 (2003).

[30] North Carolina v. League of Women Voters of N. Carolina, 135 S.Ct. 6, 6 (2014) (Ginsburg, J., dissenting).

[31] *Id.*

[32] *Id.* at 566 (Ginsburg, J., dissenting) (quoting Fannie Lou Hamer, Rosa Parks, and Coretta Scott King Voting Rights Act Reauthorization and Amendments Act of 2006, Pub. L. No. 109-246, § 2(b)(9), 120 Stat. 577, 578 (codified at 52 U.S.C. § 10301)):

[33] *Id.* at 592 (Ginsburg, J., dissenting).

In fact, as Justice Ginsburg explained in dissent, experience under the VRA demonstrated that preclearance states continued to use "second-generation barriers" to dilute the minority vote, including racial gerrymandering and at-large voting rather than district voting in cities with sizable black minorities.[34] Rather than overreach as had the majority, Justice Ginsburg parsed the congressional record in *Shelby County*. She recited a statutory history that demonstrated the tremendous support both major political parties had demonstrated for the VRA. The vote in favor of the law's reauthorization in 2006 received 390 yeas and 33 nays in the House of Representatives. The Senate vote was an even more resounding, with 98 votes for and 0 against. With this summary of its history, Ginsburg demonstrated that the majority of the Court had been activist, rather than conservative, and evinced unwillingness to defer to the people's congressional representatives.

Moreover, the resounding support reflected in the 2006 congressional vote had followed 21 Senate Judiciary Committee hearings. The total congressional record contained 15,000 pages replete with "'examples of flagrant racial discrimination' since the last reauthorization."[35] Hence, Congress had manifold reasons for relying on its enforcement authority under the Fifteenth Amendment to authorize its reenactment.[36] Justice Ginsburg wrote that the VRA's preclearance provision, Section 4(b), should have been reviewed under rational-basis scrutiny.[37] Her principle aim in the dissent was to demonstrate why the Court should have deferred to Congress's preclearance provision. Her approach also stressed the Reconstruction Amendment's grant to Congress, not to the Supreme Court, the principal authority for protecting the right to franchise without arbitrary racial exclusion.[38]

In later dissents, Justice Ginsburg continued to lament the holding in *Shelby County*. In *League of Women Voters of N.C. v. North Carolina*,[39] the

---

[34] *Shelby County*, 570 U.S. at 563.

[35] *Id.* at 565.

[36] *Id.* at 567.

[37] *Id.* at 569. Justice Ginsburg's use of the rational basis test was based on precedent: "Until today, in considering the constitutionality of the VRA, the Court has accorded Congress the full measure of respect its judgments in this domain should garner. *South Carolina v. Katzenbach* supplies the standard of review: 'As against the reserved powers of the States, Congress may use any rational means to effectuate the constitutional prohibition of racial discrimination in voting.'" 383 U.S. 301, 324 (1966). *Shelby County*, 570 U.S. at 568.

[38] *Id.* at 567–68.

[39] 769 F.3d 224 (4th Cir. 2014). For these two changes, the Fourth Circuit had concluded that the challengers were likely to prevail on the merits. *Id.* at 244–45.

Fourth Circuit had enjoined a state statute that eliminated same-day registration and prohibited the counting of out-of-precinct ballots as changes that disproportionately impacted black voters. The Supreme Court, however, stayed the mandate of the Fourth Circuit in *North Carolina v. League of Women Voters for North Carolina*.[40] In dissenting to the stay, Justice Ginsburg explained how North Carolina had responded to the holding in *Shelby County,* burdening the franchise through voter identification requirements, shortened early voting periods that restricted the length of time voting poll precincts could remain open, eliminating same-day voter registration, abolishing programs to register 16-year-old and 17-year-old high schoolers, and prohibiting the counting of ballots cast in the wrong precincts.[41] These efforts, said Ginsburg, were the consequence of a world where the preclearance requirement of the VRA played no role in changes made to voting requirements.

Elsewhere, Justice Ginsburg championed a race-conscious understanding of the VRA. For instance, she signed onto a dissent written by Justice Stevens that rejected the majority's use of strict scrutiny to review all Section 2 VRA efforts to comply with traditional districting principles.[42] She agreed with Stevens that when designing majority-minority legislative districts, the Constitution allows states to take race into account along with other considerations, such as compactness, contiguity, and respect for political subdivisions.[43] Justice Stevens and the justices that joined him argued, contrary to the holding, that "strict scrutiny does not apply where a State 'respects' or 'complies with traditional districting principles.'"[44]

Justice Ginsburg predicated her position on majority-minority voting districts on a conviction that "ethnicity itself can tie people together, as volumes of social science literature have documented—even people with divergent economic interests. For this reason, ethnicity is a significant force in political life."[45] That position did not win over a majority. The Court in *Miller v. Johnson*, for example, subjected racial policy considerations to

[40] 574 U.S. 927 (2014).

[41] *Id.* at 927.

[42] Shaw v. Hunt, 517 U.S. 899, 906–07 (1996); *Id.* at 947 n.21 (1996) (Stevens, J., dissenting), *citing* Miller v. Johnson, 515 U.S. 900, 949 (1995) (Ginsburg, J., dissenting).

[43] *Shaw*, 517 U.S. at 918–19 (Stevens, J., dissenting).

[44] *Id.* at 906.

[45] Miller v. Johnson, 515 U.S. 900, 944 (Ginsburg, J., dissenting).

strict scrutiny when regulators rely on them to subordinate "traditional race-neutral districting principles."[46] The majority warned that racial gerrymandering "may balkanize us into competing racial factions" and "carry us further from the goal of a political system in which race no longer matters."[47]

Justice Ginsburg's dissenting opinion in *Miller* argued, to the contrary, that in order to correct past racial voting injustices, "history of exclusion from state politics" required "vigilant judicial inspection to protect minority voters."[48] As a rule of thumb, Ginsburg wrote that race-based districting is permissible "so long as the delineation does not abandon familiar apportionment practices."[49] The tension between her dissent and the majority's opinion lay in their disagreement about whether the same level of exacting scrutiny should apply to policies designed benignly to advance greater voting equality as it does to policies with invidious racial provisions that prevent classes of persons from voting. Neither was she alone. In a separate dissent in *Miller*, Justice Stevens weighed in on her argument, calling on the Court to differentiate between laws designed to aid minority groups from those statutes tailored to cause them electoral harm.[50]

Justice Ginsburg more generally championed state voting rights expansion in her dissent in *Republican National Committee v. Democratic National Committee*.[51] In that case, the per curiam majority opinion stayed a trial court's preliminary injunction that had extended the time period for absentee ballots to be accepted and counted by the Wisconsin Elections Commission, even beyond the time period granted by state statute in a primary election. Ginsburg rejected the Court's opinion as wooden and insensitive to the actual needs of voters. She found that the record demonstrated that many voters never even received absentee ballots in time to meet the statutory deadline because of various delays linked to COVID-19 "pandemic-induced mail delays" rather than any fault of their own.[52] Joined by three other Justices, Ginsburg argued that the judge appropriately

[46] *Id.* at 916.

[47] *Id.*, *quoting* Shaw v. Reno, 509 U.S. 630, 657 (1993).

[48] *Id.* at 947–48 (Ginsburg, J., dissenting).

[49] *Id.* at 947 (Ginsburg, J., dissenting).

[50] *Miller*, 515 U.S. at 933 (Stevens, J., dissenting).

[51] 140 S. Ct. 1205 (2020).

[52] *Id.* 1208–09 (Ginsburg, J., dissenting).

issued the injunction to prevent the deadline from creating an unconstitutional burden on the voting rights of tens of thousands of state citizens.[53] What was most important, she explained, was the "constitutional rights of Wisconsin's citizens, [and] the integrity of the State's election process," rather than technicalities that threatened to disenfranchise them at a "most extraordinary time."[54] That opinion recognized that extraordinary times require extraordinary measures to protect the right to vote.

While most of her election opinions sought to protect the state's expansion of the franchise, Justice Ginsburg also championed the authority of Congress and the states to regulate campaign financing in elections generally and in the election of states judges, the authority of states to regulate the speech of judicial candidates. In the setting of campaign financing, she joined the lengthy, passionate dissent of Justice Stevens in *Citizens United v. Federal Election Commission*,[55] arguing that the dangers to the electoral process of unfettered corporate spending justified the narrow limits that Congress had imposed. Justice Ginsburg felt so strongly that the majority was wrong that she called *Citizens United* the worst decision that the Supreme Court had ever made.[56] Later, Ginsburg reminded the Court of the dangers of the corrupting influence of special corporate interests by making a statement in a per curiam opinion. In *Thompson v. Hebdon*,[57] the Court remanded a decision of the Ninth Circuit that had upheld Alaska's individual contribution limits. While agreeing with the remand, Justice Ginsburg took pains to point out that special circumstances that might warrant limits that were some of the lowest in the country. Since 90 percent of the revenues of the Alaska legislature came from the oil and gas industry, she believed that the Ninth Circuit might find that special circumstances warranted the low limits on individual spending in Alaska elections.

In several of her dissents, Justice Ginsburg distinguished between the voters' substantial rights to know the political leanings of candidates for legislative offices and the state's legitimate interests in limiting the speech of judicial candidates, interests that she tied to the need for an independent

---

[53] *Id.* at 1209 (Ginsburg, J., dissenting).

[54] *Id.* at 1211 (Ginsburg, J., dissenting).

[55] 558 U.S. 310, 393 (2010) (Stevens, J., dissenting).

[56] Jeffrey Rosen, *Ruth Bader Ginsburg is an American Hero: An Interview*, The New Republic, Sept. 28, 2014.

[57] Thompson v. Hebdon, 140 S.Ct. 348 (2019) (Ginsburg, J., statement).

judiciary. While the federal government sought to protect judges from influence by the appointment system, many state judges must run in periodic elections. In that setting, Justice Ginsburg took the position that elected judges must not be beholden to personal or institutional contributors to their campaigns and that judges, unlike politicians, must be free to represent the law rather than the will of their supporters or detractors.[58] She saw limits on the campaign speech of judicial candidates as a way to protect those interests.

In *Republican Party Minnesota v. White*,[59] the majority took a different position. Relying on the First Amendment and strict scrutiny, the majority struck a portion of the state's judicial ethics code that had prohibited candidates for judicial offices from announcing their views on political or legal matters.[60] The regulation subjected violators to probation, suspension, and disbarment. Rather than joining the majority's categorical understanding of free speech, Justice Ginsburg drew attention to the nuances of judicial accountability, political impartiality, and independence. She explained that unlike politicians, judges are ethically expected to engage in impartial decision-making.[61]

In her dissent to *White*, Justice Ginsburg focused on the distinct nature of judicial office, irrespective of whether a judge was elected or appointed to the bench.[62] For both, there is an imperative to act in the public trust. As she believed, therefore, a state can restrict judicial candidates from announcing their views on "disputed political or legal issues."[63] Judicial objectivity calls for independence and exercise of the rule of law.[64] Public confidence, she

---

[58] Chisom v. Roemer, 501 U.S. 380, 411 (1991) (Scalia, J., dissenting) (asserting that "judge[s] represen[t] the Law.").

[59] Republican Party of Minnesota v. White, 536 U.S. 765, 788 (2002).

[60] *Id.* at 788.

[61] *Id.* at 806 (Ginsburg, J., dissenting).

[62] *Id.* at 803 (Ginsburg, J., dissenting) ("Whether state or federal, elected or appointed, judges perform a function fundamentally different from that of the people's elected representatives.").

[63] Minn. Code of Judicial Conduct, Canon 5(A)(3)(d)(i) (2000).

[64] *White*, 536 U.S. at 804 (Ginsburg, J., dissenting) ("The guarantee of an independent, impartial judiciary enables society to 'withdraw certain subjects from the vicissitudes of political controversy, to place them beyond the reach of majorities and officials and to establish them as legal principles to be applied by the courts.'"), *quoting* West Virginia Bd. of Ed. v. Barnette, 319 U.S. 624, 638 (1943); Aharon Barak, Judicial Discretion 5 (1989).

wrote, was a compelling government interest that was within the state's power to advance.[65]

Consistent with the differentiation she articulated in *White* between judicial and political elections, in *Williams-Yulee v. Florida Bar*,[66] Ginsburg returned to the unique nature of judicial office and limitations that a state can place on judges running for election or retention. In a concurrence to *Williams-Yulee*, she again sided with states' restraints on judges' abilities to articulate campaign promises to donors.

While she agreed with the majority that it is the obligation of judges to uphold the Canon of Judicial Conduct, she parted ways with it in a key point of the decision. The majority applied the strict scrutiny standard but found that this was one of those "rare cases" in which a state government had met the demanding burden of proof.[67] Justice Ginsburg rejected the strict standard, finding that standard of review too high under the circumstances. She, moreover, continued to distance herself from the holding in *White*, articulating again that "[s]tates may regulate judicial elections differently than they regulate political elections."[68] She would have allowed states to "balance the constitutional interests in judicial integrity and free expression" rather than entirely abandoning the regulation of public participation in selecting judges.[69]

Perhaps the most partisan battle she ever heard was the case raised by then-Vice President Al Gore's challenge to the 2000 presidential election results in Florida. Less than two weeks before *Bush v. Gore*,[70] the Florida Supreme Court had ordered a limited recount of the state's popular vote, relying on a state legislative prerogative granted by the U.S. Constitution Article II, Section 1, Clause 2,[71] and a state statute that it had interpreted to authorize a contest process.[72] The state court holding provided for a central circuit court judge to review challenges and resolve intercounty

---

[65] *Republican Party of Minnesota*, 536 U.S. at 817 (Ginsburg, J., dissenting).

[66] 575 U.S. 433 (2015).

[67] 575 U.S. at 444.

[68] *Id.* at 458 (Ginsburg, J., concurring).

[69] *Id.* at 461 (Ginsburg, J., dissenting); *White*, 536 U.S. at 821 (Ginsburg, J., dissenting).

[70] 531 U.S. 98 (2000).

[71] Gore v. Harris, 772 So. 2d 1243, 1248 (Fla.), *rev'd and remanded sub nom.* Bush v. Gore, 531 U.S. 98 (2000).

[72] *Id.* at 1248–49, referring to Section 102.168 of Florida Statutes.

differences.[73] State election officials were ordered to complete manual tallies of ballots containing chads that had not fully detached from the ballot cards, resulting in ballot-counting machines to treat those ballots as containing no choice for President.

The majority in *Bush v. Gore*, by a vote of 5–4, reversed the recount order, holding that while the Florida Supreme Court had ordered that a judge discern the "intent of the voter," it failed to supply the specific, interpretive standards to assure uniform outcomes. That ambiguity, it found, violated the Equal Protection Clause of the Fourteenth Amendment.[74] In reaching that conclusion, the Court relied on its own interpretation of Florida law, violating the long-established principle that state's highest courts are final arbiters as to questions of state law[75] and declining to use the option of remanding to the Florida Supreme Court for clarification.[76]

The decision precluded an accurate determination of how Floridians had exercised the constitutional right to vote for presidential electors, and veiled by the per curiam nomenclature, the Court effectively decided the presidential contest in favor of the Republican candidate, George W. Bush.[77]

In a forceful dissent, Justice Ginsburg argued that the majority had undermined the interpretation of a state law, violating basic principles of federalism.[78] Also, under principles of comity, federal courts typically defer to the highest state supreme courts in interpretations of their own laws. That system of interpretive respect preserves state sovereignty.[79]

As Justice Ginsburg reminded her colleagues, "We have dealt with such cases [before] ever mindful of the full measure of respect we owe to

---

[73] *Id.* at 1262.

[74] Bush v. Gore, 531 U.S. 98, 105–06 (2000).

[75] Murdock v. City of Memphis, 87 U.S. (20 Wall.) 590, 626 (1874).

[76] *Id.* at 110–11.

[77] Peter M. Shane, *Disappearing Democracy: How Bush v. Gore Undermined the Federal Right to Vote for Presidential Electors*, 29 FLA. ST. U. L. REV. 535 (2001).

[78] James A. Gardner, *Forcing States to Be Free: The Emerging Constitutional Guarantee of Radical Democracy*, 35 CONN. L. REV. 1467, 1501 n. 196 (2003) ("Through more than two centuries, the principal body of law regulating federal elections has always been, and remains, state law, which governs virtually every aspect of federal elections from the drawing of district lines, to the methods of nominating candidates, to the means of casting and counting ballots.").

[79] Erie R. Co. v. Tompkins, 304 U.S. 64 (1938); *Bush*, 531 U.S. at 112 (Rehnquist, C.J., concurring).

interpretations of state law by a State's highest court."[80] She distinguished the Court's interpretation of ordinary state election law from cases that reviewed state enforcement of civil rights.[81] If anything, the *Bush* majority prevented Florida from safeguarding its citizens' civil liberties.[82] Her dissent implied that the per curiam majority had manipulated standards of review to help the Republican candidate gain political advantage.[83] Additionally, Justice Ginsburg and Justice Breyer joined Justice Stevens's separate dissent that would have found no substantial federal question at issue that could have justified the Supreme Court's review of the 2002 Presidential election in Florida.[84]

Compared to her work in other areas, Justice Ginsburg's volume of productivity on elections was measured. However, her election jurisprudence demonstrates a robust concern for representative government that is not without power to correct past disfranchisement by legislative actions and to maintain an independent judiciary. Her legacy here can be summed up as a democratically inclined approach to the right to vote.

Moreover, she distinguished political and judicial elections, given the different dynamics between the people's political choices and the importance of judge's independence. Here, she championed judicial integrity by means of politically neutral state judicial campaigns.

Most often, she made her voice heard in concurrences and dissents in matters dealing with the franchise. Perhaps Justice Ginsburg's most powerful contribution was the opposition she voiced to a majority that effectively handed a presidential election to a candidate by prohibiting a state-ordered audit to the presidential ballot to proceed. Like other parts of her jurisprudence, her election jurisprudence reveals Justice Ginsburg as a champion of civic rights and civil liberties.

---

[80] *Id.* at 137.

[81] *See, e.g.*, Cooper v. Aaron, 358 U.S. 1 (1958) (ordering the desegregation of Little Rock, Arkansas, public schools).

[82] *Bush*, 531 U.S. at 139–41.

[83] *Id.* at 136 ("There is no cause here to believe that the members of Florida's high court have done less than 'their mortal best to discharge their oath of office,' . . . and no cause to upset their reasoned interpretation of Florida law.").

[84] *See id.* at 123–29 (Stevens, J., dissenting).

3

Abortion and Sex Equality: Brief of Equal Protection Constitutional Law Scholars in *Dobbs v. Jackson Women's Health Organization*

—Reva Siegel, Melissa Murray, and Serena Mayeri

Editor's Note*

Throughout her career as an appellate lawyer and her time on the bench, Justice Ginsburg saw discrimination against pregnant women as a particularly pernicious form of sex discrimination. For Ginsburg, pregnancy and motherhood were more than just biological function or capacity. She recognized that among the political and social consequences of stereotypes about women, none worked more invidiously to cabin women's possibilities

* by Shannon Gilreath

than pregnancy discrimination. She had learned these lessons firsthand. She recalled in interviews:

> I qualified to work as a claims adjuster for the Social Security Administration at Fort Sill. . . . I told the head of the office when I started that I was 3-months pregnant. He said, "Well, we can't place you as a GS-5 because you won't be able to go to Baltimore for training. So, we will list you as a GS-2 and you'll do the work of a GS-5." It was also expected that when my child was born, I would leave. You can see why I am exhilarated by the change I have seen.[1]

Even as a lawyer and academic, the consequences of being pregnant were real for her. She recalled, "I had a year-to-year contract, and I was pretty sure that if I told them I was pregnant, I wouldn't get a contract for the next year. So I wore my mother-in-law's clothes. It was just right. She was one size larger. And I got through the spring semester. When I had the new contract in hand, I told my colleagues, when I came back in the fall, there would be one more in our family. So they stopped thinking that I was gaining a lot of weight."[2]

Because of what she observed and experienced, pregnancy discrimination as sex discrimination became essential to her view that laws enforcing traditional sex roles compromised the "equal citizenship stature" of women.[3] Beginning in the 1970s, she waged a campaign to secure the rights of citizenship for women through equal protection in cases like *Reed v. Reed,* which challenged a law that drew sex-based distinctions between male and

---

[1] Reva B. Siegel, *The Pregnant Citizen, from Suffrage to the Present*, 19TH AMEND. ED. GEO. L.J. 167 (2020) at 182; Brandon O'Connor, *Justice Ginsburg Visits West Point for Zengerle Family Lecture Series*, U.S. ARMY (Sept. 20, 2018), https://www.army.mil/article/211408/justice_ginsburg_visits_west_point_for_zengerle_family_lecture_series.

[2] *Ruth Bader Ginsburg: Justice for All*, WHAT IT TAKES (Sept. 26, 2016), https://whatittakes.simplecast.com/episodes/40ca4a6b-40ca4a6b.

[3] Justice Ginsburg used this or similar language in a variety of settings, both on and off the Court. *See, e.g.*, Gonzales v. Carhart, 127 S. Ct. 1610, 1641 (2007) (Ginsburg, J., dissenting) ("Legal challenges to undue restrictions on abortion procedures do not seek to vindicate some generalized notion of privacy; rather, they center on a woman's autonomy to determine her life's course, and thus to enjoy equal citizenship stature"); United States v. Virginia (VMI), 518 U.S. 515, 532 (1996) ("The Court has repeatedly recognized that neither federal nor state government acts compatibly with the equal protection principle when a law or official policy denies to women, simply because they are women, full citizenship stature – equal opportunity to aspire, achieve, participate in and contribute to society based on their individual talents and capacities").

female candidates to administer a decedent's estate.[4] In *Reed*, as in many of her carefully chosen early cases, Ginsburg's strategy targeted laws that imposed sex-role stereotypes on women and men without insisting that the sexes were in fact the same.[5] Of course, Ginsburg's representation of male plaintiffs in cases from this era drew harsh criticism.

But much less widely known, Ginsburg's initial campaign also singled out pregnancy discrimination.[6] In one of her first actions at the newly founded Women's Rights Project (WRP) at the American Civil Liberties Union (ACLU),[7] Ginsburg appealed a Ninth Circuit decision in *Struck v. Secretary of Defense* on behalf of an Air Force officer who was subject to automatic discharge on grounds of pregnancy or new motherhood—leaving the officer the only option of aborting the pregnancy—while male Air Force officers who were about to become fathers were not subject to a similar requirement.[8] Ginsburg contested the regulation on equal protection and substantive due process grounds.[9] She urged the Supreme Court to suspend sex-role assumptions and recognize that there were other similarly situated persons in the Air Force to whom the plaintiff could be compared: "Because pregnancy, though

---

[4] Reed v. Reed, 404 U.S. 71, 73 (1971).

[5] *See* Cary Franklin, *The Anti-Stereotyping Principle In Constitutional Sex Discrimination Law*, 85 N.Y.U.L. Rev. 83 (2010) at 86–87. For additional commentary on pregnancy and the Struck case, see *id.* at 125–28.

[6] In the early 1970s, Ginsburg authored briefs and law review articles arguing that laws according differential treatment on the basis of pregnancy should be subject to strict scrutiny under the Equal Protection Clause and under the Equal Rights Amendment. See *id.* note 163 (citing sources in addition to the *Struck* brief).

[7] *See* Amy Leigh Campbell, *Raising the Bar: Ruth Bader Ginsburg and the ACLU Women's Rights Project*, 11 Tex. J. Women & L. 157, 165 (2002) ("The ACLU's Board of Directors declared women's rights to be their top legal and legislative priority in December 1971 following the victory in Reed v. Reed. The Board hired Professor Ruth Bader Ginsburg to found and direct the Women's Rights Project (WRP) in the spring of 1972 in recognition of her successful collaboration with ACLU attorney Mel Wulf." (footnote omitted)).

[8] Brief for the Petitioner at 3–4, Struck v. Sec'y of Def., 409 U.S. 1071 (1972) (No. 72-178), 1972 WL 135840. For the regulation, see Struck v. Secretary of Defense, 460 F.2d 1372, 1374 (9th Cir. 1971). For accounts of the Struck case, see generally Neil S. Siegel & Reva B. Siegel, *Struck by Stereotype: Ruth Bader Ginsburg on Pregnancy Discrimination as Sex Discrimination*, 59 Duke Law J. (2010) and Neil S. Siegel, *The Pregnant Captain, the Notorious RBG, and the Vision of RBG: The Story of* Struck v. Secretary of Defense, *in* Reproductive Rights and Justice Stories 33 (Melissa Murray et al. eds., 2019). For an interview with the plaintiff and other commentary on the case, see Dahlia Lithwick, Loretta Ross, Neil Siegel & Reva Siegel, *Body of Law: Beyond Roe*, On the Media (Dec. 13, 2019), https://www.wnycstudios.org/podcasts/otm/episodes/on-the-media-body-law-beyond-roe.

[9] *See* Brief for the Petitioner at 7–12.

unique to women, is like other medical conditions, the failure to treat it as such amounts to discrimination which is without rational basis, and therefore is violative of the equal protection clause of the Fourteenth Amendment."[10]

Ginsburg explained that the Air Force's policy of immediately discharging pregnant-women officers who continued their pregnancies "reflect[ed] arbitrary notions of woman's place wholly at odds with contemporary legislative and judicial recognition that individual potential must not be restrained, nor equal opportunity limited, by law-sanctioned stereotypical prejudgments."[11] As she had as amicus in a more famous case challenging the unequal treatment of male and female dependents of Air Force officers,[12] in her *Struck* brief Ginsburg asked the Court to review the discharge regulation under a strict scrutiny framework.[13] Ginsburg closed her brief in *Struck*, filed just before the Court handed down *Roe v. Wade*,[14] with a due process challenge to the policy as violating Struck's "right to sexual privacy," her autonomy in deciding "whether to bear . . . a child,"[15] and her right to free exercise of religion.[16] As for Struck, "[t]he Air Force ultimately abandoned its discriminatory policy before the Supreme Court could rule on the case, perhaps aware of the optics in a case in which the government was asking a Catholic woman to have an abortion as the price for maintaining her position in the Air Force."[17] But in her *Struck* brief, Ginsburg's analysis situated pregnancy as "a locus of traditional sex-role stereotyping" requiring strict scrutiny,[18] an approach "shared by movement lawyers building sex equality jurisprudence under the [Equal Rights Amendment (ERA)]."[19]

---

[10] *Id.* at 17; Reva B. Siegel, *The Pregnant Citizen, from Suffrage to the Present*, 19TH AMEND. ED. GEO. L.J. 167 (2020) at 183.

[11] *See* Brief for the Petitioner at 14.

[12] *See* Brief of American Civil Liberties Union Amicus Curiae, Frontiero v. Richardson (1973) (No. 71-1694).

[13] Brief for the Petitioner at 26–52.

[14] 410 U.S. 113 (1973).

[15] *See* Brief for the Petitioner at 54.

[16] *Id.* at 56–58.

[17] Reva B. Siegel, *The Pregnant Citizen, from Suffrage to the Present*, 108 GEO. L.J. 19th Amend. Special Edition 167 (2020) at 183–84.

[18] *Id.* at 184.

[19] *Id.*

Given her advocacy challenging laws that regulate pregnancy, it is unsurprising that Ginsburg criticized the *Roe v. Wade* opinion for basing the right to access abortion on privacy rather than on equal protection. Ginsburg wrote that "the shape of the law on gender-based classification and reproductive autonomy indicates and influences the opportunity women will have to participate as men's full partners in the nation's social, political, and economic life."[20] Similarly, she insisted that "[a]lso in the balance is a woman's autonomous charge of her full life's course . . . her ability to stand in relation to man, society, and the state as an independent, self-sustaining, equal citizen."[21] Her analysis of the abortion question thus focused primarily not on the right to privacy, but on the "woman's equality aspect" to reproductive rights, the "equal-regard values involved in cases on abortion."[22]

Some 20 years later in a white-hot dissent, Justice Ginsburg lambasted the majority for ignoring the equality dimensions of abortion access in *Gonzales v. Carhart*, in which the Court rejected a facial challenge to the federal Partial Birth Abortion Ban of 2003.[23] "Legal challenges to undue restrictions on abortion procedures do not seek to vindicate some generalized notion of privacy," Ginsburg wrote. "[R]ather, they center on a woman's autonomy to determine her life's course, and thus to enjoy equal citizenship stature."[24] She viewed the statute under review, and the Court's defense of it, as threatening the equal citizenship of American women. Indeed, she explicitly invoked the impediments to "women's progress toward full citizenship stature throughout our Nation's history"[25] that she underscored on behalf of the Court in *United States v. Virginia*.[26] Her dissenting opinion in *Carhart* effectively concluded that the moralism and paternalism that the Act substituted for women's autonomous decision-making amounted to a violation of the Equal Protection Clause.[27]

---

[20] Ruth B. Ginsburg, *Some Thoughts on Autonomy and Equality in Relation to* Roe v. Wade, 63 N.C. L. Rev. 375 (1985) at 375.

[21] *Id.* at 383.

[22] *Id.* at 385.

[23] 550 U.S. 124 (2007).

[24] *Id.* at 172.

[25] *Id.* at 185.

[26] 518 U.S. 515 (1996).

[27] 550 U.S. at 185.

The Court's obliteration of constitutional due process protections for the abortion right in *Dobbs v. Jackson Women's Health Organization* would have undoubtedly provoked from Ginsburg a painstaking and withering dissent.[28] It is impossible to know what exactly she would have said, and the brief that follows, filed in the case by Reva Siegel, Serena Mayeri, and Melissa Murray, did not purport to speak for her. It was, however, grounded in Ginsburg's first principles of sex equality and written with her spirit as an animating guide.

[28] 142 S. Ct. 2228 (2022).

No. 19-1392

In the Supreme Court of the United States

THOMAS E. DOBBS, STATE HEALTH OFFICER OF THE MISSISSIPPI DEPARTMENT OF HEALTH, *et al.*,
Petitioners,
v.

JACKSON WOMEN'S HEALTH ORGANIZATION, *et al.*,
Respondents.

On Writ of Certiorari to the United States Court of Appeals for the Fifth Circuit

BRIEF OF EQUAL PROTECTION CONSTITUTIONAL LAW SCHOLARS SERENA MAYERI, MELISSA MURRAY, AND REVA SIEGEL AS AMICI CURIAE IN SUPPORT OF RESPONDENTS

ROBERTA A. KAPLAN
Counsel of Record
RAYMOND P. TOLENTINO
MARCELLA COBURN
RACHEL TUCHMAN
ANNA COLLINS PETERSON
Kaplan Hecker & Fink LLP
350 Fifth Avenue, 63rd Floor
New York, NY 10118
(212) 763-0883
rkaplan@kaplanhecker.com

Counsel for Amici Curiae

September 20, 2021

Becker Gallagher · Cincinnati, OH · Washington, D.C. · 800.890.5001

TABLE OF CONTENTS

Page

TABLE OF AUTHORITIES

Page(s)

CASES

v

1

INTEREST OF *AMICI CURIAE*

Amici Serena Mayeri, Melissa Murray, and Reva Siegel are professors of constitutional law and equality law. They submit this brief to identify and explain the equal protection principles that support Respondents' position and afford an independent basis on which to affirm the judgment below.[1]

Serena Mayeri is Professor of Law and History at University of Pennsylvania Carey Law School; Melissa Murray is Frederick I. and Grace Stokes Professor of Law at New York University School of Law; and Reva Siegel is Nicholas deB. Katzenbach Professor of Law at Yale Law School.[2]

SUMMARY OF ARGUMENT

The fundamental right at stake in this case matters to millions of Americans—not only to those who choose to end their pregnancies, but also to those who make life decisions secure in the understanding that they *could* make that choice if necessary. One in four women of child-bearing age in this country will have an abortion. They represent every race, religion,

---

[1] All parties have consented to the filing of this brief. No counsel for a party authored this brief in whole or in part, and no party or counsel for a party made a monetary contribution intended to fund its preparation or submission. No person other than *amici* or *amici*'s counsel made a monetary contribution to the preparation or submission of this brief.

[2] *Amici* join this brief as individuals; institutional affiliation is noted for informational purposes only and does not indicate endorsement by institutional employers of the positions advocated in this brief.

socioeconomic background, and more.[3] They often are already raising children themselves. And because our society provides such inadequate infrastructure for families and so little support for caregivers, increasingly, those who decide to end their pregnancies are living in poverty.[4]

HB 1510 impermissibly burdens the constitutional right to liberty and bodily autonomy—in direct violation of this Court's precedent in *Roe v. Wade*, 410 U.S. 113 (1973), and *Planned Parenthood of Southeastern Pennsylvania v. Casey*, 505 U.S. 833 (1992). *See* Resp. Br. 2-3, 12-15. But HB 1510 also violates another fundamental constitutional guarantee—the right to equal protection under the law. *See id.* at 36-41. As *amici* explain in this brief, the Equal Protection Clause supplies an additional, independent basis for the constitutional right to an abortion, and it forbids states like Mississippi from trampling on that right by passing laws like HB 1510.

---

[3] *See* Rachel K. Jones & Jenna Jerman, *Population Group Abortion Rates and Lifetime Incidence of Abortion: United States, 2008-2014*, 107 AM. J. PUB. HEALTH 1904, 1907 (2017) (finding that "an estimated 23.7% of women aged 15 to 44 years in 2014 will have an abortion by age 45"); *see also* Patrick T. Brown, *Catholics Are Just as Likely to Get an Abortion as Other U.S. Women. Why?*, AMERICA (Jan. 24, 2018), https://www.americamagazine.org/politics-society/2018/01/24/catholics-are-just-likely-get-abortion-other-us-women-why.

[4] *See, e.g.*, Sabrina Tavernise, *Why Women Getting Abortions Now Are More Likely to Be Poor*, N.Y. TIMES (July 9, 2019), https://www.nytimes.com/2019/07/09/us/abortion-access-inequality.html ("Half of all women who got an abortion in 2014 lived in poverty, double the share from 1994 … .").

3

Under this Court's equal protection jurisprudence, laws that classify on the basis of sex—including laws that regulate pregnancy—are subject to heightened scrutiny. *United States v. Virginia*, 518 U.S. 515, 533-34 (1996) ("*Virginia*"); *see also Nev. Dep't of Hum. Res. v. Hibbs*, 538 U.S. 721, 728-34 (2003). To survive heightened scrutiny, the State of Mississippi must offer an "exceedingly persuasive justification" for its sex-based classification: specifically, it must show that its decision to regulate by sex-discriminatory means is substantially related to the achievement of important governmental objectives. *Virginia*, 518 U.S. at 531-33. In making that showing, the State may "not rely on overbroad generalizations about the different talents, capacities, or preferences of males and females," nor may sex classifications "be used, as they once were, to create or perpetuate the legal, social, and economic inferiority of women." *Id.* at 533-34 (internal citation omitted). HB 1510 does not pass constitutional muster under this standard.

Mississippi has enacted HB 1510 to "protect[] the life of the unborn" and to "protect[] the health of women." *See* H.B. 1510 § 1(2)(b)(i)-(v), 2018 Leg., Reg. Sess. (Miss. 2018) (citations omitted). With certain narrow exceptions, the statute prohibits physicians from performing "an abortion" on a "maternal patient" after 15 weeks—singling out a pregnant woman and imposing on her the role of mother. *See id.* § 1(4). But the State denies the enormity of this imposition by expressly claiming that coercing motherhood, over a woman's objection, protects the woman in addition to any fetal life she may carry. *See id.* § 1(2)(b)(ii)-(v). The statute's paternalist justifications derive from "overbroad generalizations," *Virginia*, 518 U.S. at 533, about women as destined for motherhood that date back to nineteenth-century anti-abortion campaigns.

Relying on these antiquated sex-role stereotypes, Mississippi assumed it could fulfill *both* of its important objectives (protecting fetal life and women's health) by prohibiting abortion after 15 weeks. Because the State relied so heavily on sex-role stereotypes to achieve its two ends, it failed to explore the many less discriminatory and noncoercive ways to reduce abortion and to protect the life and health of women and future generations—such as by providing appropriate and effective sex education or assisting those who wish to bear children.

For these reasons, Mississippi has failed to offer an "exceedingly persuasive justification" for forcing a woman to continue pregnancy. *Id.* at 531. HB 1510 instead enforces a sex-based and coercive classification that "perpetuate[s] the legal, social, and economic inferiority of women." *Id.* at 534. Although people of all gender identities may become pregnant, seek abortions, or bear children, *see* Resp. Br. 13 n.3, this brief focuses on the constitutionally impermissible sex-role judgments about women that historically undergird laws regulating abortion, *see infra* Part II, including HB 1510. *See, e.g.*, Miss. H.B. 1510 § 1(2) (using language such as "maternal patient" and "women"); *see also infra* n.13 (reporting on debate among State legislators about the Mississippi women on whom the State's abortion regulations focus).[5]

---

[5] Laws that discriminate on the basis of pregnancy can involve various forms of sex-based discrimination, as this Court has

This brief proceeds in four parts. *First*, *amici* demonstrate that, under this Court's existing precedent, laws that regulate pregnancy, like HB 1510, are sex classifications subject to heightened scrutiny. *Second*, *amici* explain how HB 1510's attempt to protect both women's health and fetal life violates settled equal protection principles by relying on archaic notions about a woman's social role. *Third*, *amici* show that Mississippi relied on these impermissible assumptions to enact HB 1510's regulation on abortion and, in fact, rejected numerous other less discriminatory means of protecting women's health and fetal life. And *fourth*, *amici* explain why attempts to justify HB 1510 on equality grounds are meritless.

ARGUMENT

I. HB 1510 VIOLATES THE EQUAL PROTECTION CLAUSE

A. This Court's Precedents Recognize That Equality Principles Underlie the Constitutional Right to an Abortion

The right to make decisions about whether to end a pregnancy is grounded in both the Due Process and Equal Protection Clauses. In *Casey*, this Court acknowledged that women's talent, capacity, and right "to participate equally in the economic and social life

---

acknowledged. *Cf. Bostock v. Clayton County*, 140 S. Ct. 1731, 1744 (2020) ("In *Phillips*, the employer could have accurately spoken of its policy as one based on 'motherhood.' In much the same way, today's employers might describe their actions as motivated by their employees' homosexuality or transgender status.").

of the Nation" is dependent on "their ability to control their reproductive lives." 505 U.S. at 856. Indeed, because of the physical, emotional, spiritual, economic, and social stakes of pregnancy and motherhood, the State cannot "insist, without more, upon its own vision of the woman's role, however dominant that vision has been in the course of our history and of our culture. The destiny of the woman must be shaped to a large extent on her own conception of her spiritual imperatives and her place in society." *Id.* at 852; *see also Gonzales v. Carhart*, 550 U.S. 124, 172 (2007) (Ginsburg, J., dissenting) ("[L]egal challenges to undue restrictions on abortion procedures ... center on a woman's autonomy to determine her life's course, and thus to enjoy equal citizenship ... .").[6]

And just last Term, Justice Sotomayor recognized the equality interests at stake in accessing abortion. Justice Sotomayor observed that "[t]his country's laws have long singled out abortions for more onerous treatment than other medical procedures that carry similar or greater risks," imposing "an unnecessary, irrational, and unjustifiable undue burden on women seeking to exercise their right to choose." *FDA v. Am. Coll. of Obstetricians & Gynecologists*, 141 S. Ct. 578, 585 (2021) (Sotomayor, J., dissenting) (citing *Gonzales*, 550 U.S. at 172 (Ginsburg, J., dissenting)).

---

[6] *Cf. Lawrence v. Texas*, 539 U.S. 558, 575 (2003) ("Equality of treatment and the due process right to demand respect for conduct protected by the substantive guarantee of liberty are linked in important respects, and a decision on the latter point advances both interests.").

Those undue burdens are often most severe for low-income women and women of color. *Id.* at 582.

Accordingly, Justices of this Court have long acknowledged the fundamental equality principles that underlie the constitutional right to an abortion. Similarly, and over time, the Court has applied its prohibition on discriminatory sex-based classifications to laws regulating pregnancy. As *amici* explain in further detail below, HB 1510 violates those equality principles by imposing an unjustified and profoundly dangerous sex-based restriction on a woman's right to control her own reproductive life.[7]

B. Pregnancy Regulations Are Sex-Based Classifications Subject to Heightened Scrutiny

Throughout much of American history, belief in traditional gender roles has shaped the Nation's laws, including the assumptions that "a woman is, and should remain, 'the center of home and family life,'" and that "'a proper discharge of [a woman's] maternal

[7] Even before *Casey*, prominent legal scholars recognized that the abortion right is also protected by the Constitution's equality guarantees. *See Casey*, 505 U.S. at 928 & n.4 (Blackmun, J., concurring in part) (observing that the "assumption—that women can simply be forced to accept the 'natural' status and incidents of motherhood—appears to rest upon a conception of women's role that has triggered the protection of the Equal Protection Clause" and citing scholarship); *see also* Serena Mayeri, *Undue-ing Roe: Constitutional Conflict and Political Polarization in* Planned Parenthood v. Casey, *in* REPRODUCTIVE RIGHTS AND JUSTICE STORIES 150-52 (Melissa Murray, Katherine Shaw & Reva B. Siegel, eds. 2019) (describing role of sex equality principles in academic and judicial discourse leading up to *Casey*).

functions ... justif[ies] [protective] legislation,'" *Hibbs*, 538 U.S. at 729 (third alteration added) (citing *Hoyt v. Florida*, 368 U.S. 57, 62 (1961), and *Muller v. Oregon*, 208 U.S. 412, 422 (1908)). Those sex-role stereotypes led three members of this Court to insist that "[t]he paramount destiny and mission of woman are to fulfil the noble and benign offices of wife and mother. This is the law of the Creator." *Bradwell v. Illinois*, 83 U.S. (16 Wall.) 130, 141 (1872) (Bradley, J., joined by Swayne and Field, JJ., concurring in judgment) (upholding a state's denial of a law license to a woman because of her sex).

Fifty years ago, this Court changed course and began to strike down sex-based state action that enforced these traditional gender stereotypes as unconstitutional under the Equal Protection Clause. *See Reed v. Reed*, 404 U.S. 71, 76 (1971); *Frontiero v. Richardson*, 411 U.S. 677, 684-85 (1973) (plurality opinion) (citing *Bradwell* as evidence of the Nation's "long and unfortunate history of sex discrimination"). The Court did not initially give a clear account of how pregnancy-based regulations perpetuate these stereotypes. *See Geduldig v. Aiello*, 417 U.S. 484, 496 n.20 (1974). But as the Court gained experience interpreting the Pregnancy Discrimination Act of 1978, 42 U.S.C. § 2000e(k) (2018), it began to explain how certain laws regulating pregnancy could be based on impermissible sex-role stereotypes, *see Cal. Fed. Sav. & Loan Ass'n v. Guerra*, 479 U.S. 272, 289-90 (1987) (Marshall, J.) (upholding a state law mandating a reasonable, unpaid pregnancy disability leave as consistent with the Pregnancy Discrimination Act and Title VII because it "promotes equal employment opportunity" and "does not reflect archaic

9

or stereotypic notions about pregnancy and the abilities of pregnant workers").

The Court thereafter made clear that equal protection principles apply with equal force to pregnancy-based classifications. Justice Ginsburg's landmark decision in *United States v. Virginia* recognized that pregnancy-based regulations, too, are sex classifications subject to scrutiny under the Equal Protection Clause. *See Virginia*, 518 U.S. at 533-34 (citing *Cal. Fed.*, 479 U.S. at 289). In *Virginia*, the Court held that sex classifications cannot be justified by physical differences between men and women. The Court affirmed that the Constitution's equality guarantees extend to women as men's equals, regardless of any "inherent differences" between the sexes. Those "[i]nherent differences," the Court explained, "remain cause for celebration, but not for denigration of the members of either sex or for artificial constraints on an individual's opportunity." *Id.*

Not every sex classification, the Court reasoned, was constitutionally infirm. Sex classifications that "promot[e] equal employment opportunity" or "advance [the] full development of the talent and capacities of our Nation's people"—like the state law establishing unpaid pregnancy disability leave at issue in *Cal. Fed.*—are permissible. *Id.* at 533 (quoting *Cal. Fed.*, 479 U.S. at 289 (first alteration in original)). But the Court in *Virginia* held that the Constitution's guarantee of equal protection means that sex "classifications may not be used, as they once were ... to create or perpetuate the legal, social, and economic

10

inferiority of women." *Id.* at 534 (internal citation omitted).

Seven years later, Chief Justice Rehnquist elaborated on *Virginia*'s logic, further confirming that the Equal Protection Clause applied to laws regulating pregnancy. In *Hibbs*, the Court held that Congress could enact the Family and Medical Leave Act to remedy and prevent inequality in the provision of family leave because historically, "ideology about women's roles" had been used to justify discrimination against women particularly when they were "mothers or mothers-to-be." 538 U.S. at 736 (citation omitted).

Hibbs made clear that pregnancy-based regulations anchored in archaic stereotypes about gender roles can violate the Equal Protection Clause. As Chief Justice Rehnquist put it, the "differential [maternity and paternity] leave policies were not attributable to any differential physical needs of men and women, but rather to the pervasive sex-role stereotype that caring for family members is women's work." *Id.* at 731. Laws perpetuating such sex-role stereotypes injured women *and* men. And "[t]hese mutually reinforcing stereotypes," the Chief Justice recognized, "created a self-fulfilling cycle of discrimination that forced women to continue to assume the role of primary family caregiver." *Id.* at 736 ("Because employers continued to regard the family as the woman's domain, they often denied men similar accommodations or discouraged them from taking leave.").

Taken together, *Virginia* and *Hibbs* establish that laws regulating pregnancy are sex-based classifications that violate the Equal Protection

Clause when they are rooted in sex-role stereotypes that injure or subordinate. *See* Reva B. Siegel, *The Pregnant Citizen, from Suffrage to the Present*, 19TH AMENDMENT SPECIAL EDITION GEO. L.J. 167, 189-211 (2020); *see also id.* at 208 & n.229 (explaining *Geduldig*'s status after *Virginia* and *Hibbs*).

C. Because HB 1510 Regulates Pregnancy, It Must Satisfy Heightened Scrutiny

HB 1510 singles out pregnant women for coercive regulation. By its terms, the law is designed to deprive women, and not men, of their right to make choices about whether or not to have children.

Because Mississippi has chosen "discriminatory means" to protect health and life, the State must satisfy heightened scrutiny by offering an "exceedingly persuasive" justification for its choice of means that does not rely on "overbroad generalizations" about the differences between sexes. *Virginia*, 518 U.S. at 533. In scrutinizing sex-based state action for impermissible sex stereotyping, the *Virginia* standard examines the law's historical context and the State's decision-making in a larger policy context to ascertain whether the State's sex-based classification is being used "to create or perpetuate the legal, social, and economic inferiority of women." *Id.* at 534.[8]

[8] *See Virginia*, 518 U.S. at 535-40 (determining from historical context that stereotyped beliefs about sex roles originating in nineteenth-century ideas about women's physical and reproductive fragility underpinned the exclusion of women from VMI); *id.* at 539 (determining from policy context that VMI's

HB 1510 does not satisfy heightened scrutiny for at least two reasons. First, considered in historical context, the State's legislative findings reflect "ancient notions about women's place in the family and under the Constitution—ideas that have long since been discredited." *Gonzales*, 550 U.S. at 185 (Ginsburg, J., dissenting). *See infra* Part II. Second, relying on these traditional sex roles, the State assumed it could protect fetal life *and* the health of women by prohibiting abortion after 15 weeks. But gripped by those stereotyped beliefs, Mississippi failed to adopt many alternative, less discriminatory means of reducing abortion and supporting those who seek to raise children. *See infra* Part III.

II. MISSISSIPPI'S JUSTIFICATIONS FOR HB 1510 ARE INEXTRICABLY INTERTWINED WITH OUTDATED STEREOTYPES ABOUT WOMEN

Petitioners insist that *Roe* and *Casey* "shackle States to a view of the facts that is decades out of date." Pet. Br. 4. To the contrary, Mississippi's own logic and its laws are anchored in the past.

Today, as in the past, advocates of laws like HB 1510 argue that restricting abortion will protect fetal life *and* protect women—all while denying that limiting abortion access risks hurting women.[9] *See*

---

rejection of coeducation in 1986 did not reflect "any Commonwealth policy evenhandedly to advance diverse educational options").

[9] In the 1990s, in response to public unease with arguments against abortion that ignored or attacked women, advocates

Miss. H.B. 1510 § 1(2)(b)(i) (finding that banning abortion protects fetal life); *id.* § 1(2)(b)(ii)-(v) (finding that banning abortion protects women).

These justifications are not new. The nineteenth-century anti-abortion campaign, too, claimed that regulating abortion would protect women's physical and psychological health. The anti-abortion campaign shows how a call to protect a pregnant woman's health can function as an effort to enforce a woman's role as mother. Most importantly, the campaign demonstrates how seemingly benign concerns can be deeply entangled with wholly unconstitutional reasons for compelling a woman to bear a child. *See* Reva Siegel, *Reasoning from the Body: A Historical Perspective on Abortion Regulation and Questions of Equal Protection*, 44 STAN. L. REV. 261, 280-323 (1992) (showing how nineteenth-century doctors argued that banning abortion would protect fetal life, protect a woman's health, enforce wives' marital duties, and control the relative birthrates of "native" and immigrant populations, in order to preserve the demographic character of the nation); *see also infra* Part IV.

---

began to emphasize that restricting abortion not only protects fetal life, but also protects women's psychological and physical health. *See* Reva B. Siegel, *Why Restrict Abortion? Expanding the Frame on* June Medical, 2020 SUP. CT. REV. (forthcoming 2021) (manuscript at 20-33), https://papers.ssrn.com/sol3/papers.cfm?abstract_id=3799645 (explaining how anti-abortion movement's "pro-woman and pro-life" claims implicitly and expressly appeal to the sex role-based belief that what is best for children is best for the mother's health).

14

A. Historical Context Illustrates That Sex Stereotypes Are Interwoven into Abortion Restrictions Like HB 1510

In the nineteenth century, the physician who led the campaign to ban abortion, Dr. Horatio Storer, claimed that childbearing was "the end for which [married women] are physiologically constituted and for which they are destined by nature." *See* HORATIO STORER, WHY NOT? A BOOK FOR EVERY WOMAN 75-76 (1866); JAMES C. MOHR, ABORTION IN AMERICA: THE ORIGINS AND EVOLUTION OF NATIONAL POLICY, 1800–1900, 78, 89, 148 (1978) (recounting Storer's role in persuading Americans to ban abortion). According to Storer, avoiding this pre-ordained biological and social role would lead to a woman's physical and social ruin. *See* STORER, *supra*, at 37 ("[A]ny infringement of [natural laws] must necessarily cause derangement, disaster, or ruin."); H.S. POMEROY, THE ETHICS OF MARRIAGE 97 (1888) ("Interference with Nature so that she may not accomplish the production of healthy human beings is a physiological sin of the most heinous sort … ."). The American Medical Association's 1871 *Report on Criminal Abortion* denounced a woman who ended a pregnancy: "She becomes unmindful of the course marked out for her by Providence, she overlooks the duties imposed on her by the marriage contract." D.A. O'Donnell & W.L. Atlee, *Report on Criminal Abortion*, 22 TRANSACTIONS AM. MED. ASS'N 239, 241 (1871).

During this same time, doctors further justified controlling women's roles by asserting women's incompetence to make their own decisions about sex and childbearing. Because they understood childbearing as the "end for which [women] are psychologically constituted and for which they are destined by nature," anti-abortion advocates claimed that termination of pregnancy is "disastrous to a woman's mental, moral, and physical well-being." STORER, *supra*, at 75-76. The notion that interrupting a pregnancy produced feminine hysteria followed neatly from the premise that women lack decisional capacity to choose to avoid motherhood. *See* E.P. Christian, *The Pathological Consequences Incident to Induced Abortion*, 2 DETROIT REV. MED. & PHARMACY 145, 146 (1867) (noting that "violence against the physiological laws of gestation" would cause a "severe and grievous penalty" because of "the intimate relation between the nervous and uterine systems manifested in the various and frequent nervous disorders arising from uterine derangements"). Further, the choice to avoid motherhood was believed to confer "a moral as well as a physical taint" that "stamps its effects indelibly on the constitution of the female." J.J. Mulheron, *Foeticide: A Paper Read Before the Wayne County Medical Society*, 10 PENINSULAR J. MED. 385, 390 (1874).

And just as women's minds were supposedly irrevocably and deleteriously affected by abortion, so too were their bodies. Physicians claimed that abortion would "insidiously undermine[]" women's reproductive organs, and "permanently incapacitate[] [women] for conception." STORER, *supra*, at 50. A woman who has an abortion "destroys her health ... [and] sooner or later comes upon the hands of the physician suffering with uterine disease." O.S. Phelps, *Criminal Abortion: Read Before the Calhoun County Medical Society,* 1 DETROIT LANCET 725, 728 (1878).

According to anti-abortion advocates, these and other health issues were a "direct result of this interference with *nature's* laws." L.D. Griswold et al., *Additional Report from the Select Committee to Whom Was Referred S.B. No. 285*, 1867 OHIO SENATE J. APPENDIX 233, 234 (emphasis added). It should come as little surprise that "[s]tatements hostile to the woman's rights movement appeared in many of the anti-abortion tracts penned by America's doctors and their supporters." Siegel, *Reasoning from the Body*, *supra*, at 303; *see generally id.* at 302-14.[10]

B. HB 1510 Rests on Modern Expressions of Outdated Sex-Role Stereotypes

HB 1510 recites Mississippi's interests in banning abortion to protect fetal life and women's health. *See* Miss. H.B. 1510 § 1(2)(b)(i)-(ii). Although the State does not employ nineteenth-century rhetoric in its legislative findings, its asserted justifications for HB 1510 are a modern twist on the same old sex-role

---

[10] Emphasizing the importance of a woman's right to "voluntary motherhood" (that is, to oppose her husband's sexual advances), abolitionist and suffragist Lucy Stone remarked, "[i]t is very little to me to have the right to vote, to own property, ... if I may not keep my body, and its uses, in my absolute right." *Id.* at 305 (quoting Letter from Lucy Stone to Antoinette Brown (Blackwell) (July 11, 1855), *quoted in* ELIZABETH CAZDEN, ANTOINETTE BROWN BLACKWELL: A BIOGRAPHY 100 (1983)). Doctors leading the nineteenth-century campaign against abortion attacked arguments for voluntary motherhood on the grounds that recognizing a wife's right to refuse her husband's sexual advances would make marriage a relation of "legalized prostitution." *See id.* at 308-14. This debate over women's sexual and reproductive autonomy offered competing perspectives on the practice of abortion.

stereotypes that animated anti-abortion campaigners in centuries past.

Like nineteenth-century physicians, Mississippi assumes that women are incapable of deciding for themselves how to balance the comparative health risks and emotional burdens of continued pregnancy, childbirth, and abortion. For instance, the legislative findings in HB 1510 declare that "[a]bortion carries significant physical and psychological risks to the maternal patient," including "depression; anxiety; substance abuse; and other emotional or psychological problems." *Id.* § 1(2)(b)(ii), (iv). The State Legislature further asserts that the "medical, emotional, and psychological consequences of abortion are serious and can be lasting." *Id.* § 1(2)(b)(v) (internal quotation marks omitted); *see* Pet. Br. 8.

That unsupported assertion reflects the same stereotypical view of women's fragile, maternal psyche espoused by nineteenth-century anti-abortion advocates. Meanwhile, the mental and emotional stress of pregnancy, childbirth, and caring for children—in an economy that discriminates against mothers and pregnant people—go entirely unmentioned. *See* Stephen Benard et al., *Cognitive Bias and the Motherhood Penalty*, 59 HASTINGS L.J. 1359, 1359-61 (2008). Rather than leave judgments about how to balance these risks to *women*, Mississippi has decided to make the decision for itself, banning abortions after 15 weeks on the ground that doing so is in the psychological best interests of the "maternal patient." Miss. H.B. 1510 § 1(2)(b)(ii).

There is a second, even more fundamental, sex-role assumption underlying HB 1510. As the Court in

Virginia recounted, it was commonplace for nineteenth-century doctors to argue that women who violated sex roles (*e.g.*, by pursuing higher education) risked jeopardizing their reproductive physiology. *See Virginia*, 518 U.S. at 536-37 & n.9. The physicians in Storer's campaign repeatedly warned of the litany of health harms that would attend a woman's deviation from her reproductive destiny. *See supra* Part II.A. The reasoning Mississippi offers for banning abortion after 15 weeks—to protect the health of the "maternal patient," Miss. H.B. 1510 § 1(2)(b)(ii), (iii), echoes the sex-role assumptions of the nineteenth-century anti-abortion campaign: a pregnant woman's "health" will suffer if she deviates from her natural maternal role. But whatever health risks may be associated with abortion (on one hand) and bearing children in Mississippi (on the other), the choice of whether to assume those risks and how to weigh them belongs to women and not the State.

Moreover, when Mississippi claims that abortion in the second trimester is more dangerous than childbirth, *id.* § 1(2)(b)(iii), it appears to be making an empirical claim. In fact, Mississippi is appealing to the traditional sex-role assumption that a woman will suffer if she chooses to avoid her natural maternal role. If its claim were genuinely based in science, the State would address the scientific finding that childbirth is many times more dangerous than abortion—as this Court and others have recognized. *See Whole Woman's Health v. Hellerstedt*, 136 S. Ct. 2292, 2315 (2016) (observing that "[n]ationwide, childbirth is 14 times more likely than abortion to result in death"); Siegel, *Why Restrict Abortion?*, *supra* (manuscript at 49-50 & n.259) (describing Judge

Richard Posner and others criticizing an anti-abortion expert for persistently, and falsely, claiming that abortion is more dangerous than pregnancy). *See generally* Elizabeth G. Raymond & David A. Grimes, *The Comparative Safety of Legal Induced Abortion and Childbirth in the United States*, 119 OBSTETRICS & GYNECOLOGY 215 (2012) (concluding that the risk of death associated with childbirth is approximately 14 times higher than with abortion). *See infra* Part III.

While the justifications undergirding HB 1510 may superficially be couched in the language of health and science, even a cursory examination of the relevant historical context reveals that the State's justifications are just re-packaged versions of the same sex-role stereotypes used by nineteenth-century anti-abortion advocates. Thus, HB 1510 carries forth a long and unfortunate tradition of state-sponsored paternalism, in which the coercive control of a woman is justified as an act of benign solicitude. *See Frontiero*, 411 U.S. at 684 (explaining that traditional forms of sex discrimination were "rationalized by an attitude of 'romantic paternalism' which, in practical effect, put women not on a pedestal, but in a cage").

To be clear, Mississippi may surely protect the health of women and the next generation, but in seeking to achieve these important ends, the State may "not rely on overbroad generalizations about the different talents, capacities, or preferences of males and females." *Virginia*, 518 U.S. at 533. Those are precisely the assumptions about women on which HB 1510 relies in presenting coercion as protection. These well-worn sex-role stereotypes may be archaic, but they are anything but quaint: when these sex-role

20

stereotypes are enforced through a law restricting abortion, they can deprive a woman of her autonomy, her job, her health, and even her life.

III. RELIANCE ON IMPERMISSIBLE SEX STEREOTYPES LED MISSISSIPPI TO FOREGO LESS DISCRIMINATORY MEANS TO ACHIEVE ITS GOALS OF PROTECTING WOMEN'S HEALTH AND FETAL LIFE

Mississippi employed sex-discriminatory means to achieve its goals of protecting women's health and protecting fetal life. *Virginia* requires the State to demonstrate that its choice of sex-discriminatory means is "substantially related to the achievement of" important government ends, by advancing an "exceedingly persuasive justification" that does not rely on sex-role stereotypes. *See Virginia*, 518 U.S. at 533-34. It cannot make that showing here.

Mississippi could have employed *many* policy means to reduce abortion and protect the health of women and children. Relying on available federal funds, it could have provided appropriate and effective sex education and expanded access to contraception; it could have expanded access to health insurance and provided assistance to needy families. But instead, Mississippi has restricted abortion access.

In its belief that banning abortions at 15 weeks would protect both the fetus *and* the health of the pregnant woman—a belief that is itself rooted in stereotypes about women's roles as child bearers before all else—Mississippi pushed women who seek to end pregnancies into harm's way by compelling pregnancy and childbirth, when the State could have pursued its ends by alternate, less discriminatory means. The State singled out women who sought to end pregnancy instead of pursuing its ends by aiding those who want to avoid parenthood and supporting those who want to raise children.

Because Mississippi so heavily relied on sex-role stereotypes to enact a law that singled out and harmed women, the State has not demonstrated that its ban on abortion after 15 weeks is "substantially related" to important ends. Instead, the State's reliance on sex-role stereotypes led it to protect through coercion, which in turn "perpetuate[s] the legal, social, and economic inferiority of women." *Id.*

A. Abortion Restrictions Like HB 1510 Do Not Protect Women But Rather Expose Them to Harm

Mississippi seeks to protect women and fetal life by banning abortion after 15 weeks. But the ban it has adopted to achieve those ends actually jeopardizes, rather than protects, the health of women.

Not only does HB 1510 take from women control over their life decisions, as nineteenth-century doctors preached, it subjects women to myriad health harms in a State where the social safety net makes grossly inadequate provision for women or children. *See* Michele Goodwin, *Banning Abortion Doesn't Protect Women's Health*, N.Y. TIMES (July 9, 2021), https://www.nytimes.com/2021/07/09/opinion/roe-abortion-supreme-court.html.

The risks of compelled pregnancy are considerable, in a state where the maternal mortality rate is alarmingly high, averaging 33.2 deaths for every 100,000 live births. MISS. STATE DEP'T OF HEALTH, MISS. MATERNAL MORTALITY REPORT 10 (2019), https://msdh.ms.gov/msdhsite/index.cfm/31,8127,299,pdf/Maternal_Mortality_2019_amended.pdf.

Pregnancy in Mississippi presents particular risks for Black women, who accounted for "nearly 80 percent of pregnancy-related cardiac deaths" between 2013 and 2016. *Id.* at 16. The pregnancy-related mortality rate for Black women was nearly three times the rate for white women. *Id.* at 12 (ranging from 51.9 to 61.4 deaths per 100,000 live births compared to 18.9 to 36.7 deaths per 100,000 live births).

Forcing pregnancy and childbirth onto women against their will places their health and lives at risk. HB 1510, therefore, does not promote—let alone substantially relate to—Mississippi's claimed goal of promoting women's health.

B. Mississippi Repeatedly Rejected Nondiscriminatory Alternatives That Would Protect the Health of Women and Families

Mississippi had many policy alternatives for protecting the health of women and families. But in considering the many options before it, the State has consistently rejected noncoercive opportunities to improve the health of mothers and infants, even declining federal monies available to support these ends. The consequences are especially dire for Black mothers and infants. Despite the increased risks they face in Mississippi, the State has repeatedly declined to enact policies that could improve their health and wellbeing.

1. Access to regular health care and checkups could reduce maternal deaths by up to 60%. Emily E. Petersen et al., *Vital Signs: Pregnancy-Related Deaths, United States, 2011–2015, and Strategies for Prevention, 13 States, 2013–2017*, 68 MORBIDITY AND MORTALITY WEEKLY REPORT 423 (May 10, 2019). Lack of care can be deadly for newborns—the U.S. Department of Health and Human Services found that newborns whose mothers had no early prenatal care are almost five times more likely to die. *See* Dep't of Health & Hum. Servs. Off. on Women's Health, PRENATAL CARE, https://www.womenshealth.gov/a-z-topics/prenatal-care (Apr. 1, 2019).

Yet ensuring access to health care is largely dependent on income and insurance coverage, and Medicaid expansion under the Affordable Care Act (ACA) has been shown to reliably improve insurance access. Jamie R. Daw et al., *Medicaid Expansion Improved Perinatal Insurance Continuity for Low-Income Women*, 39 HEALTH AFFS. 1531 (Sept. 2020). Increasing access to Medicaid could not only reduce maternal and infant deaths, but could also give a pregnant person lacking alternative health insurance the security to continue an unplanned pregnancy and to cope with delivery and postpartum care.

Mississippi, however, has refused to expand Medicaid under the ACA, compromising health care access for under-resourced Mississippians. Sarah Varney, *How Obamacare Went South in Mississippi*, THE ATLANTIC (Nov. 4, 2014), https://www.theatlantic.com/health/archive/2014/11/how-obamacare-went-south-in-mississippi/382313/. This policy decision left an estimated 138,000 otherwise eligible people without health coverage and deprived the state of an estimated $1.2 billion in federal funds.

Ironically, after signing HB 1510, then-Governor Phil Bryant announced that he was "committed to making Mississippi the safest place in America for an unborn child, and this bill will help us achieve that goal." Jenny Gathright, *Mississippi Governor Signs Nation's Toughest Abortion Ban into Law*, NAT'L PUB. RADIO (Mar. 19, 2018), https://www.npr.org/sections/thetwo-way/2018/03/19/595045249/mississippi-governor-signs-nations-toughest-abortion-ban-into-law. But, in reality, Mississippi's refusal to accept federal funding to provide health care for its residents directly contributes to its startlingly high infant and maternal mortality rates, especially in communities of color.[11]

2. Lack of financial resources is among the most common reasons that women provide for ending a pregnancy. *See* M. Antonia Biggs et al., *Understanding Why Women Seek Abortions in the US*, 13 BMC WOMEN'S HEALTH 29 (2013), https://www.ncbi.nlm.nih.gov/pmc/articles/PMC3729671. The Temporary Assistance for Needy Families (TANF) program, which provides grants to support low-income families with children, enables Mississippi to channel

---

[11] In 2018, the State ranked worst in the nation for infant mortality, with a rate of 8.43 infant deaths per 1,000 live births. MISS. STATE DEP'T OF HEALTH, INFANT MORTALITY REPORT 1 (2019), https://msdh.ms.gov/msdhsite/_static/resources/8431.pdf. Black infants constitute most infant deaths in Mississippi and are almost twice as likely to die as white infants. *Id.* at 8.

federal monies to its low-income residents. Participating in TANF offers a clear, noncoercive means of empowering people to choose to continue pregnancy with resources to support dependent family members.

Remarkably, despite this opportunity to support at least some women in choosing to continue pregnancies and to reduce the nation's highest child poverty rate, in 2019, Mississippi spent only about five percent of its TANF funds on direct assistance to families. Ali Safawi, *Mississippi Raises TANF Benefits but More Improvements Needed, Especially in South*, CTR. FOR BUDGET & POL'Y PRIORITIES (May 4, 2021), https://www.cbpp.org/blog/mississippi-raises-tanf-benefits-but-more-improvements-needed-especially-in-south. And the number of poor families receiving TANF has declined precipitously: less than 3,000 families received the maximum benefit of $170 per month by 2021, down from 23,700 families in 1999. *See* Anna Wolfe, *Mississippi Found 'Absurd' Ways to Spend Welfare on Anything but the Poor. These Bills Would Put More Money into Families' Pockets*, MISS. TODAY (Jan. 29, 2021), https://mississippitoday.org/2021/01/29/mississippi-found-absurd-ways-to-spend-welfare-on-anything-but-the-poor-these-bills-would-put-more-money-into-families-pockets.[12] Until 2021,

[12] TANF money has also been blatantly wasted in the State. Beginning in 2016, the director of the Mississippi Department of Human Services spearheaded the "largest public embezzlement scheme in state history." Anna Wolfe, *Embattled Welfare Group Paid $5 Million for New USM Volleyball Center*, MISS. TODAY (Feb. 27, 2020), https://mississippitoday.org/2020/02/27/welfare-program-paid-5-million-for-new-volleyball-center/. Millions of

Mississippi maintained the lowest TANF benefit levels in the nation, refusing for decades even to adjust for inflation. *Id.*

Moreover, many women who decide to end a pregnancy are poor and low-income mothers who fear that having another child will compromise their ability to provide for the children they already have. Mississippi preserves policies that reinforce those genuine concerns. For instance, the State maintains a family cap, limiting TANF benefits for additional children born into families that receive public assistance. Mississippi's family cap survives despite evidence that these policies "harm children's health" and "deepen poverty," evidence that has prompted their repeal in many states. Teresa Wiltz, *Family Welfare Caps Lose Favor in More States*, PEW STATELINE (May 3, 2019), https://www.pewtrusts.org/en/research-and-analysis/blogs/stateline/2019/05/03/family-welfare-caps-lose-favor-in-more-states.

3. Information about and access to contraception lowers rates of unplanned pregnancies. But rather than provide effective sex education and contraceptive access, Mississippi continues to promote abstinence-only sex education. Chris Elkins, *More Than 'Just Say No' Needed in Sex Ed*, DAILY J. (Dec. 13, 2012), https://www.djournal.com/opinion/other-opinion-more-than-just-say-no-needed-in-sex-ed/article_

---

dollars meant for TANF instead were diverted to "a new volleyball stadium, a horse ranch for a famous athlete, multi-million dollar celebrity speaking engagements, high-tech virtual reality equipment, luxury vehicles, steakhouse dinners and even a speeding ticket." Wolfe, *Mississippi Found 'Absurd' Ways to Spend Welfare on Anything but the Poor*, *supra*.

db4f2969-e2b8-5950-8fd7-f46d551cb742.html. For example, instead of using federal monies to implement comprehensive sex education at no cost to the state, Mississippi funded a "Teen Pregnancy Prevention Summit" featuring pamphlets discouraging the use of contraceptives because they supposedly harm girls' "physical[,] emotional and spiritual well-being." Andy Kopsa, *Sex Ed Without Condoms? Welcome to Mississippi*, THE ATLANTIC (Mar. 7, 2013), https://www.theatlantic.com/national/archive/2013/03/sex-ed-without-condoms-welcome-to-mississippi/273802; *see also* Alana Semuels, *Sex Education Stumbles in Mississippi*, L.A. TIMES (Apr. 2, 2014) (recounting a public school sex education curriculum which instructed students to unwrap a piece of chocolate, pass it around the class, and observe how dirty it became to "show that a girl is no longer clean or valuable after she's had sex").

The consequences of these policies for women's and children's health are severe: Mississippi boasts some of the nation's highest rates of teen pregnancy, gonorrhea, chlamydia, and syphilis. Sarah Fowler, *Mississippi Has the Highest Rate of this STD, Ranks 3rd for Two Others*, MISS. CLARION LEDGER (Oct. 15, 2019), https://www.clarionledger.com/story/news/local/2019/10/15/gonorrhea-std-rate-mississippi-highest-chlamydia-syphillis-access-to-care-factor/3932140002/. Nevertheless, Mississippi continues to rely on a mode of protecting women's health and fetal life that is rooted in impermissible sex stereotypes, and does so by restricting access to reproductive health care.

Mississippi objects that *Casey*'s protections for women's decision-making "prevent[] States from providing health benefits and protections that they can provide in other contexts." Pet. Br. 41-42. But Mississippi has a wealth of policy options for reducing the incidence of abortion in the state and protecting women's health. *See* Emily Wax-Thibodeaux & Ariana Eunjung Cha, *The Mississippi Clinic at the Center of the Fight to End Abortion in America*, THE WASH. POST (Aug. 24, 2021) (recounting story of a young woman receiving follow up care after abortion in the state's only remaining clinic who said "that because Mississippi teaches only abstinence in public schools, no one explained to her how to prevent pregnancy if she had sex").

In short, Mississippi could provide care and support for individuals who wish: to avoid pregnancy, to bear children who will not languish in poverty, to preserve their own or their children's health, or to safeguard their ability to provide for existing children. Instead, Mississippi chooses to prevent women from making the most intimate, consequential decisions for themselves and to coerce women into giving birth under dangerous, demeaning conditions.[13] HB 1510 thus functions more as a tool of control than as an

---

[13] For a debate among white and Black Mississippi lawmakers about the women regulated by the State's abortion restrictions, including remarks by Republican Sen. Joey Fillingane, co-sponsor of HB 1510, *see* Emily Wagster Pettus, *Mississippi Considers Abortion Ban After Fetal Heartbeat*, ABC NEWS, (Feb. 5, 2019), https://abcnews.go.com/us/wirestory/mississippi-considers-abortion-ban-fetal-heartbeat-60864978.

expression of care for Mississippi's women and children. *See* Pet. App. 46a n.22.

IV. HB 1510 DOES NOT ADVANCE EQUALITY INTERESTS

Increasingly, those who support abortion restrictions take the extraordinary position that laws like HB 1510 actually *promote* equality under the law by preventing abortion from being used for eugenic purposes. In his separate concurrence in the judgment below, Judge Ho, drawing on a concurrence by Justice Thomas, asserts "that abortion 'has proved to be a disturbingly effective tool for implementing the discriminatory preferences that undergird eugenics'" and notes that "the current 'abortion ratio ... among black women is nearly 3.5 times the ratio for white women.'" Pet. App. 35a (quoting *Box v. Planned Parenthood of Ind. & Ky., Inc.*, 139 S. Ct. 1780, 1790-91 (2019) (Thomas, J., concurring)).

Such efforts to link abortion to eugenics ignore the fundamental differences between a state-sponsored program of eugenic regulation designed to control the demographic character of the community and a law protecting an individual's decision to terminate a pregnancy. In the former, decisional authority rests with the state. In the latter, the state protects the authority of an individual to make reproductive decisions consistent with her individual beliefs and circumstances.

Without acknowledging these differences, abortion opponents insist that, today, *Roe* and the constitutional law of abortion rights are being used as a tool of eugenic manipulation. There is a certain irony here: If there is any historical association between abortion law and projects of demographic control, it lies in the nineteenth-century campaign to criminalize abortion itself.

The nineteenth-century campaign unfolded during an era of nativist, anti-immigrant, anti-Catholic feeling. *See* ERIKA LEE, AMERICA FOR AMERICANS: A HISTORY OF XENOPHOBIA IN THE UNITED STATES 42-44 (2019). Storer and others blamed abortion for the differences in birth rate between "native" (*i.e.*, Protestant) women and "foreign" women. *See* STORER, *supra*, at 62-63; *id.* at 64-65 (observing that "abortions are infinitely more frequent among Protestant women than among Catholic [women]"); *see also, e.g.*, William McCollom, *Criminal Abortion*, TRANSACTIONS VT. MED. SOC'Y 40, 42 (1865) ("Our own population seem to have a greater aversion to the rearing of families than ... the French, the Irish and the Germans."); L.C. Butler, *The Decadence of the American Race,* 77 BOS. MED. & SURGICAL J. 89, 93-94 (Sept. 5, 1867) (comparing Protestant and Catholic doctrine on abortion with attention to the relevant reproductive rates of Protestants and Catholics). Storer tied Protestant families' declining size to Protestant women exercising reproductive autonomy; he thus sought abortion bans to increase the number of Protestants. He questioned whether "the great territories of the far West, just opening to civilization, and the fertile savannas of the South" would be filled by "our own children, or by those of aliens? This is a question that our own women must answer; upon their loins depends the future destiny of the nation." STORER, *supra*, at 85. His words resonated with at least some state lawmakers enacting abortion restrictions. *See* L.D. Griswold et al., *supra*, at 235 ("Shall we permit our broad and fertile prairies to be settled only by the children of aliens?"). Doctors leading the campaign to criminalize abortion sought to wrest control of the reproductive decisions of "our own women" to protect fetal life, to enforce marital roles, and to preserve the demographic character of the nation. Siegel, *Reasoning from the Body*, *supra*, at 297-300.

Interest in eugenics—"'the science of improving stock' by giving 'the more suitable races or strains of blood a better chance of prevailing speedily over the less suitable'"—became more popular in the nineteenth and early twentieth century. DOROTHY ROBERTS, KILLING THE BLACK BODY 24, 59 (2d ed. 2017). Eugenicists argued that "society should encourage the procreation of those of superior lineage, while discouraging procreation among—and public support for—those of inferior lineage." Melissa Murray, *Race-ing Roe: Reproductive Justice, Racial Justice, and the Battle for* Roe v. Wade, 134 HARV. L. REV. 2025, 2036-37 (2021).

But the twentieth century eugenics movement did not focus on abortion as a way to control the population. It turned to laws permitting sterilization of the "feebleminded" and "habitual criminals," as well as laws criminalizing miscegenation and interracial marriage. *Id.* at 2037. By the mid-twentieth century, policies of reproductive control primarily targeted impoverished communities of color perceived as threats to the public fisc by *curtailing* individuals' ability to make decisions about their reproductive lives. *Id.* at 2047.

Mississippi's own history is instructive. In the 1950s and 1960s, state lawmakers prescribed sterilization as a punishment for nonmarital childbearing. *See id.* at 2042 (describing 1964 Student Nonviolent Coordinating Committee pamphlet *Genocide in Mississippi*). Civil rights leader Fannie Lou Hamer famously estimated that six in ten Black women who gave birth in Sunflower County Hospital during this period underwent post-partum sterilization without their consent, and often without their knowledge, a practice so common it was colloquially called a "Mississippi appendectomy." CHANA KAI LEE, FOR FREEDOM'S SAKE: THE LIFE OF FANNIE LOU HAMER 21-22, 80 (1999); REBECCA M. KLUCHIN, FIT TO BE TIED: STERILIZATION AND REPRODUCTIVE RIGHTS IN AMERICA, 1950-1980 at 93-94 (2009). As history makes clear, there is simply no comparison between state policies of reproductive control aimed at limiting birth among marginalized groups and the individual right to make reproductive decisions free from state coercion.

Further, when abortion opponents point to the incidence of abortion among minority communities as evidence that abortion is rife with "eugenic potential," they ignore the "structural impediments communities of color face in reproductive decisionmaking." Murray, *supra*, at 2090-91. For many people of color, "the decision to terminate a pregnancy is shot through with concerns about economic and financial insecurity, limited employment options, diminution of educational opportunities, and lack of access to health care and affordable quality childcare." *Id.* at 2090-91. Efforts to associate abortion with eugenics obscure how Mississippi's own policy choices, by failing to support families, perpetuate the conditions that lead increasing numbers of poor women and women of color to decide to end their pregnancies. *See supra* Part III. Rather than link abortion rates to the policy choices that perpetuate poverty, opponents shift blame on to women who make decisions about abortion in a nation that provides scarcely any support for those who conceive, bear, and raise children.

* * *

For a half century, this Court has affirmed that the Equal Protection Clause forbids the State from imposing traditional gender roles. *See also* Ruth Bader Ginsburg, *Sex Equality and the Constitution: The State of the Art*, 4 WOMEN'S RTS. L. REP. 143, 143-44 (1978). HB 1510 does just that. It discriminates on the basis of sex, enforcing nineteenth-century sex-role stereotypes that compel a woman to continue pregnancy while the State foregoes alternative nondiscriminatory means to achieve the same ends.

In *Casey*, the Court explained that a pregnant woman's "suffering is too intimate and personal for the State to insist, without more, upon its own vision of the woman's role, however dominant that vision has been in the course of our history and our culture." *Casey*, 505 U.S. at 852. Mississippi has banned abortion after 15 weeks to protect the life and health of the fetus and the "maternal patient." Miss. H.B. 1510 § 1(2)(b)(ii)-(v). The statute addresses a pregnant woman as a mother, but in the same breath, it deprives her of control over whether to become a mother—all while claiming to act in the name of her "physical and psychological" "health." *See id.* Mississippi offers no persuasive justification for its ready embrace of sex-based coercive means to protect life and health when less discriminatory means were available.

At the heart of both the Due Process Clause and the Equal Protection Clause is the individual's right to be free from state imposition of traditional gender roles. HB 1510 denies that fundamental constitutional guarantee.

CONCLUSION

For the foregoing reasons, the judgment below should be affirmed.

Respectfully submitted,

ROBERTA A. KAPLAN
Counsel of Record
RAYMOND P. TOLENTINO
MARCELLA COBURN
RACHEL TUCHMAN
ANNA COLLINS PETERSON
Kaplan Hecker & Fink LLP
350 Fifth Avenue, 63rd Floor
New York, NY 10118
(212) 763-0883
rkaplan@kaplanhecker.com

September 20, 2021 *Counsel for Amici Curiae*

4

Justice Ginsburg's Cautious Legacy for the Equal Rights Amendment

—Julie C. Suk[1]

This chapter explores the legacy of Ruth Bader Ginsburg for inclusive constitutional change, unearthing her lifelong commitment to the Equal Rights Amendment (ERA), which was adopted over 50 years ago by Congress in 1972. It took nearly half a century for the Amendment to be ratified by the 38 states required by Article V, with Virginia becoming the last state to ratify it in 2020—the year of Justice Ginsburg's death. Because the

 Many thanks to law school audiences at events and panels featuring my research on the Equal Rights Amendment's legislative history and recent resurgence, recounted in greater detail for a general audience in *We the Women: The Unstoppable Mothers of the Equal Rights Amendment.* This piece grew out of reflections on the challenging questions raised at those events, including at Harvard Law School's Nineteenth Amendment and Equal Rights Amendment event, Columbia Law School's launch of the new Equal Rights Amendment Project, Boston College Law School's Constitution Day event, and the University of Virginia Law Review's symposium titled *From the ERA to Black Lives Matter.* Many thanks to Joseph Blocher, Pamela Bookman, David Pozen, and Reva Siegel; to the participants in the Yale Law School ACS Progressive Scholarship workshop for critical comments and suggestions that have greatly improved the piece; and to Varshini Parthasarathy and A. Lulu Zhang for excellent research assistance.

last three ratifications occurred decades after congressionally imposed time limits, Justice Ginsburg publicly expressed doubts about the viability of the ERA as it was being disputed in Congress and in the courts. This chapter unpacks Justice Ginsburg's ambivalent stance toward the ERA, tracing it to her commitment to greater inclusion in the process of constitutional change, analyzed in her legal scholarship of the 1970s.

As a scholar, Ginsburg focused not only on sex discrimination, but also on legal procedure. She was keenly aware that the procedural paths toward important socio-legal changes, including women's equal citizenship, would shape their potential to endure as law. This chapter puts the spotlight on Ginsburg's often-neglected writings as a scholar before her judicial career. Ginsburg's transformative vision of constitutional gender equality had an institutional and procedural dimension that accompanied its ambitious substantive ideals. A modern constitutional democracy would fully include women in the rights and responsibilities of citizenship and power by eliminating gender stereotypes from the law and by implementing public policies to enable the participation of people of all genders.

To Ginsburg, legislatures rather than courts are best equipped to complete this project. To legitimize such large-scale constitutional change, Ginsburg viewed Congress as the appropriate institutional driver of the constitutional amendment process. Accordingly, Congress had plenary power over the procedural incidents of constitutional amendments such as the ERA, including ratification time limits and rescissions. Ginsburg's legislative constitutionalism on both the substance and the procedure of the ERA point to cautiously viable paths forward for both the resurgent ERA and for future amendments that aim to secure the inclusion of previously disempowered people in our democracy.

I. Introduction

History will remember the late Justice Ruth Bader Ginsburg as America's "founding mother" of constitutional gender equality,[2] who in 2020 died

[2] *See 'The Most Important Woman Lawyer in the History of the Republic': How Did Ruth Bader Ginsburg Change America? More Than 20 Legal Thinkers Weigh In*, POLITICO (Sept. 18, 2020, 11:59 PM), https://www.politico.com/news/magazine/2020/09/18/ruth-bader-ginsburg-legacy-418191 [https://perma.cc/LG6U-YPVD] (compiling opinions of twenty legal thinkers, including Kenji Yoshino, who called her the "founding mother – or simply founder – of our nation's sex equality jurisprudence"). Throughout Justice Ginsburg's career, the laws that

an immortal feminist and pop culture icon.[3] This chapter unpacks Justice Ginsburg's legacy for the future of women's constitutional rights, including her lifelong commitment to the ERA.

Over half a century ago, Congress adopted the Equal Rights Amendment (ERA), the Amendment that would have guaranteed that equal rights could not be abridged on account of sex. The ERA embodied the constitutional principle Ginsburg embraced while litigating the sex discrimination cases that made her famous. In the year immediately preceding her death, however, she criticized efforts to revive the ERA ratification process.[4] Justice Ginsburg's seemingly ambivalent stance toward the ERA has deep roots in her thinking as a legal scholar whose work focused not only on sex discrimination, but also on civil procedure. Particularly in the setting of important socio-legal changes, Justice Ginsburg had a heightened appreciation for the challenges of establishing their procedural legitimacy. A constitutional transition toward a more inclusive democracy faced enormous procedural barriers, and thus necessitated exceptional paths whose legitimacy would be questioned. Months after Justice Ginsburg's death, her landmark sex equality opinion in *United States v. Virginia*[5] reached its 25th anniversary. Meanwhile, a global pandemic laid bare the fragility of women's progress toward equal participation in the workforce and the nation's economy, given women's disproportionate responsibility for childcare.[6] As

---

advanced women's rights used the term "sex," such as the Nineteenth Amendment of the U.S. Constitution (guaranteeing that the right to vote would not be abridged "on account of sex"), U.S. CONST. amend. XIX, Title VII of the Civil Rights Act of 1964 (prohibiting discrimination in employment "because of . . . sex"), 42 U.S.C. § 2000e-2(a)(1), and Title IX of the Education Amendments Act of 1972 (prohibiting exclusion from educational opportunities in federally funded institutions "on the basis of sex"), 20 U.S.C. § 1681(a). Justice Ginsburg explained decades later that she chose to use the term "gender" in lieu of "sex" in her briefs, in part to deflect male audience attention away from the ordinary associations with the word "sex." *See Columbia Law School Honors Justice Ginsburg*, C-SPAN, at 41:25-42:15 (Nov. 19, 1993), https://www.c-span.org/video/?53194-1/columbia-law-school-honors-justice-ginsburg [https://perma.cc/S9D6-CLJ8].

[3] *See* Linda Greenhouse, *Ruth Bader Ginsburg, Supreme Court's Feminist Icon, Is Dead at 87*, N.Y. TIMES (Sept. 24, 2020), https://www.nytimes.com/2020/09/18/us/ruth-bader-ginsburg-dead.html.

[4] *See* sources cited *infra* note 13.

[5] 518 U.S. 515 (1996).

[6] *See generally* Titan Alon, Sena Coskun, Matthias Doepke, David Koll & Michèle Tertilt, *From Mancession to Shecession: Women's Employment in Regular and Pandemic Recessions* (Nat'l Bureau of Econ. Rsch., Working Paper No. 28632, 2021).

efforts to add the ERA to the Constitution continue in Congress and the courts,[7] Ginsburg's body of work as a legal scholar sheds crucial light on the unfinished project of constitutional gender equality as well as the role of courts and constitutional amendments in constraining or facilitating it.[8]

Although Ginsburg spent the last 40 years of her career as a judge, including as a Justice of the highest court of the land, she established her legacy for women's rights in the decade before she became a judge through her transformative work as a lawyer and law professor in the 1970s. As a legal scholar, her 1970s writings created an intellectual architecture to support constitutional gender equality, featuring a strong case for the ERA.[9] Ginsburg's background as scholar of comparative law and civil procedure[10] shaped her approach to gender equality under the law, both what it could mean substantively as well as how it could be achieved procedurally.[11]

---

[7] *See* 166 CONG. REC. H1140 (daily ed. Feb. 13, 2020) (statement of Rep. Scott) (discussing the House floor vote on H.J. Res. 79, removing the deadline for the ratification of the ERA); Virginia v. Ferriero, 525 F. Supp. 3d 36 (D.D.C. 2021) (hearing lawsuit by three states seeking declaratory judgment that the ERA is part of the Constitution, with five intervening states seeking declaration that ERA has expired). New resolutions have been introduced in the 117th Congress to remove the deadline for ERA ratification. *See* H.R.J. Res. 17, 117th Cong. (2021); S.J. Res. 1, 117th Cong. (2021). For a narrated account of the ERA's legislative history from its introduction in 1923 through its ratifications by Nevada, Illinois, and Virginia, see JULIE C. SUK, WE THE WOMEN: THE UNSTOPPABLE MOTHERS OF THE EQUAL RIGHTS AMENDMENT (2020).

[8] Surely, the future of law and policy around gender justice will be concerned with the gendered economic effects of the COVID-19 pandemic, especially on working mothers. *See* Eleni X. Karageorge, *COVID-19 Recession Is Tougher on Women*, U.S. BUREAU OF LAB. STAT. (Sept. 2020), https://www.bls.gov/opub/mlr/2020/beyond-bls/covid-19-recession-is-tougher-on-women.htm [https://perma.cc/DR6A-HRBN].

[9] *See, e.g.*, Ruth Bader Ginsburg, Comment, *The Equal Rights Amendment Is the Way*, 1 HARV. WOMEN'S L.J. 19, 25–26 (1978) [hereinafter Ginsburg, *Equal Rights Amendment Is the Way*]; Ruth Bader Ginsburg, *Gender and the Constitution*, 44 U. CIN. L. REV. 1, 27 (1975) [hereinafter Ginsburg, *Gender and the Constitution*]; Ruth Bader Ginsburg, *The Need for the Equal Rights Amendment*, 59 A.B.A. J. 1013, 1013 (1973); Ruth Bader Ginsburg, *Let's Have E.R.A. as a Signal*, 63 A.B.A. J. 70, 70 (1977) [hereinafter Ginsburg, *ERA as a Signal*].

[10] *See* RUTH BADER GINSBURG & ANDERS BRUZELIUS, CIVIL PROCEDURE IN SWEDEN (1965). For an account of the influence of Swedish developments in gender equality on Ruth Bader Ginsburg during this period, see Cary Franklin, *The Anti-Stereotyping Principle in Constitutional Sex Discrimination Law*, 85 N.Y.U. L. REV. 83, 97–105 (2010).

[11] *See* Ruth Bader Ginsburg, *The Status of Women: Introduction*, 20 AM. J. COMPAR. L. 585, 585–86 (1972); Ruth Bader Ginsburg, Observation, *Ratification of the Equal Rights Amendment: A Question of Time*, 57 TEX. L. REV. 919, 920 (1979) [hereinafter Ginsburg, *Ratification of the Equal Rights Amendment*].

Despite her ardent support of the ERA for half a century,[12] Justice Ginsburg publicly expressed doubts about the process by which the ERA was returning to the political hopper in 2020.[13] As the ERA's viability is being considered by Congress and courts, this chapter unites the contrasting dimensions of Justice Ginsburg's gender equality legacy—one substantive, the other procedural—to synthesize a viable, if unprecedented, path for the ERA and for inclusive constitutional change under a constitution made exclusively by white men in the eighteenth century.

Popular books[14] and acclaimed films[15] have made the American public well aware of Ginsburg's contributions as an advocate for women's rights throughout the 1970s. She pursued, to great success, a strategy of incremental litigation that expanded the Fourteenth Amendment's guarantee of equal protection of the laws, one case at a time, to invalidate governmental

---

[12] *See* sources cited *supra* note 9. In the last decade of her life, Justice Ginsburg gave many public interviews and speeches in which she said that the ERA is the first amendment she would choose to add to the Constitution if she could. *See, e.g.*, *Justices Scalia and Ginsburg on the First Amendment and Freedom*, C-SPAN (Apr. 17, 2014), https://www.c-span.org/video/?404745-1/radio-justices-scalia-ginsburg-amendment-freedom [https://perma.cc/HZ5R-RFHR]; *Justice Ruth Bader Ginsburg Discusses* Roe v. Wade, *Her Legal Career, and Women on the Supreme Court*, NYU L. NEWS (Feb. 20, 2018), https://www.law.nyu.edu/news/Ruth-Bader-Ginsburg-Kenji-Yoshino-Center-for-Diversity-Inclusion-and-Belonging [https://perma.cc/6PKR-RCYX]; *Video Clip: Justice Ruth Bader Ginsburg and the Equal Rights Amendment*, C-SPAN, at 2:46-2:54 (Feb. 1, 2018), https://www.c-span.org/classroom/document/?8979 [https://perma.cc/VER9-KZLF] ("And so I would like to see an Equal Rights Amendment in our Constitution . . . ."). She has argued that the interpretation of the Fourteenth Amendment to include sex equality has gotten "almost" to an ERA but cannot substitute for the ERA because of the importance of being able to see the principle of equal citizenship stature between women and men in the text of one's pocket constitution. *See What Ginsburg Wants to Tell Her Granddaughters*, CNN, at 00:40-00:45, https://www.cnn.com/videos/us/2018/02/11/rbg-on-equal-rights-amendment.cnn/video/playlists/supreme-court-justice-ruth-bader-ginsburg/ [https://perma.cc/9PAY-7MF6] (last visited May 2, 2022) ("But it's important to have an Equal Rights Amendment in the Constitution . . . .").

[13] *See* Searching for Equality: The Nineteenth Amendment and Beyond, A Conversation Between United States Supreme Court Justice Ruth Bader Ginsburg and Ninth Circuit Court of Appeals Judge M. Margaret McKeown (Feb. 10, 2020), *in* 108 GEO. L.J. 5, 11 (2020) [hereinafter Searching for Equality]; *see also infra* note 46 and accompanying text.

[14] *See, e.g.*, IRIN CARMON & SHANA KNIZHNIK, NOTORIOUS RBG: THE LIFE AND TIMES OF RUTH BADER GINSBURG (1st ed. 2015); REBECCA GIBIAN, THE RBG WAY: THE SECRETS OF RUTH BADER GINSBURG'S SUCCESS (2019); POCKET RBG WISDOM: SUPREME QUOTES AND INSPIRED MUSINGS FROM RUTH BADER GINSBURG (2019).

[15] RBG (CNN Films 2018); On the Basis of Sex (Focus Features 2018); RUTH: Justice Ginsburg in Her Own Words (Sanders and Mock Productions 2019).

sex discrimination.[16] As a law professor, she brought courses on women and the law, including sex discrimination, into the law school curriculum, authoring the first textbook on the subject.[17] As a scholar, she imagined a constitutional landscape beyond incremental litigation, and she justified an amendment to the Constitution, the ERA, as "a clear statement of the nation's moral and legal commitment to a system in which women and men stand as full and equal individuals before the law."[18] She brought her intuitions about procedural fairness to her testimonies as a scholarly expert in congressional hearings on extending the deadline on ERA ratification, urging that "[i]t would be the bitterest of ironies if the equal rights amendment were to become the first proposed amendment in this Nation's history to die because [of] a procedural time bar. . . . No amendment to date has failed for that reason."[19] Although the ERA ratification deadline expired in 1982, she continued to say in public interviews and speeches in the past decade that the ERA was the amendment that she most hoped would be added to the Constitution one day. Justice Ginsburg believed it was important for future generations to see the ERA in their pocket constitutions, to be assured of our polity's fundamental commitment to the inclusion of women as fully equal citizens. Making such a commitment in a constitution was as important, in her view, to enshrining other human rights, such as free speech.[20] But as the ERA appeared to inch closer to inclusion in the Constitution by way of post-deadline ratifications, Justice Ginsburg questioned the irregularity of the process as threatening the ERA's legitimacy.

Part I provides an overview of the ERA's procedural history: its adoption by Congress, its failed ratification in the 1970s, and the ongoing legal and political controversies about recent efforts to revive it. Opponents of the ERA have argued that it is no longer needed because the Supreme

---

[16] *See, e.g.*, Reed v. Reed, 404 U.S. 71 (1971); Frontiero v. Richardson, 411 U.S. 677 (1973); Weinberger v. Wiesenfeld, 420 U.S. 636 (1975); Califano v. Goldfarb, 430 U.S. 199 (1977).

[17] *See* KENNETH M. DAVIDSON, RUTH BADER GINSBURG & HERMA HILL KAY, TEXT, CASES AND MATERIAL ON SEX-BASED DISCRIMINATION (1974).

[18] Ginsburg, *Gender and the Constitution*, *supra* note 9.

[19] *See Equal Rights Amendment Extension: Hearings on S.J. Res. 134 Before the Subcomm. on the Const. of the S. Comm. on the Judiciary*, 95th Cong. 262–71 (1978) [hereinafter *Equal Rights Amendment Extension Senate Hearings*] (testimony and written statement of Ruth Bader Ginsburg).

[20] *See What Ginsburg Wants to Tell Her Granddaughters*, *supra* note 12.

Court's sex equality jurisprudence, mostly achieved because of Ginsburg's advocacy under the Fourteenth Amendment, now functions as the ERA was intended to.

Part II identifies the more ambitious goals of the ERA that have not been fully achieved through Equal Protection sex equality jurisprudence to date. The ERA's framers, and Justice Ginsburg, intended the ERA to trigger transformative legislation to fully realize women's stature as equal citizens. Women's second-class status resulted from the disadvantages and dangers they faced because they were mothers, actual or potential. Robust policies to secure women's equal participation in the rights and duties of citizenship would be needed.

Part III turns to Justice Ginsburg's sex equality opinions on the Supreme Court, including *United States v. Virginia*,[21] to highlight her awareness of the secondary role of courts in making equality real.

Part IV turns to Ginsburg's contributions to the ERA deadline extension debates in the late 1970s, which affirmed the power of Congress—rather than courts—not only to implement the substance of the ERA, but also to drive the ERA's procedural path to legitimacy. Of particular importance is Justice Ginsburg's analysis of the unique challenges facing human rights amendments pursued under the rigid Article V process. In the long run, with a willing political majority, the ERA may be saved by a synthesis of Ginsburg's revolutionary vision of constitutional gender equality with her incremental approach to the process of transformative constitutional change.

II. The Fall and Rise of the Equal Rights Amendment

The ERA has taken a strange procedural path across a century, with recent events raising unprecedented constitutional questions. Although an ERA proposal was introduced in every Congress since 1923, it did not win the two-thirds vote of both houses of Congress necessary under Article V until

[21] 518 U.S. 515 (1996).

1972.[22] Thirty-five states ratified the Amendment between 1972 and 1977.[23] But the congressional resolution adopting the Amendment included a time limit on ratification, anticipating that the ERA would "be valid to all intents and purposes as part of the Constitution when ratified by the legislatures of three-fourths of the several States within seven years from the date of its submission by the Congress."[24]

Since 1918, Congress has often imposed seven-year time limits on the ratification of constitutional amendments, but these provisions were not a necessary feature of amendment proposals. The Nineteenth Amendment, proposed in 1919 and ratified in 1920, had no ratification deadline because its proponents feared that a deadline would unduly stymie an amendment procuring suffrage for women.[25] For most of its history, the ERA was introduced without a ratification deadline; it was adopted by one chamber of Congress without a deadline in 1950, 1953, and 1970.[26] But the preamble of the resolution proposing the ERA in 1971 included the seven-year ratification deadline, mostly to quiet the small but vocal opposition in the Senate, which included a segregationist who had filibustered the Civil Rights Act.[27] Thus, the ERA that both houses of Congress adopted in 1972—by over 90 percent of the vote in both chambers—included the language declaring that the Amendment would be valid "when ratified . . . within seven years."[28]

---

[22] Article V of the U.S. Constitution provides, in relevant part, "The Congress, whenever two thirds of both Houses shall deem it necessary, shall propose Amendments to this Constitution . . . which . . . shall be valid to all Intents and Purposes, as Part of this Constitution, when ratified by the Legislatures of three fourths of the several States . . . ." U.S. CONST. art. V; *see* H.R.J. Res. 208, 92d Cong. (1972) (proposing the Equal Rights Amendment). There were hearings from 1925 through 1971, and the Senate voted twice by a two-thirds vote on a different version of the ERA in 1950 and 1953, but the House did not follow. *See generally* SUK, *supra* note 7 (compiling this history).

[23] Julie C. Suk, *The Trump Administration Says the ERA Is Dead on Arrival. It Isn't*, WASH. POST (Jan. 21, 2020), https://www.washingtonpost.com/outlook/2020/01/21/trump-administration-says-era-is-dead-arrival-it-isnt/.

[24] H.R.J. Res. 208.

[25] *See* SUK, *supra* note 7, at 18–20.

[26] *See id.* at 55, 58–61 (detailing the 1950, 1953, and 1970 adoptions in one chamber).

[27] *See id.* at 62–66, 84 (quoting Martha Griffiths' explanation for why she accepted the seven-year time limit).

[28] H.R.J. Res. 208.

In 1978, the seventh year, Congress extended the deadline to 1982.[29] But no additional states ratified the Amendment between 1977 and 1982. Because 38 states are needed to make three-fourths of the states, the ERA was three states short of the three-fourths required for ratification as of both the 1979 and 1982 deadlines. Furthermore, five states that ratified the ERA from 1972 to 1977 took further action intending to rescind their prior ratifications.[30] After the extended deadline elapsed in 1982, the ERA was presumed dead.[31]

Over three decades later, three additional states—Nevada, Illinois, and Virginia—ratified the ERA, in 2017, 2018, and 2020 respectively.[32] The ratification count stands at 38, if rescissions are ignored.[33] After Virginia became the thirty-eighth state to ratify the ERA in January 2020, a majority of the House voted to remove the deadline immediately and to recognize the ERA part of the Constitution "whenever ratified by the legislatures of three-fourths of the several States."[34] But the Senate did not follow.[35] In the 117th Congress, the House voted again to remove the deadline for ERA

---

[29] H.R.J. Res. 638, 95th Cong., 92 Stat. 3799 (1978).

[30] The legislatures of Nebraska, Kentucky, Tennessee, Idaho, and South Dakota took action to rescind their prior ratifications. Idaho brought a federal lawsuit seeking a judicial declaration of the validity of rescission. Although a district court validated rescission, Idaho v. Freeman, 529 F. Supp. 1107, 1155 (D. Idaho 1981), and the Supreme Court granted certiorari, the Supreme Court dismissed the case as moot after the June 30, 1982, ratification deadline expired. Nat'l Org. for Women, Inc. v. Idaho, 459 U.S. 809, 809 (1982).

[31] Assuming that ratification of the ERA adopted by Congress in 1972 could not continue past the prior deadline, the ERA was reintroduced in both houses of Congress in 1983. For an account of the debates surrounding these new ERA proposals in the 1980s, see generally Serena Mayeri, *A New E.R.A. or a New ERA? Amendment Advocacy and the Reconstitution of Feminism*, 103 Nw. U. L. Rev. 1223 (2009).

[32] For a detailed account of the legislative debates leading up to these states' ratifications, see Suk, *supra* note 7, at chs. 10–12.

[33] One federal district court concluded that states may rescind their ratifications up until the time of the amendment's ultimate certification and addition to the Constitution. *Freeman*, 529 F. Supp. at 1155. Virginia, Nevada, and Illinois argue that the text and history of Article V prohibit states from rescinding their ratifications. *See* Complaint at 15, Virginia v. Ferriero, 525 F. Supp. 3d 36 (D.D.C. 2021) (No. 1:20-cv-00242).

[34] H.R.J. Res. 79, 116th Cong. (2020).

[35] S.J. Res. 6, 116th Cong. (2019) had 48 cosponsors, but the Senate Judiciary Committee did not hold hearings or report the resolution. *See S.J. Res. 6 (116th): A Joint Resolution Removing the Deadline for the Ratification of the Equal Rights Amendment.*, GovTrack.us, govtrack.us/congress/bills/116/sjres6/cosponsors [https://perma.cc/4BB7-H2DF] (last visited May 2, 2022) (listing cosponsors).

ratification in March 2021.[36] A bipartisan resolution to the same effect was introduced again in the Senate.[37] Although it appeared that the Democratic majority in the Senate supported removing the ERA deadline,[38] the resolution did not come to a vote in the Senate, as the Senate filibuster rule[39] prevented serious consideration of any legislative proposals that were not supported by a supermajority of 60 senators. As of the writing of this article, there have been no Senate hearings, floor debates, or votes on the deadline removal resolution.

A few months before her death, and over 40 years after she testified before Congress to keep the ERA alive, Justice Ginsburg surprised legal observers and media commentators by publicly questioning the wisdom of these recent efforts to resurrect the ERA.[40] She expressed her preference for a "new beginning" for the ERA.[41] At a public event commemorating the centennial of women's suffrage at Georgetown University Law School in February 2020, Judge Margaret McKeown brought Virginia's recent

---

[36] H.R.J. Res. 17, 117th Cong. (2021).

[37] S.J. Res. 1, 117th Cong. (2021).

[38] The 2020 House vote was 232–183 in support of removing the deadline. *See* 166 Cong. Rec. H1142-43 (daily ed. Feb. 13, 2020). No Democrat opposed it, and five Republicans voted in favor of it. *See id.* In the Senate, no Democrat opposed the ERA deadline removal in the 116th Congress; there were 44 Democratic cosponsors and two Republican cosponsors. *See S.J.Res.6 – A Joint Resolution Removing the Deadline for the Ratification of the Equal Rights Amendment.*, Congress.Gov, https://www.congress.gov/bill/116th-congress/senate-joint-resolution/6/cosponsors?searchResultViewType=expanded (last visited May 2, 2022). Vice President Kamala Harris explicitly supported passing the ERA as a presidential candidate, and the Biden presidential campaign's women's agenda explicitly supported congressional removal of the time limit. *See The Biden Agenda for Women*, Biden Harris Democrats, https://perma.cc/6DPW-HVJ5 (last visited August 27, 2024).

[39] S. Doc. No. 113-18, at 16 (2013). For an account of the emergence of the "stealth filibuster," see generally Catherine Fisk & Erwin Chemerinsky, *The Filibuster*, 49 Stan. L. Rev. 181 (1997).

[40] *See* David G. Savage, *Ratification of Equal Rights Amendment Runs into Opposition — from Trump, Sure, but Ruth Bader Ginsburg?*, L.A. Times (Feb. 13, 2020, 4:00 AM), https://www.latimes.com/politics/story/2020-02-13/ratification-of-era-looks-doubtful-ginsburg-skepticism; Ian Millhiser, *Ruth Bader Ginsburg Probably Just Dealt a Fatal Blow to the Equal Rights Amendment*, Vox (Feb. 11, 2020, 12:30 PM), https://www.vox.com/2020/2/11/21133029/ruth-bader-ginsburg-equal-rights-amendment-supreme-court [https://perma.cc/YH46-KTZN]; Russell Berman, *Ruth Bader Ginsburg Versus the Equal Rights Amendment*, Atlantic (Feb. 15, 2020), https://www.theatlantic.com/politics/archive/2020/02/ruth-bader-ginsburg-equal-rights-amendment/606556/; Joseph Guzman, *Did Ruth Bader Ginsburg Just Kill the Equal Rights Amendment?*, Hill (Feb. 12, 2020), https://thehill.com/changing-america/respect/equality/482744-ginsburg-says-process-to-ratify-equal-rights-amendment [https://perma.cc/Z4AF-MFSG].

[41] Berman, *supra* note 40.

ratification to Justice Ginsburg's attention and asked for her prognosis on when we would obtain an ERA on the federal level.[42] Justice Ginsburg replied, "I would like to see a new beginning. I'd like it to start over."[43] She was concerned that there was "too much controversy about a latecomer [like] Virginia ratifying long after the deadline passed."[44] Pointing out that several states had rescinded their ratifications, she invoked a basic intuition about treating opposing sides fairly: "If you count a latecomer on the plus side, how can you disregard states that said, 'We've changed our minds'?"[45] These comments sounded in concerns about procedural fairness and public acceptance of the Amendment's legitimacy. She made such suggestions a year before, also at a Georgetown event, when she said, "I hope someday [the ERA] will be put back in the political hopper, starting over again collecting the necessary number of states to ratify it."[46]

But moments prior to questioning the procedural legitimacy of the ERA's recent resurrection, at the event with Judge McKeown, Justice Ginsburg unequivocally supported the substance of an Equal Rights Amendment:

> The Constitution's Preamble says, "We the People . . . in Order to form a more perfect Union." The Union will be more perfect if we added this clarion statement to our fundamental instrument of government: Men and women are persons of equal-citizenship stature. . . . Why should the rest of the world have the equivalent of an ERA while the United States lags behind?[47]

Nonetheless, the ERA's opponents embraced Justice Ginsburg's remarks questioning the ERA revival on the House floor three days later during the floor debate on the resolution, *Removing the Deadline for Ratification of Equal Rights Amendment*, which the House Judiciary Committee had

---

[42] Searching for Equality, *supra* note 13.

[43] *Id.*

[44] *Id.*

[45] *Id.*

[46] Georgetown Law, *Justice Ginsburg to Address New Georgetown Law Students*, FACEBOOK, at 1:03:42-1:03:54 (Sept. 12, 2019), https://www.facebook.com/georgetownlaw/videos/2325195750861807 [https://perma.cc/W73G-RSL8].

[47] Searching for Equality, *supra* note 13.

reported out in January 2020.[48] Doug Collins of Georgia quoted Justice Ginsburg's reference to "too much controversy" about the late ratifiers such as Virginia and about the rescissions.[49] But beyond these concerns about procedural legitimacy, he and others voting against the deadline removal registered their substantive opposition to the ERA, stating that, "[i]f ratified, the ERA would be used by pro-abortion groups to undo pro-life legislation."[50] Nonetheless, a majority of the House voted to remove the deadline in 2020 and 2021.[51] The resolution would have recognized the ERA as valid to all intents and purposes as part of the Constitution "whenever ratified" by three-fourths of the states.[52] Notwithstanding any time limits imposed by the 1972 resolution introducing the ERA, the 2020 resolution, if the Senate had adopted the same—would have recognized the ERA as part of the Constitution consequent to Virginia becoming the thirty-eighth state to ratify it.[53]

Before the House voted to remove the deadline, Virginia, Nevada, and Illinois—the states that recently ratified—filed a lawsuit against the National Archivist seeking mandamus relief requiring the Archivist to publish and certify the ERA as part of the Constitution immediately.[54] These states contended that Congress's deadline on ERA ratification could not bind the states under Article V.[55] Invoking their power to ratify amendments under Article V and their sovereignty under the Tenth Amendment, these states contended that their ratifications completed the Article V process of making an Article V amendment, and that enforcing the deadline would be unconstitutional.[56] The district court dismissed the suit for lack of standing,

---

[48] 166 Cong. Rec. H1129 (daily ed. Feb. 13, 2020).

[49] *Id.* at H1129-30 (remarks of Rep. Doug Collins).

[50] *Id.* at H1130 (remarks of Rep. Debra Lesko).

[51] In floor debates in 2021, opponents of the ERA deadline removal again quoted Ginsburg's wish for a "new beginning" to argue that it was too late to revive the ERA legally. *See* 167 Cong. Rec. H1421 (daily ed. Mar. 17, 2021) (remarks of Rep. Debra Lesko).

[52] H.R.J. Res. 79, 116th Cong. (2020).

[53] *See id.*

[54] *See* Complaint, *supra* note 33, at 16.

[55] *See id.* at 13.

[56] *See* Virginia v. Ferriero, 466 F. Supp. 3d 253, 254 (D.D.C. 2020) (order granting motion to intervene). Alabama, Louisiana, and South Dakota brought an earlier action against the National Archivist in an Alabama federal court before Virginia's ratification of the ERA, seeking a declaratory judgment rejecting late ratifications and seeking return of the rescinding

holding that because the Constitution assigns no legally significant role to the Archivist in the amendment process,[57] the Archivist's failure to publish the ERA was not an injury in fact to the late-ratifying states. If the ERA has been validly ratified, it is part of the Constitution regardless of whether the Archivist acts. If it has not been validly ratified, the Archivist's publication could not make the ERA part of the Constitution.

Two never-ratified states (Alabama and Louisiana) and three states that attempted to rescind or sunset their ratifications of the ERA in the 1970s (Nebraska, Tennessee, and South Dakota) intervened in the litigation.[58] The district court granted their summary judgment motion, agreeing that Congress's legally binding seven-year deadline expired in 1979.[59] The court explicitly declined to rule on the validity of rescissions. In addition, the court stated in no uncertain terms that its judgment did not determine the validity of past or future congressional action to extend the ratification deadline: "In light of its decision on the deadline issue, the Court does not reach the question of whether states can validly rescind prior ratifications. Nor does the Court make any statement on whether Congress's extension of the ERA deadline was constitutional."[60] Because Congress had not yet passed legislation in both chambers "to revive the ERA despite both deadlines' expirations," the district court was "not confronted with that difficult issue either," and therefore there was no holding on it.[61]

Two of the late-ratified states, Nevada and Illinois, pursued an appeal of the district court's decision at the D.C. Circuit, which was argued and is pending as of this writing. Throughout this litigation and debates in Congress about the ERA, it is the ERA's opponents, not its proponents, who invoke and embrace Justice Ginsburg, quoting her Georgetown interview in

state's ratification documents. *See* Complaint, Alabama v. Ferriero, No. 7:19-cv-02032, 2019 WL 6894418 (N.D. Ala. Dec. 16, 2019). The plaintiff states voluntarily dismissed that suit in February 2020 and filed a motion to intervene in the ratifying states' lawsuit in the D.C. federal court. *See id.*; Partially Opposed Motion to Intervene and Supporting Statement of Points and Authorities, Virginia v. Ferriero, No. 1:20-cv-00242-RC (D.D.C. filed Feb. 19, 2020).

[57] Virginia v. Ferriero, 525 F. Supp. 3d 36, 47 (D.D.C. 2020).

[58] *See* Intervenors' Motion for Summary Judgment and Supporting Memorandum of Points and Authorities, *Ferriero*, 525 F. Supp. 3d 36 (No. 1:20-cv-00242-RC).

[59] Virginia v. Ferriero, 466 F. Supp. 3d 253, 254 (D.D.C. 2020).

[60] *Ferriero*, 525 F. Supp. 3d at 61.

[61] *Id.*

their briefs, hearings, and floor proceedings.[62] To make their case against the ERA, its opponents have relied not only on Justice Ginsburg's doubts about the procedural fairness of removing the deadline while ignoring states' efforts to rescind their ratifications, but also on her past achievements as an advocate for women's rights. Indeed, Representative Debra Lesko (R-AZ), one of several Republican Congresswomen opposing the ERA deadline removal in the House, argued that the bill was "not necessary," again relying on Justice Ginsburg's words. "The ACLU women's rights director wrote: 'It has been clearly understood that the 14th Amendment prohibits discrimination based on sex.'"[63] During the Nevada Senate's debates leading to its ratification vote in 2017, opponents argued that the ERA was no longer needed because the Equal Protection Clause had achieved the ERA's goals. Nevada Senator Roberson quoted Justice Ginsburg's acknowledgment, shortly after *United States v. Virginia* was decided, that "There is no practical difference between what has evolved and the ERA."[64]

The "de-facto ERA," as the legal scholars that he cited call it, is the body of Supreme Court precedents that have outlawed governmental sex discrimination under the Fifth and Fourteenth Amendments, largely resulting from Ginsburg's successful litigation strategy of the 1970s. It began with her brief for *Reed v. Reed* in 1971, which persuaded the Supreme Court to strike down a state statutory preference for men in appointing the administrator of a deceased person's estate,[65] and culminated in her 1996 opinion as a Justice on behalf of a Supreme Court majority in *United States v. Virginia* in 1996, invalidating the Virginia Military Institute's longstanding policy of excluding women from admission.[66] These cases now firmly require courts

---

[62] *See* Partially Opposed Motion to Intervene and Supporting Statement of Points and Authorities, *supra* note 56, at 5.

[63] 166 CONG. REC. H1130 (daily ed. Feb. 13, 2020) (remarks of Rep. Debra Lesko).

[64] S. 2017-024, 79th Sess., at 12 (Nev. 2017) (remarks of Sen. Roberson). Senator Roberson was quoting at length from Reva B. Siegel, *Constitutional Culture, Social Movement Conflict and Constitutional Change: The Case of the De Facto ERA*, 94 CALIF. L. REV. 1323, 1333-34 (2006) (discussing David A. Strauss, *The Irrelevance of Constitutional Amendments*, 114 HARV. L. REV. 1457 (2001); CASS R. SUNSTEIN, THE SECOND BILL OF RIGHTS: FDR'S UNFINISHED REVOLUTION AND WHY WE NEED IT MORE THAN EVER (2004); and quoting Justice Ginsburg in Jeffrey Rosen, *The New Look of Liberalism on the Court*, N.Y. TIMES (Oct. 5, 1997), https://www.nytimes.com/1997/10/05/magazine/the-new-look-of-liberalism-on-the-court.html.

[65] *See* Brief for Appellant, Reed v. Reed, 404 U.S. 71 (1971) (No. 70-4), 1971 WL 133596; *Reed*, 404 U.S. at 77.

[66] United States v. Virginia, 518 U.S. 515, 519–58 (1996).

to scrutinize governmental use of sex classifications and to strike down those that perpetuate gender stereotypes or women's inferior status without an "exceedingly persuasive" justification.[67]

Are twenty-first-century ERA opponents correct that the ERA is no longer necessary because of Justice Ginsburg's successes in establishing gender equality as a requirement of the constitutional equal protection guarantees in the Fifth and Fourteenth Amendments? Independently of procedural fairness, is a guarantee of sex equality in the Constitution's text *substantively* obsolete, unnecessary, and illegitimate? Yes, the Equal Protection Clause now requires the equal protection of women under the law. But Ginsburg's early writings on the ERA, consistent with its legislative history and her sex equality jurisprudence as a Justice, show that there is much more to constitutional sex equality than what the Supreme Court has established through its sex equality decisions.

History establishes the close link between the ERA and Ginsburg's successes at the Supreme Court. To be sure, the equal protection cases Ginsburg litigated, and her landmark opinion in *United States v. Virginia*, were monumental achievements for women's rights that should not be diminished. A steady line of Supreme Court decisions applied heightened scrutiny to laws that treated men and women differently.[68] This jurisprudence, however, depended in part on the momentum generated by the ERA as it was making its way through Congress and the states. The House of Representatives adopted the ERA on October 12, 1971, by a vote of 354–24,[69] just one week before the Supreme Court heard oral arguments in *Reed v. Reed*—the first Supreme Court decision to strike down a sex-discrimination law based on the Equal Protection Clause of the Fourteenth Amendment.[70] During hearings on the ERA in March 1971,[71] as well as in floor debates that October,[72] Congresswoman Martha Griffiths, the primary sponsor of the ERA

[67] *Id.* at 533.

[68] *See, e.g.*, *Reed*, 404 U.S. 71; Frontiero v. Richardson, 411 U.S. 677 (1973); Weinberger v. Wiesenfeld, 420 U.S. 636 (1975); Califano v. Goldfarb, 430 U.S. 199 (1977).

[69] *See* 117 Cong. Rec. 35,815 (1971).

[70] *Reed*, 404 U.S. 71, was argued on October 19, 1971, and decided on November 22, 1971.

[71] *Equal Rights for Men and Women 1971: Hearings on H.R.J. Res. 35,208, and Related Bills and H.R. Res. 916 and Related Bills Before the Subcomm. No. 4 of the H. Comm. on the Judiciary*, 92d Cong. 1-310 (1971) [hereinafter *1971 House Judiciary Committee ERA Hearings*].

[72] *See* 117 Cong. Rec. 35,298 (1971) (document submitted by Rep. Martha Griffiths).

in the House, sharply criticized the Idaho statute that gave a preference to men over women as executors of estates and pointed out that the ERA was necessary because the Supreme Court had, to date, never ruled in favor of a woman challenging a sex-discrimination law under the Equal Protection Clause.[73] Griffiths had joined an amicus brief for the National Organization of Women Legal Defense and Education Fund for Mrs. Reed in the pending Supreme Court case.[74]

The primary brief attacking the Idaho law was Ginsburg's brief for the ACLU. It was the first of her several meticulously researched and thoroughly reasoned Supreme Court briefs arguing that sex discrimination violated the Equal Protection Clause. The *Reed* brief detailed the history of sex discrimination in equal protection jurisprudence, the long movement for women's suffrage, and the Nineteenth Amendment.[75] It cited the West German Constitutional Court's decisions within the last decade striking down similar laws preferring sons to daughters in property inheritance.[76] Ginsburg also cited the U.N. Charter and a lecture on gender emancipation by the Swedish Prime Minister.[77] Her brief situated the constitutional sex equality principle in a global context, invoking two bodies of law—the West German Constitution and the U.N. Charter—that had been discussed in the congressional ERA hearings of decades past.

Ginsburg also listed pioneering Black civil rights attorney Pauli Murray and the ACLU women's rights lawyer Dorothy Kenyon as coauthors of the brief, even though neither of them had written any part of it.[78] In citing these women, Ginsburg wanted to acknowledge her intellectual debt to ideas they had developed in earlier briefs and law review articles.[79] The House adopted

[73] *1971 House Judiciary Committee ERA Hearings*, *supra* note 71, at 36 (statement of Rep. Martha Griffiths).

[74] *See* Joint Brief of Amici Curiae American Veterans Committee, Inc. & Now Legal Defense and Education Fund, Inc., *Reed*, 404 U.S. 71 (No. 70-4), 1971 WL 133600.

[75] *See* Brief for Appellant, *supra* note 65, at 24–41.

[76] *Id.* at 55.

[77] *Id.* at 55 n.52.

[78] *See id.* at 68.

[79] *See id.* Pauli Murray was invited to testify before the Senate Judiciary Committee's ERA hearings, and she submitted written testimony arguing that Black women had the most to gain from an ERA. *See Equal Rights 1970: Hearings on S.J. Res. 61 and S.J. Res. 231 Before the S. Comm. on the Judiciary*, 91st Cong. 427–33 (1970) [hereinafter *Equal Rights 1970 Senate Hearings*] (statement of Pauli Murray). For an assessment of Murray's written testimony and

the ERA in October 1971, and one month later, the Supreme Court decided the case in Mrs. Reed's favor, striking down the Idaho law that had favored her ex-husband as the executor of their deceased son's estate. The Senate then adopted the ERA and sent it to the states for ratification, three months after the Supreme Court's decision in *Reed*. *Reed*'s trajectory illustrated the dialogue between Congress and the Court about the constitutional status of sex discrimination, beginning with members of Congress opining on a pending case and the Court producing a judgment that appeared responsive. The ERA's support in Congress nudged the Court to scrutinize patriarchal laws, and the Court's first step toward sex equality signaled to Congress its receptiveness to further development. The significant social and political change that the ERA entailed could not be achieved by one of these bodies alone.

The Justices' responsiveness to congressional support for the principle of sex equality became more explicit in later decisions. In *Frontiero v. Richardson*, Ginsburg's first Supreme Court oral argument, the Court invalidated a rule that automatically allowed male military personnel to receive dependent benefits for their wives, while requiring female military personnel to prove that the husband was actually dependent on her for over a year and a half to qualify for the same benefits.[80] *Frontiero* repudiated the nineteenth-century Supreme Court cases that reinforced sexist attitudes toward women. A four-Justice plurality concluded: "There can be no doubt that our Nation has had a long and unfortunate history of sex discrimination. Traditionally, such discrimination was rationalized by an attitude of 'romantic paternalism' which, in practical effect, put women, not on a pedestal, but in a cage."[81] Justice Brennan invoked Congress's adoption of the ERA as a partial justification for scrutinizing laws that treated the sexes unequally:

---

its resonances with the debates surrounding the ERA's resurgence nearly five decades later, see Julie C. Suk, *A Dangerous Imbalance: Pauli Murray's Equal Rights Amendment and the Path to Equal Power*, 107 Va. L. Rev. Online 3 (2021). Serena Mayeri details Pauli Murray's development, with Dorothy Kenyon, of a Fourteenth Amendment strategy, and how they both came to support the ERA after initial skepticism. *See* Serena Mayeri, *Constitutional Choices: Legal Feminism and the Historical Dynamics of Change*, 92 Calif. L. Rev. 755, 797–98, 798 n.203 (2004).

[80] *See* 411 U.S. 677 (1973) (plurality opinion).

[81] *Id.* at 684 (footnote omitted).

> And § 1 of the Equal Rights Amendment, passed by Congress on March 22, 1972, and submitted to the legislatures of the States for ratification, declares that "[e]quality of rights under the law shall not be denied or abridged by the United States or by any State on account of sex." Thus, Congress itself has concluded that classifications based upon sex are inherently invidious, and this conclusion of a coequal branch of Government is not without significance to the question presently under consideration.[82]

The Supreme Court developed its skepticism of laws that discriminated against women with awareness that a democratically elected Congress supported such an approach as evidenced by both houses' votes for the ERA by overwhelming majorities. Justice Brennan affirmed the ERA's democratic political legitimacy and relied on it to bring the ERA's normative aspirations into judicial interpretation of existing constitutional guarantees. A partially completed amendment was sufficient, at least for Justice Brennan, to take the principle of sex equality seriously in interpreting the Fifth and Fourteenth Amendments.[83]

Although the majority of Justices agreed to invalidate the sex classification in the military benefits scheme in *Frontiero*, they could not agree on the standard of review for sex classifications in the law. In contrast to Justice Brennan's reliance on the ERA as authority to regard sex classifications as inherently invidious, Justice Powell, writing for three Justices, refrained from approaching sex as a suspect classification because the ERA was pending ratification in the states and therefore could not yet be relied upon as a full constitutionalization of sex equality:

> The Equal Rights Amendment, which if adopted will resolve the substance of this precise question, has been approved by the Congress and submitted for ratification by the States. If this Amendment is duly adopted, it will represent the will of the people accomplished in the manner prescribed by the Constitution. By acting prematurely and unnecessarily, as I view it, the Court has assumed a decisional responsibility at

---

[82] *Id.* at 687–88 (alteration in original) (footnote omitted) (citation omitted).

[83] *See generally* Rosalind Dixon, *Partial Constitutional Amendments*, 13 U. Pa. J. Const. L. 643 (2011) (arguing that proposed amendments carry positive significance and should be used in common law constitutional interpretation).

> the very time when state legislatures, functioning within the traditional democratic process, are debating the proposed Amendment. It seems to me that this reaching out to pre-empt by judicial action a major political decision which is currently in process of resolution does not reflect appropriate respect for duly prescribed legislative processes.[84]

Justice Powell warned that a judicial attempt to enshrine sex equality as a constitutional principle would weaken democratic institutions and usurp the role of representatives elected by the people in deciding "sensitive issues of broad social and political importance."[85] The Court's enforcement of ERA principles in equal protection cases made the ERA itself less necessary to challenge sex-discriminatory laws.[86]

Additional cases that Ginsburg argued before the Court throughout the 1970s reinforced sex equality as an equal protection principle.[87] Those cases developed the intermediate scrutiny standard,[88] restyled as "skeptical scrutiny" to invalidate the Virginia Military Institute's (VMI) policy of excluding women in 1996.[89] In the six cases Ginsburg argued before the Supreme Court from 1972 to 1978, each case had a male plaintiff, and four of these cases involved governmental benefits schemes that treated men and women differently on the assumption that men were breadwinners and women were their caregiving dependents.[90] As Cary Franklin has detailed, Ginsburg's time in Sweden, where she began her career as a legal scholar of comparative civil procedure, shaped her vision of emancipation from gender

---

[84] *Frontiero*, 411 U.S. at 692 (Powell, J., concurring).

[85] *Id.*

[86] It is noteworthy that, decades later, state legislators such as Senator Roberson in Nevada, and congressional opponents such as Representative Collins, have pointed to the evolution of the Supreme Court's sex equality jurisprudence under the Equal Protection Clause as evidence the ERA is no longer necessary, echoing the scholars who celebrate the "de facto" ERA. *See* S. 2017–024, 79th Sess., at 11–12 (Nev. 2017) (statement of Sen. Roberson); 166 Cong. Rec. H1129-30 (daily ed. Feb. 13, 2020) (remarks of Rep. Doug Collins, R-GA).

[87] Reed v. Reed, 404 U.S. 71 (1971); *Frontiero*, 411 U.S. 677; Weinberger v. Wiesenfeld, 420 U.S. 636 (1975); Califano v. Goldfarb, 430 U.S. 199 (1977).

[88] *See* Craig v. Boren, 429 U.S. 190, 199 (1976) (recognizing an "important governmental objective" that was "substantially related to achievement of that goal").

[89] United States v. Virginia, 518 U.S. 515, 518 (1996).

[90] *See, e.g.*, *Reed*, 404 U.S. 71; *Frontiero*, 411 U.S. 677; *Weinberger*, 420 U.S. 636; *Califano*, 430 U.S. 199; Kahn v. Shevin, 416 U.S. 351 (1974); Duren v. Missouri, 439 U.S. 357 (1979).

stereotypes.[91] On June 8, 1970, Olof Palme, then Swedish Prime Minister, gave a speech called "The Emancipation of Man"[92] at the Women's National Democratic Club in Washington, D.C.—a speech that Ginsburg quoted in her landmark *Reed* brief.[93] Palme said, "The greatest disadvantage with the male sex-role is that the man has too small a share in the upbringing of the children."[94] This increased the burden for women, who often had two roles, one in the home and one in the labor market—whereas men only had one—and also harmed men. Palme and Ginsburg argued that such gendered expectations constrained men's opportunities to lead fulfilling lives in the home and family. In *Weinberger v. Wiesenfeld* and *Califano v. Goldfarb*, the Supreme Court struck down provisions of the Social Security Act that allowed widows, but not widowers, to collect survivors' benefits accrued by their spouses who worked prior to their deaths.[95] These cases established, as a rule of constitutional law, that government may not distribute benefits and burdens based on stereotyped assumptions about men's and women's proper roles in the family.[96]

Nonetheless, the Court stopped short of striking down all gender classifications based on assumptions about men's and women's proper roles. *Rostker v. Goldberg* upheld the Military Selective Service Act,[97] which required all men, but not women, to register for the military draft. Although the draft has not been utilized since 1973, the male-only registration requirement continued to be contested in litigation and in Congress, relying mostly on the Supreme Court's landmark sex equality decision, *United States v. Virginia*, authored by Justice Ginsburg.[98]

---

[91] *See* Franklin, *supra* note 10.

[92] Olof Palme, Swedish Prime Minister, Address at the Women's National Democratic Club: The Emancipation of Man (June 8, 1970).

[93] Brief for Appellant, *supra* note 65, at 55 n.52.

[94] Palme, *supra* note 92, at 7.

[95] 420 U.S. 636, 638–39 (1975); 430 U.S. 199, 201–02 (1977).

[96] *See Califano*, 430 U.S. at 205–06.

[97] 453 U.S. 57, 83 (1981). The Supreme Court reasoned that, in the event of a military draft, the military primarily needed persons eligible for combat roles, and because women were not included in combat roles at the time, treating men and women the same for the purposes of registration for the military draft would fail to meet military needs. *See id.* at 80–82.

[98] 518 U.S. 515 (1996). The Department of Defense ended its exclusion of women from combat roles in 2013. *See* Ernesto Londoño, *Pentagon Removes Ban on Women in Combat*, WASH. POST. (Jan. 24, 2013), https://www.washingtonpost.com/world/national-security/

In *United States v. Virginia*, the Supreme Court required the state's premier military academy to open its doors to females.[99] The VMI's long-standing policy of excluding women was premised on the rationale that fundamental differences between women and men made men, and not women, suited for the "adversative" training for military combat that the school required of its students.[100] The Supreme Court, in a 7–1 judgment authored by Justice Ginsburg, held that Virginia had no "exceedingly persuasive justification" for excluding all women from the "citizen-soldier training afforded by VMI."[101]

Excluding women from an opportunity violated equal protection when premised on "generalizations about 'the way women are.'"[102] At the same time, Justice Ginsburg's opinion leaves space for the law to generalize about women's experience of subordination and disadvantage. For over a century since the founding, "women did not count among voters composing 'We the People,'" she noted.[103] She declared, "Sex classifications may be used to compensate women 'for particular economic disabilities [they have] suffered,'" or "to advance full development of the talent and capacities of our Nation's people," citing, among other cases, the *Cal Fed* case of 1987, which validated a gender-differentiated maternity leave policy.[104] But *United States v. Virginia* made clear that the Fourteenth Amendment prohibited the use of gender lines to "create or perpetuate the legal, social, and economic inferiority of women."[105]

---

pentagon-to-remove-ban-on-women-in-combat/2013/01/23/6cba86f6-659e-11e2-85f5-a8a9228e55e7_story.html. The male-only draft registration statute was challenged again in litigation, but the Fifth Circuit upheld it in 2020, Nat'l Coal. for Men v. Selective Serv. Sys., 969 F.3d 546 (5th Cir. 2020), and the Supreme Court declined to review it, deferring to Congress. Nat'l Coal. for Men v. Selective Serv. Sys., 141 S. Ct. 1815, 1816 (2021) (mem.).

[99] 518 U.S. 515, 518 (1996).

[100] An expert testified at the district court level, "'[m]ales tend to need an atmosphere of adversativeness,' while '[f]emales tend to thrive in a cooperative atmosphere.'" *Id.* at 541.

[101] *Id.* at 534.

[102] *Id.* at 550.

[103] *Id.* at 531.

[104] *Id.* at 533–34 (citing Cal. Fed. Sav. & Loan Ass'n v. Guerra, 479 U.S. 272, 289 (1987). Reva Siegel argues that the citation to *Guerra* in *United States v. Virginia* recognized the regulation of pregnancy as a sex-based classification worthy of heightened scrutiny. Reva B. Siegel, *The Pregnant Citizen, from Suffrage to the Present*, 19 Geo. L.J. 167, 205 (2020).

[105] 518 U.S. at 534.

III. The Unfinished Business of Equal Protection

Did *United States v. Virginia* achieve the ERA's goals? It did invalidate laws that excluded women from benefits and opportunities on the basis of sex, while preserving the possibility of laws designed to overcome women's disadvantages.[106] Old male bastions of power, such as VMI, were opened up to women. But the ERA's framers and founders in Congress demanded more governmental action to overcome women's second-class status in society.[107] The fundamental problem was women's lack of power in a legal order that assumed they were not entitled to any, and that presumed that their place was in the home. Solving it would require addressing the burdens women sustained because of their traditional role within the family, beyond merely declaring sex equality under the law. As Florence Dwyer, a Republican from New Jersey put it, "[W]omen want only what is their due. They want to be treated as whole citizens. They want to be recognized as having a full stake in the life of our nation. Consequently, they also want the means necessary to fulfill this role. . . ."[108]

A. Motherhood and the ERA

Congresswomen from both political parties converged in their concern for the economic security of mothers. Martha Griffiths, a Democrat from Michigan and the primary sponsor of the ERA in the House, invoked the needs of wives, abandoned wives, and widows for equal opportunities to support their families.[109] Florence Dwyer predicted that the ERA would "give new dignity" to the roles of homemaker and mother.[110] By guaranteeing non-abridgment of equal rights based on sex, the ERA would strike at

[106] Professor Thomas Emerson of Yale Law School, along with several students, authored an article that was quoted extensively throughout the 1971–1972 legislative debates about the ERA detailing the ERA's intended and likely effects on the law. *See* Barbara A. Brown, Thomas I. Emerson, Gail Falk & Ann E. Freedman, *The Equal Rights Amendment: A Constitutional Basis for Equal Rights for Women*, 80 YALE L.J. 871 (1971).

[107] *See* SUK, *supra* note 7, at 78–82; *see also infra* text accompanying notes 135–139.

[108] 116 CONG. REC. 27,770 (1970) (statement of Rep. Florence Dwyer). Pauli Murray gave a full account in her September 1970 written testimony to Congress on the ERA as being really about equal power for women. *See Equal Rights 1970 Senate Hearings*, *supra* note 79, at 433.

[109] 116 CONG. REC. 27,999 (1970) (statement of Rep. Martha Griffiths).

[110] 116 CONG. REC. 28,004 (1970) (statement of Rep. Florence Dwyer).

inequalities attributable to government action *and* inaction on issues that shaped women's prospects for political and economic power, especially in light of the disadvantages women faced because of motherhood. The disadvantages stemming from women's role within the family—beyond legal discrimination and exclusion—were not addressed adequately by the Supreme Court's equal protection jurisprudence.

These disadvantages shaped Ginsburg's personal and professional life as she began litigating against sex discrimination.[111] At her Supreme Court confirmation hearings in 1993, Ginsburg drew attention to her brief in *Struck v. Secretary of Defense*,[112] a case that the government settled before the Supreme Court could issue a decision.[113] Captain Susan Struck was an Air Force officer who was discovered to be pregnant while stationed in Vietnam.[114] The Air Force fired her, giving her the option of remaining employed if she terminated her pregnancy.[115] Struck refused to have an abortion, hoping instead to use the disability leave she had earned to give birth and "surrender [the] child[] for adoption" and arguing that her leave of absence would be no different from those taken by temporarily disabled men.[116] Ginsburg's brief argued that pregnancy discrimination violated equal protection of the laws under the Fifth Amendment.[117] But the Air Force rehired Struck and the case became moot.[118] Thus, Ginsburg's opportunity to anchor the unfair treatment of pregnancy and maternity within equal protection jurisprudence was lost.

---

[111] *See* CARMON & KNIZHNIK, *supra* note 14, at 33, 39.

[112] *See Nomination of Ruth Bader Ginsburg, to be Associate Justice of the Supreme Court of the United States: Hearings Before the S. Comm. on the Judiciary*, 103d Cong. 205–06 (1993) [hereinafter *Ginsburg Confirmation Hearings*]; Brief for the Petitioner at *3, Struck v. Sec'y of Def., 409 U.S. 1071 (1972) (No. 72-178), 1972 WL 135840. For a commentary on the *Struck* case as it concerned gender stereotyping, see generally Neil S. Siegel & Reva B. Siegel, *Struck by Stereotype: Ruth Bader Ginsburg on Pregnancy Discrimination as Sex Discrimination*, 59 DUKE L.J. 771 (2010).

[113] *Struck*, 409 U.S. at 1071.

[114] *See Ginsburg Confirmation Hearings*, *supra* note 112, at 206; Brief for the Petitioner, *supra* note 112.

[115] Brief for the Petitioner, *supra* note 112, at *4, *14.

[116] *Id.* at *4, *8.

[117] *Id.* at *12–14.

[118] *Ginsburg Confirmation Hearings*, *supra* note 112, at 206.

A few years later, in 1974, the Supreme Court held in *Geduldig v. Aiello* that a governmental temporary disability benefits scheme that excluded normal pregnancy and childbirth from coverage was consistent with equal protection.[119] Two years later, in *Gilbert v. General Electric*, the Court additionally held that Title VII's prohibition of discrimination because of sex did not prohibit discrimination because of pregnancy, and upheld the legality of a private employer's temporary disability benefits scheme that covered all temporary work-disabling conditions except pregnancy and childbirth.[120] Ginsburg's scholarly writings were critical of these decisions.[121] Her criticism of the Supreme Court's reluctance to recognize pregnancy discrimination as a constitutional violation pointed her to the conclusion that the Equal Rights Amendment was needed.[122]

Working with sparse text in the Equal Protection Clause, an all-male Supreme Court could not agree to the standard of scrutiny for sex classifications in *Frontiero*, nor could these Justices fully grasp pregnancy

---

[119] *See* 417 U.S. 484, 497 (1974).

[120] 429 U.S. 125, 139–40 (1976). For a history of this litigation, see Deborah Dinner, *The Costs of Reproduction: History and the Legal Construction of Sex Equality*, 46 HARV. C.R.-C.L. L. REV. 415, 423–24 (2011).

[121] *See, e.g.*, Ruth Bader Ginsburg, *From No Rights to Half Rights to Confusing Rights: For Women, the Supreme Court's Decisions Are a Study in Male Hesitation and Legal Timidity*, 7 HUM. RTS. 12, 14 (1978) [hereinafter Ginsburg, *From No Rights*] ("It may be that the woman disabled by pregnancy is not trusted by the Justices. (Is she really sick or does she just want to malinger and stay at home with the baby?)"); Ruth Bader Ginsburg, *Gender in the Supreme Court: The 1973 and 1974 Terms*, 1975 SUP. CT. REV. 1, 11 [hereinafter Ginsburg, *Gender in the Supreme Court*] (proposing "rigorous review of employment practices which place women at a disadvantage in the labor market, not the restrained equal protection review applied in *Aiello*."); Ruth Bader Ginsburg, *Sex Equality and the Constitution*, 52 TUL. L. REV. 451, 461 (1978) ("Decisions relating to other problems encountered by pregnant women have taken a meandering course.")

[122] *See* Ginsburg, *From No Rights*, *supra* note 121, at 47. Ginsburg explained the pregnancy cases as the Court's hesitation about making new doctrine without firm textual authority for constitutional sex equality:

> The historic fact that our 18th- and 19th- century Constitution-makers had women's emancipation nowhere on their agenda is an obvious source of the Justices' uneasiness, and their reluctance to provide the firmer guidance lower courts seek.
> The Equal Rights Amendment probably would relieve the Court's anxiety and end its hesitancy to shape new constitutional doctrine, for the E.R.A. would provide a firm root for that doctrine in the nation's fundamental instrument of government.

Id.; *see also* Ginsburg, *Gender in the Supreme Court*, *supra* note 121, at 10 n.59 (explaining that the ERA would alter the Title VII holding in *Aiello*).

discrimination as sex discrimination. Ginsburg read these decisions as evidencing a weak and disorganized doctrinal development of a principle—sex equality—in part because it was not clearly enshrined in the eighteenth-century and nineteenth-century constitutional text. The ERA and its legislative history would provide judges with the direction to build sex equality doctrine. In expressing her views about what the ERA would do as law, including doctrinal changes that would occur, Ginsburg often cited the ERA as discussed in Congress[123] rather than her own normative views as the main source. She did not argue that the ERA would necessitate specific outcomes on specific doctrinal questions—rather, her argument for the ERA was mostly process-based. Its presence in the Constitution would signal to judges and legislatures that they must think hard about what it means for the law to treat women as fully equal citizens.[124] Existing sex equality law—including Title VII—was built more tentatively on the deliberate doctrinal development of race equality.[125]

As of 2021, the United States remained one of the few countries in the world lacking a legal guarantee of paid maternity leave[126] for the majority of working mothers, as only 16 percent of American workers in the private industry have access to paid leave.[127] In the early 1970s, one avenue to paid maternity leave was coverage under temporary disability benefit programs, but a California statute excluded pregnancy and childbirth from its disability

---

[123] *See, e.g.*, Ginsburg, *Ratification of the Equal Rights Amendment*, *supra* note 11, at 937 (arguing that the "congressional history" did not suggest ERA would authorize homosexual marriage); Ginsburg, *Equal Rights Amendment Is the Way*, *supra* note 9, at 22 ("Yes, there will be some work in this for the judiciary, but most jurists seem reliable enough to interpret the ERA in the spirit of its legislative history.").

[124] *See* Ginsburg, *ERA as a Signal supra* note 9, at 73 ("It would serve as a forthright statement of our moral and legal commitment to a system in which neither sons nor daughters are pigeon-holed by government because of their sex.").

[125] On race-sex analogies, see generally SERENA MAYERI, REASONING FROM RACE: FEMINISM, LAW, AND THE CIVIL RIGHTS REVOLUTION (2011).

[126] *See* ORG. FOR ECON. CO-OPERATION & DEV., FAM. DATABASE: PARENTAL LEAVE SYSTEMS 3, 7 (2021), https://www.oecd.org/els/soc/PF2_1_Parental_leave_systems.pdf [https://perma.cc/L37R-TF8V].

[127] This number is current as of March 2018. *See Access to Paid and Unpaid Family Leave in 2018*, U.S. BUREAU OF LAB. STAT.: ECON. DAILY (Feb. 27, 2019), https://www.bls.gov/opub/ted/2019/access-to-paid-and-unpaid-family-leave-in-2018.htm [https://perma.cc/R86T-LP3M]. At that time, seventeen percent of all civilian employees and twenty-five percent of state and local government workers had access to paid family leave. *Id.*

scheme.[128] The lack of paid leave causes economic detriment to working mothers who typically need to take some time off to give birth and care for a newborn. But *Geduldig* insisted that the Equal Protection Clause did not protect pregnant women from discrimination,[129] and the Supreme Court has not invoked the de facto ERA to otherwise scrutinize inequalities women face because of childbearing and childrearing.

In the years following the ERA's adoption by Congress, the number of women elected to Congress doubled, and they formed a bipartisan Congresswomen's Caucus in 1977, which organized efforts to advance legislation on women's issues,[130] including pregnancy discrimination and the ERA deadline extension. Congress overruled *Gilbert v. General Electric* by adopting the Pregnancy Discrimination Act in 1978[131] in the same month that it voted to extend the ERA deadline.[132] The statute provided that discrimination because of sex under Title VII encompassed discrimination because of pregnancy, childbirth, or related medical conditions.[133] But the statutory intervention did not change the status of pregnancy discrimination under the Equal Protection Clause. Meaningfully addressing disadvantages women face because of childbearing and childrearing requires more than a judicially enforceable right against the government's unequal treatment of women and men. Ginsburg's reading of the text and legislative history of the ERA pointed to legislatures, rather than judges, as primary actors in eradicating these disadvantages.

B. The Framers' Institutional Vision for Legislatures

The ERA's congressional framers hoped the ERA would reduce the barriers women faced because they were mothers, mothers-to-be, or potential mothers. But these barriers resulted from a range of complex social, cultural, and institutional dynamics. Thus, no constitutional provision, whether it was the Equal Protection Clause or the ERA, would sufficiently address these

---

[128] *See* Geduldig v. Aiello, 417 U.S. 484, 488–89 (1974) (citation omitted). A generation later, in 2002, California became the first state in the United States to pass legislation guaranteeing paid family leave. *See* S.B. 1661, 2002 Reg. Sess. (Cal. 2002).

[129] *See supra* note 119 and accompanying text.

[130] *See* Irwin N. Gertzog, Congressional Women: Their Recruitment, Treatment, and Behavior 182–85 (1984).

[131] *See* Pub. L. No. 95-555, 92 Stat. 2076.

[132] H.R.J. Res. 638, 95th Cong. (1978).

[133] 42 U.S.C. § 2000e(k).

problems if courts and judges were the primary enforcers. Public policies at both the federal and state levels were needed, and they would have to provide more remedies than any that courts could order. That's why the ERA's framers envisioned Congress and state legislatures tackling gender inequalities in the first instance, not the Supreme Court.

Congresswoman Patsy Takemoto Mink, a Japanese-American from Hawaii, became the first nonwhite woman elected to Congress.[134] Elected in 1964, Mink advanced this legislative vision of the ERA while centering her work as a legislator on the employment opportunities of working mothers.[135] In floor debates on the ERA in 1970 and 1971,[136] in judiciary subcommittee hearings in 1971,[137] and in a law review article published that same year,[138] Congresswoman Mink emphasized the need for robust legislation beyond the ERA to make equality a reality for women. The ERA would provide clear constitutional authority for Congress to regulate the sources of women's disadvantage, independently of the limited powers that the Supreme Court attributed to Congress in the Commerce Clause and the Fourteenth Amendment. The ERA would also serve as a political catalyst for such legislation. In the House Judiciary Committee's 1971 hearing on the ERA, Mink said that there were three general approaches to remedy injustice: "(1) adoption of an equal rights amendment to the U.S. Constitution . . . (2) judicial attack[s] on discriminatory laws . . . under the fifth

---

[134] *See* Judy Tzu-Chun Wu, *The Dead, the Living, and the Sacred: Patsy Mink, Antimilitarism, and Reimagining the Pacific World*, 18 Meridians 304, 305 (2019).

[135] Patsy Mink actively opposed the nomination of Judge Harrold Carswell for a seat on the Supreme Court in 1970 because of his refusal to grant a rehearing en banc in the Fifth Circuit's decision in Phillips v. Martin Marietta Corp., 416 F.2d 1257 (5th Cir. 1969), which had declined to recognize discrimination against the mother of young children as sex discrimination under Title VII. *See Nomination of George Harrold Carswell, of Florida, to Be Associate Justice of the Supreme Court of the United States: Hearings Before the S. Comm. on the Judiciary*, 91st Cong. 81–88 (1970) (statement of Rep. Patsy T. Mink). Betty Friedan argued that Carswell was unfit to be on the Supreme Court because his decision went against "4 million working mothers" in the United States. *Id.* at 89 (testimony of Betty Friedan, Nat'l President, Nat'l Org. for Women).

[136] *See* 117 Cong. Rec. 35, 318–19 (1971). For a narrative account of Mink's contribution to the floor debates on the ERA, see Suk, *supra* note 7, at 68–82.

[137] *See 1971 House Judiciary Committee ERA Hearings*, *supra* note 71, at 521 (statement of Rep. Patsy T. Mink).

[138] *See* Patsy T. Mink, *Federal Legislation to End Discrimination Against Women*, 5 Val. U. L. Rev. 397, 410–11 (1971).

and 14th amendments; and (3) passage of Federal and State legislation to prohibit overt discrimination and to eliminate situations which are discriminatory in effect."[139] Mink noted, "While these approaches are not mutually exclusive—and, indeed, could be attempted simultaneously—it is my belief that the most immediate progress is attainable through the third alternative, direct legislative enactments."[140] In floor debates about the ERA, Mink described the Amendment as constitutional "backing"[141] for these legislative projects, and the legislatures would be looking not only to repeal laws that distinguished by sex overtly but also to change situations where women were disparately impacted or burdened.

Mink, like Ginsburg, was one of few women of their generation who graduated from one of the nation's best law schools. Mink graduated from the University of Chicago School of Law in 1951,[142] and like Ginsburg, faced discrimination in her quests for law firm employment, not only because she was a woman, and a nonwhite one no less, but also because she was a mother of a young child.[143] Concerns about working motherhood animated Mink's leadership on comprehensive childcare legislation concurrent with her vocal support for the ERA. The childcare bill—which would have created federally funded childcare options for all, regardless of ability to pay—was passed with bipartisan support by both houses of Congress, but was vetoed by Nixon in 1971.[144] In a law review symposium piece published in 1971, Mink argued that "[l]ack of child care facilities is a major tool of discrimination."[145] She noted that "[t]he lack of day care facilities is a major obstacle to an overwhelming number of women who are employed or who, more importantly, desire employment."[146]

---

[139] *1971 House Judiciary Committee ERA Hearings*, *supra* note 71, at 521 (statement of Rep. Patsy T. Mink).

[140] *Id.*

[141] 117 CONG. REC. 35,319 (1971).

[142] *See* Interview by Michael J. Murphy, Office of the Historian, U.S. House of Representatives, with Gwendolyn Mink (March 14, 2016), https://history.house.gov/Oral-History/Women/Gwendolyn-Mink/ [https://perma.cc/3PXV-CXM8].

[143] *Id.*

[144] *See generally Comprehensive Preschool Education and Child Day-Care Act of 1969: Hearings on H.R. 13520 Before the Select Subcomm. on Educ. of the H. Comm. on Educ. And Lab.*, 91st Cong. 8 (1970) (testimony of Patsy T. Mink).

[145] Mink, *supra* note 138, at 411.

[146] *Id.*

Ginsburg contributed to the same symposium. So did pioneering African-American civil rights attorney Pauli Murray, whom Justice Ginsburg often recognized as the intellectual architect of the sex equality litigation strategies that succeeded in the 1970s.[147] Ginsburg's symposium contribution criticized the lack of attention in law school curricula to sex-based discrimination in the law, noting specifically, inter alia, that "the proposed Equal Rights Amendment, although it has been in the congressional hopper for decades, is not mentioned"[148] in courses on constitutional law. Pauli Murray's contribution analyzed the barriers to equal opportunity for women in employment and education and emphasized that "congressional action with adequate funding"[149] was necessary to overcome them. Among her proposals was the bill that became Title IX, which goes beyond prohibiting discrimination and requires recipients of federal funding to eliminate disparities.[150]

Patsy Mink sponsored Title IX, and after her death in 2002, the statute was named for her, recognizing that she was the "[m]other of Title IX."[151] Pauli Murray had testified in writing to support the ERA in the Senate Judiciary Committee hearing in 1970, arguing that the ERA could go beyond the concerns of litigation under the Equal Protection Clause: "Quite apart from the legal implications discussed in the various statements by attorneys, there are strong policy considerations which impel support of the Equal Rights Amendment in 1970."[152] She also described Congress as "a political body which must be responsive to rapid social change."[153] The ERA would engender legislative transformation. It would establish that "the sole purpose of

---

147 Ginsburg famously included Pauli Murray as a coauthor on her landmark brief in *Reed*. *See* Brief for Appellant, *supra* note 65.

148 Ruth Bader Ginsburg, *Treatment of Women by the Law: Awakening Consciousness in the Law Schools*, 5 VAL. U. L. REV. 480, 484 (1971) (footnote omitted).

149 Pauli Murray, *Economic and Educational Inequality Based on Sex: An Overview*, 5 VAL. U. L. REV. 237, 277 (1971).

150 *See generally Discrimination Against Women: Hearings on Section 804 of H.R. 16098 Before the Special Subcomm. on Education of the H. Comm. on Education and Labor, Parts I & II*, 91st Cong. 434 (1971) (statement of Patsy Mink); 20 U.S.C. § 1681.

151 *See The 14th Amendment and the Evolution of Title IX*, U.S. COURTS, https://www.uscourts.gov/educational-resources/educational-activities/14th-amendment-and-evolution-title-ix [https://perma.cc/WV65-9XHS] (last visited May 7, 2022).

152 *See Equal Rights 1970 Senate Hearings*, *supra* note 79, at 431.

153 *Id.*

governments is to create the conditions under which the uniqueness of each individual is cherished and is encouraged to fulfill his or her highest creative potential."[154] Murray, like Mink, saw the ERA as the political catalyst that would legitimize ambitious legislation creating the actual conditions of equal opportunity.[155] Judicial doctrines developed under the Equal Protection Clause were more limited, in part because the precedents requiring state action for a violation[156] (also textually enshrined in the ERA) would make it difficult to challenge the exclusions of women by private institutions. Also, "the traditional attitude of judges in the federal courts"[157] limited the possibilities of change through adjudication. Thus, the more ambitious goals of constitutional sex equality would be implemented by legislation rather than by litigation.

In later scholarly work, Ginsburg embraced and defended the primacy of legislatures as implementers of the ERA. On her reading, Section 3 of the ERA, which creates a two-year delay between the date of ratification and the effective date of the Amendment, "gives our legislators a two-year period to update laws now lagging behind social change."[158] While acknowledging that legislators could update laws without the ERA, "history strongly suggests that the task will continue to be relegated to a legislative back burner absent the propelling force supplied by the Amendment."[159]

The ERA "should end legislative inertia that retards social change by keeping obsolete laws on the books, so the Amendment should relieve judicial uneasiness in the gray zone between interpretation and amendment of the Constitution."[160] This article, in the inaugural issue of *Harvard Women's Law Journal*, concluded with an explicit understanding of legislatures as the

[154] *Id.* at 433.

[155] In another law review article about African-American women and the ERA, Murray argued, "Consideration of the amendment by state legislatures would stimulate a detailed review of all state laws and policies affecting women. No comparable political activity would focus nationwide attention upon the need to modernize and extend state labor standards." Pauli Murray, *The Negro Woman's Stake in the Equal Rights Amendment*, 6 Harv. C.R.-C.L. L. Rev. 253, 258 (1971).

[156] Murray, *supra* note 149, at 270–71.

[157] *Id.* at 271.

[158] Ginsburg, *Equal Rights Amendment Is the Way*, *supra* note 9, at 23 (referencing Section 3 of the ERA).

[159] *Id.*

[160] *Id.* at 25.

first movers of equal rights, and with a role for judges only in the event of legislative failure:

> With the Equal Rights Amendment, we may expect Congress and the state legislatures to undertake in earnest, systematically and pervasively, the law revision so long deferred. And in the event of legislative default, the courts will have an unassailable basis for applying the bedrock principle: All men and all women are created equal.[161]

It is noteworthy that before these words were published in a law journal, Ginsburg had delivered them as a speech to judges and lawyers at the Second Circuit Judicial Conference in 1976,[162] essentially asking the bench and the bar to defer to elected lawmakers and to step in only if they defaulted in their duties. Legislatures should repeal laws that treated men and women differently and make the policy judgment about whether to abolish a burden imposed on one gender, such as the military draft, or to impose the same burden on both genders equally. The substantive goals of the ERA could not be fulfilled by litigation and judicial interpretation alone.[163] Judges could invalidate legislation but could not rewrite it. So even if it can be said that *United States v. Virginia* achieved the ERA's goals, such a view would only encompass the negative goals of dismantling discrimination, not the positive goals of establishing a gender-equal legal order.

The legislative project of the ERA was partially realized while the ERA was being ratified in the 1970s, even without its complete ratification: Title IX was adopted by Congress and signed into law in June 1972.[164] Congress passed comprehensive federal childcare legislation, but President Nixon vetoed it in 1971.[165] Despite Patsy Mink's declaration that same year that

161 *Id.* at 26.

162 *See id.* at 19 n.*.

163 *See* Ruth Bader Ginsburg, *Sexual Equality Under the Fourteenth and Equal Rights Amendments*, 1979 WASH. U. L.Q. 161, 173 ("Framed as a basic human rights norm, the ERA has two offices. First, it directs federal and state legislatures to undertake conforming legislative revision. The Amendment stipulates a two-year period for this mop, broom, and paint operation. Second, it directs the judiciary to a clear source for the constitutional principle, men and women are equal before the law." (footnotes omitted)).

164 20 U.S.C. § 1681.

165 Jack Rosenthal, *President Vetoes Child Care Plan as Irresponsible: He Terms Bill Unworkable and Voices Fear It Would Weaken Role of Family*, N.Y. TIMES, Dec. 10, 1971, at 1.

"[t]his decade must and will see the child care situation resolved,"[166] five decades have gone by without federal childcare policy.

This history seems to confirm Ginsburg's prediction that, absent the ERA, the task of legislating equality policy would remain on a "legislative back burner."[167] Viewing the ERA's function as similar to international human rights norms, Ginsburg noted that even when an international human rights norm lacked clear force of law and judicial enforcement, it still shaped the law's development: "Authoritative formulation of the basic norm is an indispensable step toward defense and fulfillment of [a] human right," she argued. "Only upon official commitment to the norm can we proceed securely to 'measures of implementation,' arrangements designed to promote effective application of the norm."[168] In invoking the human rights model, Ginsburg suggested that "we"—the people and lawmaking bodies—needed the ERA as a guiding principle as much as courts needed it to anchor a more comprehensive doctrinal development.

The twenty-first-century resurrection of the ERA that took its first significant step when Nevada ratified it in 2017 paid homage to Justice Ginsburg's legislative constitutionalism. Senator Pat Spearman, the leading cosponsor of the ratification bill, opened the floor debate and quoted Ginsburg's concluding paragraph from *Harvard Women's Law Journal* above:

> With the Equal Rights Amendment, we may expect Congress and the State legislatures to undertake in earnest, systematically and pervasively, the law revision so long deferred. And in the event of legislative default, the courts will have an unassailable basis for applying the bedrock principle: All men and all women are created equal.[169]

In the same legislative session, the legislators who sponsored and defended the ERA also passed legislation guaranteeing reasonable accommodations for pregnant workers[170] and nursing mothers,[171] as well as

[166] Mink, *supra* note 138, at 411.

[167] Ginsburg, *Equal Rights Amendment Is the Way*, *supra* note 9, at 23.

[168] *Id.*

[169] S. 2017–024, 79th Sess., at 5 (Nev. 2017) (statement of Sen. Pat Spearman).

[170] S.B. 253, 2017 Leg., 79th Sess. (Nev. 2017).

[171] Assemb. B. 113, 2017 Leg., 79th Sess. (Nev. 2017).

legislation protecting domestic violence victims from adverse employment actions.[172]

Shortly after *United States v. Virginia*, the Supreme Court's Fourteenth Amendment jurisprudence diminished Congress's power to legislate aggressively against some of the manifestations of women's unequal status. In *United States v. Morrison*, the Supreme Court held, over a four-Justice dissent joined by Justice Ginsburg, that Section 5 of the Fourteenth Amendment did not authorize Congress to legislate remedies for sexual assault by private individuals and other forms of gender-based violence.[173] *Morrison* relied on a long history of interpreting Section 5 of the Fourteenth Amendment narrowly since the *Civil Rights Cases* in 1883.[174] With the Fourteenth Amendment alone, the legitimacy of Congress's power to regulate the broad range of dynamics that abridge women's equal status would be in question. Because the ERA's framers explicitly referenced the need for equality-promoting legislation, the ERA would go beyond Fourteenth Amendment precedent to legitimize such legislation. Patsy Mink characterized the ERA as a reaction to the "lack of action by our executive, legislative, and judicial bodies to put into effect the equal rights safeguards already in the Constitution"; therefore, "[a]doption of the amendment would . . . leave us the formidable task of seeking extensive legislation and judicial actions."[175]

IV. Further Limits of Adjudicating Socio-Legal Change

A. *A Silence of Equal Protection Law:* **Sessions v. Morales-Santana**

Congress's power to legislate gender equality under the ERA is crucial in light of Justice Ginsburg's understanding that courts, as compared to legislatures, are constrained in their ability to deliver full equality. In *Sessions v. Morales-Santana*, the Supreme Court invalidated the different treatment of men and women under the Immigration and Nationality Act's provisions

[172] S.B. 361, 2017 Leg., 79th Sess. (Nev. 2017).

[173] 529 U.S. 598, 617–27 (2000).

[174] *See generally* The Civil Rights Cases, 109 U.S. 3 (1883).

[175] 117 Cong. Rec. 35,318 (1971).

on the acquisition of U.S. citizenship for a child born abroad.[176] If the child was born to unmarried parents and the mother was a U.S. citizen, the statute required the mother to live continuously in the United States for one year before the child's birth for the child to obtain citizenship.[177] If the father was the U.S. citizen, he must have lived in the United States for at least ten years before the child's birth, at least five of which had to be after the age of fourteen, to pass on his citizenship to the child.[178] The case grew out of a deportation proceeding against a criminal defendant who claimed that he was a U.S. citizen despite being born abroad because his father, though unmarried to his mother, was a U.S. citizen.[179] Because the defendant's father had not met the statute's residency requirement, whether Morales-Santana was a U.S. citizen was in question, with direct implications for his deportability.

Justice Ginsburg, writing for the Supreme Court majority, held that the gender line Congress drew was incompatible with the Fifth Amendment's requirement that the government accord all persons "equal protection of the laws."[180] The Court concluded that gender-differentiated treatment in the statute was based on "overbroad generalizations about the way men and women are"[181] and could not be sustained under *United States v. Virginia*.[182] At the same time, the Court refrained from thus concluding that Morales-Santana was a U.S. citizen as he would have been under the statute if the parent with U.S. citizenship had been his mother rather than his father.[183] Justice Ginsburg acknowledged that, although "the equal protection infirmity" in treating unwed fathers and mothers differently was "clear, this Court is not equipped to grant the relief Morales-Santana seeks."[184] The

---

176 137 S. Ct. 1678, 1700–01 (2017). For an account of the remedy in this case, see Cary Franklin, *Biological Warfare: Constitutional Conflict Over "Inherent Differences" Between the Sexes*, 2017 SUP. CT. REV. 169, 202–04; and Kristin A. Collins, *Equality, Sovereignty, and the Family in* Morales-Santana, 131 HARV. L. REV. 170, 171, 176 (2017).

177 *Morales-Santana*, 137 S. Ct. at 1687 (citing 8 U.S.C. § 1401(a)(7)).

178 *Id.*

179 *Id.*

180 *Id.* at 1689.

181 *Id.*

182 518 U.S. 515 (1996).

183 *Morales-Santana*, 137 S. Ct. at 1701.

184 *Id.* at 1698.

Court could not extend to his father, and derivatively to him, the benefit that an unwed mother enjoyed.

The Court could invalidate unequal treatment, but it was not free to make the policy choice between two radically different ways of treating men and women equally. Ending unequal treatment could mean requiring the longer physical presence requirement for unwed mothers to make them equal to unwed fathers or shortening the physical presence requirement for unwed fathers to make them equal to unwed mothers. Quoting precedent, Justice Ginsburg wrote, "How equality is accomplished . . . is a matter on which the Constitution is silent."[185] Furthermore, how equality was accomplished was a matter for Congress rather than the Court, and in this case, the Court's job was to guess, based on available legislative evidence, the path to equality that Congress would likely choose.

Congress's role in making a policy decision to extend, rather than to extinguish, a benefit enjoyed by one gender to achieve equal treatment was a subject of ERA discussion, both in congressional debates as well as in Ginsburg's scholarly writings. One of the most contentious questions about the ERA was whether it would require women to be drafted, just like men.[186] It was related to the question of protective labor legislation for women only. If there were laws that protected women from overtime work, for instance, would women lose such protections under the ERA or would men gain them?[187] Patsy Mink, along with Shirley Chisholm, the first African-American woman elected to Congress,[188] at various moments advanced the view that the ERA would require leveling up.[189] Women were exempt from compulsory military service; extending that exemption to men would mean eliminating the draft and moving toward the policy of relying on volunteer-only

[185] *Id.* at 1698 (alteration in original) (quoting Levin v. Com. Energy, Inc., 560 U.S. 413, 426–27 (2010)).

[186] *See* 117 Cong. Rec. 35,296 (1971) (statement of Martha Griffiths).

[187] For decades, social reformers and labor unions had opposed the ERA out of fear that it would erode labor protections for women. That fear was expressed by union leader Myra Wolfgang even in the 1970 hearings. *See Equal Rights 1970 Senate Hearings*, *supra* note 79, at 31 (statement of Myra Wolfgang).

[188] Jennifer Steinhauer, *2019 Belongs to Shirley Chisholm*, N.Y. Times (July 6, 2019), https://www.nytimes.com/2019/07/06/sunday-review/shirley-chisholm-monument-film.html.

[189] 116 Cong. Rec. 28, 028–29 (1970). Initially, Mink argued that the ERA should specifically state that any rights, benefits, or privileges conferred on one sex should be construed to apply to both sexes equally. However, she later voted for the ERA without such clarifying language, trusting that legislative history would make the framers' intentions clear.

military service.[190] If women were protected from certain forms of overwork, men, too, would get those protections under the ERA.[191] Martha Griffiths, the primary sponsor of the ERA in the House, argued that it would be Congress, rather than the courts, that would decide how to replace laws that discriminated on the basis of sex while acting to repeal them.[192] Legislatures, rather than courts, could thoughtfully redesign policy, taking many competing priorities into account, beyond the interests of parties to a litigation. If real equality requires thoughtful and data-driven public policy that is responsive to the needs of many, courts are ill-equipped for the systematic revision of the law that the ERA intended to bring about.

It is worth taking a moment to consider seriously how Justice Ginsburg's account of Section 3 of the ERA, which created a two-year delay between the ERA's ratification and legal effect, would have worked and what difference it might have made to the statute at issue in *Morales-Santana*. Congress and state legislatures would use the time—before the ERA could be enforced in courts—to review all the laws on the books that might deny or abridge equal rights on account of sex. Indeed, Ginsburg herself had compiled these laws into a volume titled *Sex Bias in the U.S. Code* in 1977 for the U.S. Commission on Civil Rights.[193] The Introduction to that compilation noted that Congresswoman Martha Griffiths, the ERA's chief sponsor, called for every standing committee of Congress to examine the laws in force within their respective jurisdictions for their effects on women.[194] Studying the laws' operation through this lens, legislators would have to assess whether they abridged equal rights, including whether sex inequality would be exacerbated by the law's repeal. With legislative power at its disposal, a legislature could then replace the repealed law with one respectful of equal rights,

---

[190] *See* Wu, *supra* note 134, at 327.

[191] *See* 116 CONG. REC. 28,029 (1970).

[192] *1971 House Judiciary Committee ERA Hearings*, *supra* note 71, at 51 (statement of Martha Griffiths) ("[E]ven if the 14th amendment is determined to apply at last to women, I still think it would be a good idea to pass this amendment because you will have to go time and time and time again to the Supreme Court to make that 14th amendment really function where women are concerned. But if you pass this amendment, you are going to have every legislature in this country looking at their own laws to determine how they distinguish between men and women, and you will have this body doing something about it and it should do something about it.").

[193] *See* U.S. COMM'N ON C.R., SEX BIAS IN THE U.S. CODE: A REPORT OF THE U.S. COMMISSION ON CIVIL RIGHTS, at iii (1977).

[194] *See id.* at 7.

in consideration of the resources available and competing policy priorities. If a ratified ERA had triggered a legislative process of systematic review, repeal, and replacement of the laws that abridged equal rights on account of sex, judicial review would likely operate differently in enforcing the ERA as compared to equal protection. Ginsburg had suggested that judges should act only in the event of legislative default.[195] Although she did not spell out what that meant, a reasonable approach would be for courts to defer to Congress's judgments as to whether an existing law was worth repealing because of its sex-discriminatory effects, as well as to Congress's policy choices with regard to replacing any laws rendered obsolete by the ERA. What might emerge from the ERA is a more collaborative dialogue between Congress and the Supreme Court over the meaning of sex equality and what it requires.

B. Justice Ginsburg's Dialogue with Congress

Justice Ginsburg's dissenting opinions in statutory sex discrimination cases reveal her efforts at a dialogue with Congress. In 2007, Justice Ginsburg read her dissent in *Ledbetter v. Goodyear Tire & Rubber Co.* from the bench.[196] In a 5–4 decision, the Supreme Court rejected a female retiree's Title VII and Equal Pay Act claims on the grounds that they were time-barred.[197] She alleged pay discrimination over the course of an entire career, but the Supreme Court held that only the allegedly discriminatory paychecks within 180 days of her filing at the Equal Employment Opportunity Commission (EEOC) were timely.[198] Justice Ginsburg viewed the Court's interpretation of Title VII as straying far away from fidelity to the statute's core purpose: "This is not the first time the Court has ordered a cramped interpretation of Title VII, incompatible with the statute's broad remedial purpose. Once again, the ball is in Congress's court. As in 1991, the Legislature may act to correct this Court's parsimonious reading of Title VII."[199] Congress listened

[195] Ginsburg, *Equal Rights Amendment Is the Way*, *supra* note 9, at 25.

[196] *See* Linda Greenhouse, *In Dissent, Ginsburg Finds Her Voice at Supreme Court*, N.Y. Times (May 31, 2007), https://www.nytimes.com/2007/05/31/world/americas/31iht-court.4.5946972.html.

[197] *See* Ledbetter v. Goodyear Tire & Rubber Co., 550 U.S. 618, 632 (2007).

[198] *Id.* at 628.

[199] *Id.* at 661 (Ginsburg, J., dissenting) (citations omitted).

and, in 2009, passed the Lilly Ledbetter Fair Pay Act, overruling the Supreme Court majority and establishing that every discriminatory paycheck can keep the claims of past violations timely.[200]

In 2009, Justice Ginsburg dissented in yet another sex discrimination case, this one involving pregnancy discrimination. Again, she criticized her colleagues' highly constrained interpretation of Congress's intent in adopting the Pregnancy Discrimination Act of 1978 (PDA).[201] In *AT&T Corp. v. Hulteen*, female employees challenged their employer's retirement credit policies, adopted before the PDA, which awarded fewer pension credits for pregnancy leave than for medical leave generally.[202] Although the employer equalized the pension credits between pregnancy and disability leave following the enactment of the PDA, the female employees argued that the employer's failure to correct the credits awarded under the old pre-PDA formula for the purposes of pension payments years later violated the statute.[203] The Court allowed the old, pre-PDA formula to be used, finding no PDA violation and viewing it as a bona fide seniority system under Title VII.[204] Justice Ginsburg noted:

> [The PDA] does not oblige employers to make women whole for the compensation denied them when, prior to the Act, they were placed on pregnancy leave, often while still ready, willing, and able to work, and with no secure right to return to their jobs after childbirth. But the PDA does protect women, from and after April 1979, when the Act became fully effective, against repetition or continuation of pregnancy-based disadvantageous treatment.[205]

Justice Ginsburg's dissent focused on the Supreme Court's prior insistence that pregnancy discrimination was not sex discrimination in *Gilbert* while "disregarding the opinions of other courts [and] of the agency that

[200] Pub. L. No. 111-2, 123 Stat. 5.

[201] Pub. L. No. 95-555, 92 Stat. 2076.

[202] 556 U.S. 701, 704 (2009).

[203] *Id.* at 705–07.

[204] *Id.*

[205] *Id.* at 719 (Ginsburg, J., dissenting) (footnote omitted).

superintends enforcement of Title VII."[206] Eventually Congress recognized that pregnancy was the root cause of discrimination against women in the paid labor force.[207] There was a certain outlandishness to the Court's insistence—despite other institutional voices to the contrary—that pregnancy discrimination was distinct from sex discrimination. Perhaps it revealed the limits of the legal reasoning at which courts excel compared to the political branches. Justice Ginsburg quoted a district court judge in a pregnancy discrimination case from 1974:

> [I]t might appear to the lay mind that we are treading on the brink of a precipice of absurdity. Perhaps the admonition of Professor Thomas Reed Powell to his law students is apt; "If you can think of something which is inextricably related to some other thing and not think of the other thing, you have a legal mind."[208]

For Justice Ginsburg, the majority of the Justices in *Hulteen* "erred egregiously," while Congress "made plain its view" that it "intended no continuing reduction of women's compensation, pension benefits included, attributable to their placement on pregnancy leave."[209] She wrote the *Ledbetter* and *Hulteen* dissents during the time when she was the only woman on the Supreme Court, when it appeared that her colleagues on the Court could not see the dynamics of gender inequality that were more visible to Congress—a political and democratically elected branch.

Justice Ginsburg appreciated the comparative institutional competence of legislatures versus courts in implementing the socio-legal changes that came along with fully integrating women in citizenship and power. From her ERA scholarship in 1978 to her judicial opinions and writings 40 years later, her belief in the limited ability of courts to order social change is clear.[210] While she criticized the Supreme Court's decisions on pregnancy, it

---

[206] *Id.* at 723.

[207] *Id.* at 719.

[208] *Id.* at 727 (alteration in original) (quoting Wetzel v. Liberty Mut. Ins. Co., 372 F. Supp. 1146, 1157 (W.D. Pa. 1974), *aff'd*, 511 F.2d 199 (3d Cir. 1975), *vacated and remanded*, 424 U.S. 737 (1976)).

[209] *Id.* at 723.

[210] *See* Ruth Bader Ginsburg, Address, *Some Thoughts on Judicial Authority to Repair Unconstitutional Legislation*, 28 CLEV. ST. L. REV. 301, 301, 303 (1979) (recognizing difficulties

was surely not lost on her that those cases involved benefits schemes, about which Justices expressed reluctance to rewrite policies in a manner that would increase expenditures of public resources—a function more suited to the legislature.[211] Just before she was nominated to the Supreme Court, Ginsburg publicly criticized *Roe v. Wade* for rewriting policy beyond merely invalidating one abortion law. *Roe* endeavored "to fashion a regime blanketing the subject, a set of rules that displaced virtually every state law."[212] The *Roe* Court "invited no dialogue with legislators," and "seemed entirely to remove the ball from the legislators' court."[213] Ginsburg believed that *Roe* halted state legislatures' marked trend toward the liberalization of abortion statutes and incited a backlash in the form of a successful right-to-life movement. A more restrained judicial role, she suggested, might have resulted in state legislative action with greater long-term stability in legitimizing access to abortion.[214]

Her cautionary criticism of *Roe* points to the possibility of courts nudging Congress and state legislatures without displacing their norm-implementing role. In this vein, the Supreme Court has recently declined to resolve the ERA's most hotly contested issue, denying a certiorari petition challenging the Military Selective Service Act's male-only draft registration requirement, suggesting that it is for Congress, not the Court, to specify how the genders should be treated equally.[215] As the parties challenging the law acknowledged, gender-equal treatment can mean requiring everyone to register regardless of gender, abolishing the draft registration requirement altogether, or replacing the draft registration requirement with a nonmilitary and nondiscriminatory national service scheme.[216] Congress has wide

---

courts face in ordering inclusion of persons left out by a legislature, due to courts' lack of power over the purse).

[211] *See* Geduldig v. Aiello, 417 U.S. 484, 494 n.18, 495–96 (1974) (noting the increased cost of covering normal pregnancy, deferring to the state's policy judgment, and that the "courts will not interpose their judgment" on these resource-allocation decisions).

[212] Ruth Bader Ginsburg, *Speaking in a Judicial Voice*, 67 N.Y.U. L. Rev. 1185, 1199 (1992).

[213] *Id.* at 1205.

[214] *See id.* at 1186, 1191.

[215] *See* Nat'l Coal. for Men v. Selective Serv. Sys., 141 S. Ct. 1815 (2021) (Sotomayor, J., respecting the denial of certiorari) (acknowledging the "deference to Congress on matters of national defense and military affairs . . . while Congress actively weighs the issue.").

[216] *See* Petition for a Writ of Certiorari at 36–37, *Nat'l Coal. for Men*, 141 S. Ct. 1815 (No. 20-928).

latitude, whereas the Court's role would be limited to striking down a gender-unequal scheme without replacing it with a regime of gender equality.

Furthermore, in the twenty-first century, the public meaning of the phrase "on account of sex" has evolved since the ERA's introduction and adoption. When the ERA was adopted by Congress in 1972, the abridgment of equal rights on account of sex was mostly understood to mean discrimination against women in favor of men.[217] A generation later, as the legislative debates in the Nevada and Virginia ratifications make clear, discrimination against LGBTQ and other gender-nonconforming people is understood to be a form of sex discrimination.[218] However, as the economic disadvantages faced by working mothers differ from homophobia and the forms of exclusion experienced by transgender people, a range of policies sensitive to the complex and evolving dynamics of inequality is required to implement equal rights for all genders. That, too, is more suited to legislatures rather than to courts. Courts might pull the brakes on discriminatory laws, but the equality of women and disfavored sexual minorities would require further interventions that only a lawmaking body can deliver.

V. Congress's Legitimizing Role in the Amendment Process

A. Justice Ginsburg on the 1978 ERA Deadline Extension

Ginsburg's appreciation of Congress as the primary guardian of the ERA's *substance* in her 1970s scholarly writings was also reflected in her vision of Congress's role in the *process* of making the ERA part of the Constitution. Her heightened concern for the process by which the ERA became part of the Constitution explains her most recent remarks in 2020 favoring "a new beginning" for the ERA. These remarks should be read in the context of her more thoroughly reasoned account of the Article V amendment process in her written and oral testimony before the House and Senate Judiciary Committees in 1977 and 1978 supporting the extension of the ERA's ratification

[217] *See* Suk, *supra* note 7, at 57–82.

[218] *See id.* at chs. 10, 12; *see also id.* at 161–62 (describing efforts like those led by Danica Roem, "Virginia's first transgender delegate," to recognize "the equal rights of all sexes and genders, beyond male and female"). The Supreme Court affirmed this meaning of discrimination because of "sex" in Title VII in Bostock v. Clayton County, 140 S. Ct. 1731, 1754 (2020).

deadline.[219] In those hearings, she argued that Congress had the authority to extend the ratification deadline and to reject states' efforts to rescind.[220] But she did not argue that Congress was legally required by Article V to act one way or another on these political questions. Although Ginsburg's 1970s scholarly publications and congressional testimonies on the ERA deadline are seldom read or quoted today, they represent her last work as a publicly engaged scholar before she became a judge on the D.C. Circuit, and they reflect her efforts to balance procedural fairness with substantive equality in a constitutional democracy.

This synthesis is directly relevant to the forward trajectory of the ERA. The question of whether the ERA ratification deadline *can* be changed by Congress as a legal matter is distinct from the question of whether the ERA ratification deadline *should* be changed by Congress as a political or moral matter. Justice Ginsburg did not articulate a position on whether the ERA *must* start over, or on whether the Constitution *permits* late ratifications or rescissions *as a matter of law*. Justice Ginsburg did make public extemporaneous remarks that she would "*like* to see a new beginning" for the ERA and she questioned, "If you count a latecomer on the plus side, how can you disregard states that said, 'We've changed our minds'?"[221] At that moment,

[219] *See Equal Rights Amendment Extension: Hearings on H.R.J. Res. 638 Before the Subcomm. on Civ. & Const. Rts. of the H. Comm. on the Judiciary*, 95th Cong. 121–30 (1978) [hereinafter *Equal Rights Amendment Extension House Hearings*] (testimony of Ruth Bader Ginsburg); *Equal Rights Amendment Extension Senate Hearings*, *supra* note 19, at 262–71. Ginsburg testified in support of congressional action to extend the ratification deadline, as did constitutional law experts Professor Thomas I. Emerson of Yale Law School, Professor Laurence H. Tribe of Harvard Law School, and Professor Jules Gerard of the Washington University in St. Louis Law School. *See Equal Rights Amendment Extension Senate Hearings*, *supra* note 19, at 114, 144, 238. Patricia Wald, who went on to be Ginsburg's judicial colleague on the D.C. Circuit, also testified in favor of the deadline extension in her capacity as an Assistant Attorney General in the Justice Department. *Id.* at 54. Former Harvard Law School Dean and Solicitor General Erwin Griswold testified against the deadline extension. *Equal Rights Amendment Extension House Hearings*, *supra*, at 108. Griswold is familiar to the fans of Notorious RBG and the biopic On the Basis of Sex as the law dean who asked all the women in Ginsburg's law school class to justify their taking the law school spots of men. *See* CARMON & KNIZHNIK, *supra* note 14, at 34.

[220] *See Equal Rights Amendment Extension House Hearings*, *supra* note 219, at 128; *Equal Rights Amendment Extension Senate Hearings*, *supra* note 19, at 265, 267–68.

[221] Searching for Equality, *supra* note 13 (emphasis added).

states filed federal lawsuits in Alabama[222] and the District of Columbia[223]—raising precisely those legal questions—so a seasoned and cautious judge like Justice Ginsburg could not possibly be offering her legal opinion in a public speech on pending litigation initiated with the intention of eventually landing in the Supreme Court. Thus, her remarks must be understood as the expression of her personal wishes for how history might unfold, having been asked for a "prognosis"[224] rather than a reasoned legal opinion. Her personal preference for a "new beginning" is consistent with the reasoned legal position she advanced in a 1979 *Texas Law Review* article that built on her 1977 and 1978 ERA deadline testimonies. She proffered that Congress had the constitutional authority to reasonably set and revisit ratification timelines as part of its Article V power to "propose amendments."[225] Congress, she urged, was also the body best positioned to determine whether rescissions should be effective, with an eye to establishing the ERA's procedural legitimacy.[226]

B. "The Idea Generates Fears": The Case for More Time

In her careful reading of the history of constitutional amendments, Ginsburg suggested that seven-year ratification windows may be inappropriate for amendments proposing human rights guarantees involving significant social transformations.[227] Prior rights amendments were added to the Constitution as a consequence of violent revolution and war. The Bill of Rights grew out of the American Revolution, and the Thirteenth, Fourteenth, and Fifteenth Amendments grew out of the Civil War. Without waging a violent

---

[222] Alabama and Louisiana—two unratified states—and South Dakota, a rescinding state, sued the National Archivist in anticipation of Virginia's ratification of the ERA, seeking a judicial declaration that the ERA had expired. Complaint, *supra* note 56. After Virginia, Nevada, and Illinois brought suit in D.C. District Court, Alabama, Louisiana, and South Dakota voluntarily dismissed their action in Alabama, and moved to intervene in the D.C. litigation. *See* Joint Stipulation & Plaintiffs' Notice of Voluntary Dismissal, State v. Ferriero, No. 7:19-cv-02032-LSC (N.D. Ala. Feb. 27, 2020); Partially Opposed Motion to Intervene and Supporting Statement of Points and Authorities, *supra* note 56.

[223] *See* Complaint, *supra* note 33.

[224] Searching for Equality, *supra* note 13.

[225] Ginsburg, *Ratification of the Equal Rights Amendment*, *supra* note 11, at 929.

[226] *See id.* at 941.

[227] *Id.* at 922.

armed conflict, the drive for women's right to vote took much longer, having been launched in 1848 and succeeding with the Nineteenth Amendment's ratification some 72 years later.[228] In addition, unlike the rights protections that emerged from violent revolution and war, the Nineteenth Amendment succeeded only after its goals were already partially met, as a significant number of states had already extended the right to vote to women.

The women's suffrage amendment took generations of local campaigns to succeed. Placing the ERA within this historical context, Ginsburg noted that, although the ERA was first introduced in 1923, it was not even taken seriously for several decades because "[t]he idea generates fears and attracts resistance of a kind that the vote for eighteen-year-olds and proposals concerning the structure and powers of government do not encounter."[229] No amendment that had successfully been added to the Constitution had taken more than four years to ratify after congressional proposal, but perhaps short time frames skewed constitutional amendments away from transformative human rights provisions, she suggested.[230]

How much time is reasonable? Relying on the Supreme Court's decision in *Coleman v. Miller*, Ginsburg argued that "Congress is uniquely equipped to decide the timeliness question," because ultimately, it required political, rather than legal, judgments.[231] The determination of how much time the states should take to ratify an amendment and therefore legitimize its place in the Constitution, *Coleman v. Miller* acknowledged, required "full knowledge and appreciation . . . of the political, social and economic conditions which have prevailed during the period since the submission of the amendment."[232] Furthermore, fundamental human rights guarantees like the ERA tended, in Ginsburg's view, to generate confusion, misunderstanding, and contestation, which Congress should take into account in setting a ratification timeline.[233] Ginsburg acknowledged that "[o]ur grandest constitutional guarantees, like the ERA, would make soft targets for fear campaigns,

228 *Id.*

229 *Id.* (footnote omitted).

230 *Id.* at 221–22 ("Acceptance of a broad human rights norm that breaks with tradition takes time to achieve.").

231 *Id.* at 924.

232 *Id.* (quoting Coleman v. Miller, 307 U.S. 433, 454 (1939)).

233 *Id.* at 932–33.

because they are stated at the level of majestic generality."[234] Because of this problem, it made sense for Congress to propose an amendment with an "initial judgment" as to the ratification timeline, acknowledging the possibility of miscalculation and retaining the option of revisiting and extending the timeline, informed by the initial experience of the ratification debates.[235] A key question for Congress to consider in deciding whether to change its initial judgment about the ratification timeline was whether the time that had elapsed had allowed for full and fair debate to address the complex issues raised by the amendment proposal.

Ginsburg parsed both the text of Article V and the text of the ERA resolution to show how Congress had proceeded in this way with regard to the ERA. As Virginia, Nevada, and Illinois have argued in litigation, Article V is silent about timelines for ratification.[236] While they argue that this silence precludes Congress from imposing ratification deadlines that would bind the states, Ginsburg read this silence through the lens of Article V's delegation of the power to "propose" amendments to Congress. Congress elected to impose seven-year deadlines on state ratification of the Eighteenth, Twentieth, Twenty-First, Twenty-Second, Twenty-Third, Twenty-Fourth, Twenty-Fifth, and Twenty-Sixth Amendments, and Ginsburg posited that Congress's power to "propose" amendments under Article V gave it plenary power to regulate the amendment process. She described the ratification deadline as a "casual, procedural measure," the functional equivalent of a legislative measure imposing a statute of limitations.[237]

Unlike the deadlines Congress imposed on the ratification of constitutional amendments in the first half of the twentieth century, the ERA deadline could be revisited and extended. Ginsburg was one of several witnesses that supported this argument as a textual matter during the 1977 and 1978 congressional hearings on the ERA deadline extension. The first constitutional amendment that Congress proposed with a ratification deadline was the Eighteenth Amendment, which prohibited the sale and manufacture of alcoholic beverages.[238] The deadline was inserted into the text of the

[234] *Id.* at 933.

[235] *See Equal Rights Amendment Extension Senate Hearings*, *supra* note 19, at 268.

[236] *See* Complaint, *supra* note 33, at 13–14.

[237] *Equal Rights Amendment Extension Senate Hearings*, *supra* note 19, at 266.

[238] The deadline was introduced by then-Senator Warren Harding of Ohio, as a subtle attempt to derail the Prohibition Amendment. For an account of the Prohibition deadline's origins, see

constitutional amendment itself; Section 3 of the Eighteenth Amendment provides, "This article shall be inoperative unless it shall have been ratified as an amendment to the Constitution by the legislatures of the several States, as provided in the Constitution, within seven years from the date of the submission hereof to the States by the Congress."[239]

The same language, "inoperative unless" ratified within seven years, was inserted into the text of the Twentieth, Twenty-First, and Twenty-Second Amendments.[240] Ginsburg pointed out, as did a few other witnesses during the ERA extension hearings, that Congress changed its practice with regard to the seven-year deadline beginning with the Twenty-Third Amendment, which provided for the representation of non-state districts (such as the District of Columbia) by electors in presidential elections.[241] When Congress proposed that Amendment, it responded to concerns that seven-year deadlines would "clutter up" the text of the Constitution, by placing the ratification time limit in the resolution proposing the Amendment rather than in the Amendment text.[242] Therefore, it was not part of the Amendment that was ratified, and thus would not be subject to the procedural requirements for proposing a constitutional amendment under Article V if a change in deadline were to be proposed.

Nonetheless, Congress used similarly conditional language in the resolutions introducing the Twenty-Third and Twenty-Fourth Amendments. Those resolutions provided that the Amendments would be valid "only if" ratified within seven years.[243] Congress changed the language of the Deadline Clause in the resolutions introducing the Twenty-Fifth and Twenty-Sixth Amendments, which adopted the same language used in the 1972 resolution adopted to propose the ERA. These resolutions stipulated that the proposed

---

David E. Kyvig, *Historical Misunderstandings and the Defeat of the Equal Rights Amendment*, PUB. HISTORIAN, Winter 1996, at 45, 55–56.

[239] U.S. CONST. amend. XVIII, § 3 (repealed 1933).

[240] U.S. CONST. amend. XX, § 6; *id.* amend. XXI, § 3; *id.* amend. XXII, § 2.

[241] U.S. CONST. amend. XXIII.

[242] *Equal Rights Amendment Extension House Hearings*, *supra* note 219, at 42, 247. The text and history of the seven-year deadlines in the Twentieth, Twenty-Second, and Twenty-Third Amendments are discussed in an Office of Legal Counsel memo that was submitted during the House Judiciary Subcommittee on Civil and Constitutional Rights' deadline extension hearings in 1977. *See id.* at 11 (reprinting Memorandum from John M. Harmon, Assistant Att'y Gen., DOJ, to Robert J. Lipshultz, Counsel to the President (Oct. 31, 1977)).

[243] *Id.* at 12.

Amendment would be effective "when ratified" by three-fourths of the states within seven years,[244] not "only if." "When ratified" meant that if the Amendment were ratified within that time frame, Congress was agreeing in advance that the Amendment would be valid. But if the Amendment were not ratified, the consequence had not been spelled out. Ginsburg read this language as Congress reserving its authority to revisit the issue of timeliness in the event that the Amendment took longer than seven years to ratify. She invoked the well-established "general rule that extensions [of] statutes of limitation may be directed by the legislature."[245]

Coleman v. Miller explained why, as a normative matter, Congress is best placed to judge the timeliness of an amendment.[246] It was a political judgment about the political, social, and economic conditions pertinent to whether the amendment was necessary.[247] Indeed, with regard to Congress's Article V power to propose amendments that it deems "necessary," the Supreme Court already held that the necessity of an amendment was a purely political question for Congress, not subject to judicial scrutiny or review.[248] Legislators elected by the people rather than by judges appointed for life were likely to be more in touch with the lived political, social, and economic conditions experienced by their constituents.

In her statements to the House and Senate Judiciary Subcommittees in 1977 and 1978, Ginsburg described Congress as the "director of the amendment process" under our constitutional scheme.[249] Thus, Congress was free to take a range of approaches to any time limits for ratification, which was "the functional equivalent of a statute of limitations associated with a legislative measure," an "incidental, procedural facet of the amendment process."[250] Congress could choose to have no time limit whatsoever, or specify a tight time frame, such as seven years expressed in the amendment text itself. The middle course, according to Ginsburg, was to approach time

---

[244] *Id.*

[245] *Id.* at 129 (statement of Ruth Bader Ginsburg).

[246] 307 U.S. 433, 454 (1939).

[247] *Id.*

[248] Laurence Tribe cautioned against judicial supervision of Article V, because amendments are independent from normal legal processes. *See* Laurence H. Tribe, *A Constitution We Are Amending: In Defense of a Restrained Judicial Role*, 97 HARV. L. REV. 433, 444 (1983).

[249] *Equal Rights Amendment Extension Senate Hearings*, *supra* note 19, at 265.

[250] *Id.* at 268.

limits as "a procedural facet of the amendment process."[251] By phrasing it in tentative language, "when ratified," Congress expressed an "initial judgement as to time."[252]

But putting that judgment into the resolution rather than into the amendment text, in light of the option to choose the latter, indicated an intent to separate that initial judgment from the text submitted to the states for ratification, so that Congress could retain its authority to extend the time period, "should 'the public interests' and 'relevant conditions' so warrant."[253] In Ginsburg's view, Congress was wise to extend the deadline in 1978 because "[t]he debate on the equal rights amendment, far more complex than those attending other recent amendments, has not run its course and should be allowed to continue."[254] Finally, Ginsburg also argued that it would be up to Congress after the thirty-eighth state ratification to decide, in its political discretion, whether to count the rescinding states as ratified states.[255] The question was premature until then, when only Congress could decide, as it had with the Fourteenth Amendment. As Ginsburg noted, "An informed judgment cannot be made by crystal ball, but only by focusing on the precise situation existing when the ratification process is completed."[256]

Consider Justice Ginsburg's spontaneous 2020 remarks in the context of her account of Congress's role: "[i]f you count a latecomer on the plus side, how can you disregard states that said, 'We've changed our minds'?" and "[t]here's too much controversy about a latecomer [like] Virginia ratifying long after the deadline passed."[257] These are political controversies that Congress must resolve, not courts. Congress may have reasons to make a different determination in 2023 than it might have made at earlier historical moments about whether more time for debate about the ERA was needed or whether it is fair to ignore states' wishes to withdraw their approvals. With historical hindsight, Congress may also develop more thorough understandings of both the substantive need for the ERA and the procedural barriers

---

[251] *Id.*

[252] *Id.*

[253] *Equal Rights Amendment Extension House Hearings*, *supra* note 219, at 128.

[254] *Id.* at 129.

[255] *See* Ginsburg, *Ratification of the Equal Rights Amendment*, *supra* note 11, at 941.

[256] *Equal Rights Amendment Extension Senate Hearings*, *supra* note 19, at 271.

[257] Searching for Equality, *supra* note 13.

that prevented its full and proper consideration within the original time limit in the past. Congress's political assessment of the political pros and cons of starting anew may be different from Justice Ginsburg's hope for a brand-new ERA. But Ginsburg believed, from the 1970s to 2020, that Congress, not the judiciary, was the primary driver of constitutional equality and the director of the amendment process.

VI. The Special Procedural Challenges of Constitutional Inclusion

A. The Difficulty of Amendment Under Article V

Justice Ginsburg's thinking about the ERA deadline extension also shed light on the special challenges facing amendments related to significant social change. Indeed, the U.S. Constitution has not been amended since 1992. In fact, the Amendment that was ratified in 1992 was adopted by two-thirds of both houses of Congress in 1789. It was written by founding father James Madison and proposed to the states with the original Bill of Rights.[258] When ratifications by 38 states, accumulated over 203 years, were completed, each chamber of Congress passed a concurrent resolution affirming the Twenty-Seventh Amendment (prohibiting Congress from giving itself a raise before an election cycle has run its course).[259]

The lack of amendments in nearly three decades may speak more to Article V's obsolescence than it does to the Constitution's perfection or suitability to twenty-first-century conditions.[260] The last time both houses of Congress voted by a two-thirds majority to adopt a constitutional amendment was in 1978, when it sent the District of Columbia voting rights amendment to the states for ratification.[261] That amendment would have provided the District of Columbia with the same representation in Congress that it would have had if it were a state—one representative and two Senators.[262] Adopted by Congress in August 1978 between the House and Senate votes

---

[258] *See Madison Amendment Surprises Lawmakers*, 48 Cong. Q. Almanac 58, 58–59 (1992).

[259] *See* 138 Cong. Rec. 11,869 (1992) (Senate); 138 Cong. Rec. 12,052 (1992) (House).

[260] *See* Richard Albert, *Constitutional Disuse or Desuetude: The Case of Article V*, 94 B.U. L. Rev. 1029, 1031–32, 1073 (2014).

[261] Proposing an Amendment to the Constitution to Provide for Representation of the District of Columbia in Congress, H.R.J. Res. 554, 95th Cong., 92 Stat. 3795 (1978).

[262] *Id.* § 1.

to extend the deadline on ERA ratification in 1978, Congress placed the seven-year ratification deadline in the text of the proposed D.C. amendment itself,[263] rather than in the resolution introducing the amendment, as it had done with the ERA and the Twenty-Fifth and Twenty-Sixth Amendments. Section 4 of the D.C. voting rights amendment mirrored the conditional language of the deadline in the Eighteenth, Twentieth, Twenty-First, and Twenty-Second Amendments, reading, "[t]his article shall be inoperative, unless it shall have been ratified as an amendment to the Constitution by the legislatures of three-fourths of the several States within seven years from the date of its submission."[264]

Ginsburg, testifying in ERA deadline hearings in the Senate Judiciary Committee just three weeks before the Senate's vote on the D.C. amendment, had argued that the different language used for the ERA deadline language, "valid 'when ratified . . . within seven years,'" reserved Congress's power to change it.[265] This contrast supported Ginsburg's view that the ERA deadline could be changed by Congress, whereas the strong language placed in the text of an amendment could not be. Because only 16 states ratified the D.C. voting rights amendment by August 1985,[266] it, too, was presumed dead. But Congress's choice of the within-amendment conditional deadline language for the only amendment it adopted after adopting the ERA affirms Ginsburg's understanding, which was that different language gives rise to different legal consequences for the possibility of changing the deadline. The text of the D.C. amendment supports Ginsburg's Article V theory: that Congress chose language in the ERA deadline that retained the power of a future Congress to revisit and change the deadline.

B. Lessons from the Nineteenth Amendment

The political process by which three additional states ratified the 1970s ERA decades after the deadline should be understood as a different kind of new beginning for the ERA, one that responds pragmatically to the exclusionary barriers Article V imposes, by design, on any constitutional

---

[263] *Id.* § 4.

[264] *Id.*

[265] *See Equal Rights Amendment Extension Senate Hearings*, *supra* note 19, at 268.

[266] *See* Jessie Kratz, *Unratified Amendments: DC Voting Rights*, NAT'L ARCHIVES: PIECES OF HIST. (June 17, 2020), https://prologue.blogs.archives.gov/2020/06/17/unratified-amendments-dc-voting-rights/ [https://perma.cc/525S-DNH8].

amendments to empower the disempowered. This new beginning renews the work of past generations without discarding the necessary political power that past generations accumulated incrementally under conditions of second-class citizenship. For people who have had to participate in our constitutional democracy without fully equal rights, building the consensus necessary to change the constitution *asynchronously* across generations has been the only plausible path. The women constitution makers who laid the groundwork for the ERA did not live to see the ERA ratified by 38 states.[267] One explanation for why it took so long is that the very problem that the ERA was designed to correct—the long and unfortunate history of women's second-class citizenship thoroughly chronicled in Ginsburg's *Reed v. Reed* brief—was made difficult to correct through the procedures specified by Article V.[268] The long history of the Nineteenth Amendment, the first step toward correcting women's second-class status as citizens, illustrates this as well.

Article V requires the mobilization of large supermajorities of Congress (two-thirds of both houses) and the state legislatures (three-fourths)—a far greater consensus than that required to amend most state constitutions and constitutions around the world.[269] Article V entrusts amendments to Congress and the states rather than to "We the People."[270] The people who are

---

[267] *See generally* Suk, *supra* note 7, at 2–3 (describing the century-long ongoing effort across generations to enshrine the ERA in the U.S. Constitution).

[268] Brief for Appellant, *supra* note 65.

[269] *See* Richard Albert, Constitutional Amendments: Making, Breaking, and Changing Constitutions 96 (2019) (noting that comparative constitutional scholars identify the U.S. Constitution as the world's most difficult to amend). As for state constitutions, the New York state constitution, for instance, requires identical versions of a proposed constitutional amendment to be passed by a majority of each house in two consecutive legislative sessions before it is placed on the ballot for a statewide referendum. When a majority of voters approve, it becomes an amendment. N.Y. Const. art. XIX, § 1. Although this procedure is fairly common, some states require the legislature to vote by three-fifths supermajority only once before the measure goes on the ballot for a voter referendum. In some states, the voters must vote by a three-fifths supermajority to approve an amendment. Forty-nine states reserve some role for voters in the amendment process, and some states provide a procedural option for voters to propose amendments through ballot initiatives. *See* Jennie Drage Bowser, *Constitutions: Amend with Care*, State Legislatures, Sept. 2015, at 14, 16.

[270] Article V names four paths to amendment. A proposal by Congress, a two-thirds vote in both houses, ratification by three-fourths of the state legislatures, or by state ratifying conventions in three-fourths of the states. All the amendments, except the Twenty-First Amendment, have followed the first path, with the Twenty-First Amendment being the sole amendment that has been ratified by ratifying conventions. *See* Kenneth D. Rose, American Women and the

excluded from voting for representatives have no say in the amendment process. Therefore, any amendment seeking to end the disfranchisement of such people is subject to the power and generosity of the people who are already rightsholders and who may benefit from the continued exclusion of others. Given Article V's design, it is not surprising that the constitutional amendments that sought to overcome past exclusions of African-Americans and women, and to integrate them into the equal rights of citizenship, have faced real difficulties meeting the requirements of Article V. The Thirteenth, Fourteenth, and Fifteenth Amendments required a civil war, and many commentators have suggested that these Amendments did not clearly meet the requirements of Article V.[271] Indeed, any understanding of the Fourteenth Amendment as an Article V amendment must assume that Article V authorizes Congress to disregard ratifying states' subsequent efforts to rescind their ratifications.[272] Without such flexible readings of Article V, in the direction of making it easier rather than harder to amend the Constitution to include the disempowered, it is hard to consider the constitutional amendments that have included African-Americans in full citizenship as Article V amendments.

The Nineteenth Amendment met the requirements of Article V with congressional adoption in 1919 and ratification by three-fourths of the states by 1920.[273] And even when it did, people with legal training filed a lawsuit claiming that it violated Article V. In *Leser v. Garnett*, a male voter who had been a state judge in Maryland argued that extending suffrage to women radically enlarged the electorate so as to alter the representation of

---

REPEAL OF PROHIBITION 1 (1996). Article V also allows for amendments to be proposed by a convention formed by Congress upon petition by two-thirds of the state legislatures. Such amendments then have to be ratified either by state legislatures or by state ratifying conventions, the mode being determined by Congress. Amendments that alter the representation of the states in the Senate must be approved by every state whose representation is reduced. In addition, the slave trade was made unamendable until 1808. *See* U.S. CONST. art. V.

[271] *See, e.g.*, 2 BRUCE ACKERMAN, WE THE PEOPLE: TRANSFORMATIONS 110–13 (1998); David E. Pozen & Thomas P. Schmidt, *The Puzzles and Possibilities of Article V*, 121 COLUM. L. REV. 2317, 2347–51 (2021); John Harrison, *The Lawfulness of the Reconstruction Amendments*, 68 U. CHI. L. REV. 375, 456–57 (2001). Others suggest that constitutional amendment validity need not be judged solely by adherence to Article V. *See generally* Akhil Reed Amar, *Philadelphia Revisited: Amending the Constitution Outside Article V*, 55 U. CHI. L. REV. 1043 (1988).

[272] *See* ACKERMAN, *supra* note 271, at 111.

[273] Ginsburg, *Ratification of the Equal Rights Amendment*, *supra* note 11, at 921.

the states in the Senate.[274] Under Article V, any reduction of the equal representation of the states in the Senate must be consented to individually by each state.[275] The Supreme Court rejected this theory, but the very making of a colorable argument regarding the Nineteenth Amendment's procedural validity under Article V suggests tensions, real and perceived, between Article V and inclusive constitutional change. A fully ratified amendment under Article V actually took generations—nearly a century—after suffragists first demanded women's right to vote. Neither Elizabeth Cady Stanton nor Susan B. Anthony, the women widely acknowledged to be the "founding mothers" of women's suffrage, lived to see the women's suffrage amendment adopted and ratified,[276] even though they testified in Congress when the amendment was proposed for the first time in 1878.[277]

In supporting the extension of the ERA deadline in the late 1970s, Ginsburg pointed out that suffragists had resisted a seven-year deadline for the Nineteenth Amendment, and that those who survived to the 1970s argued against a time limit for the ERA.[278] The seven-year ratification deadline on the women's suffrage amendment was proposed in Congress but rejected.[279] Suffrage leader Carrie Chapman Catt testified in Congress against the seven-year deadline, urging that such a deadline was "two amendments bound up in one"[280]—it amended Article V by making it even harder to change the Constitution than it already was. One congressman during floor debates predicted that a ratification deadline would prolong the fight for the suffrage amendment.[281] Many states imposed waiting periods between a failed vote on a federal constitutional amendment and the next reintroduction of

---

[274] 258 U.S. 130, 133 (1922).

[275] U.S. CONST. art. V.

[276] *See* CARRIE CHAPMAN CATT & NETTIE ROGERS SHULER, WOMAN SUFFRAGE AND POLITICS: THE INNER STORY OF THE SUFFRAGE MOVEMENT 107–08 (1923).

[277] *See Prohibiting the Several States from Disfranchising United States Citizens on Account of Sex and Protest Against Women's Suffrage: Arguments Before the S. Comm. on Privileges & Elections*, 45th Cong. 4–17 (1878) (statement of Elizabeth Cady Stanton).

[278] Ginsburg, *Ratification of the Equal Rights Amendment*, *supra* note 11, at 921.

[279] *Id.* at 921 n.7.

[280] *Extending the Right of Suffrage to Women: Hearings on H.R.J. Res. 200 Before the H. Comm. on Women Suffrage*, 65th Cong. 36 (1918) [hereinafter *Extending the Right of Suffrage to Women*] (statement of Carrie Chapman Catt, President, National American Women's Suffrage Association).

[281] 56 CONG. REC. 808 (1918) (statement of Rep. French).

that same amendment.[282] A ratification deadline would wipe out the ratifications achieved within seven years and require the process to start all over again in Congress, which could delay a women's suffrage amendment for decades more.

Ginsburg appreciated how long it took for the transgenerational process of making the Nineteenth Amendment part of the Constitution to succeed. Thomas I. Emerson, a professor at Yale Law School, also testified in the deadline extension hearings before the House and Senate Judiciary Committees.[283] Complementing Ginsburg's view that human rights guarantees simply took longer than other kinds of amendments, Emerson argued that "a long period of time is necessary for the nation to make up its mind with respect to fundamental changes in the status of large groups in the population."[284] Both Emerson and Ginsburg referenced the distortions in the debate about the ERA that warranted a congressional change in the ratification timeline. Distortions occurred, according to Emerson, because of high levels of discomfort and resistance to the fundamental social change that the Amendment represented, akin to the Fourteenth Amendment and going beyond the Nineteenth Amendment.[285] Such significant changes gave rise to "scare stories" and misunderstandings about what the Amendment would do.[286] Ginsburg believed that Congress would have to consider all this in determining whether to change the deadline or accept rescissions.[287] And surely, as she acknowledged toward the end of her life, Congress would also have to consider the perceptions of unfairness arising not only from these "scare stories," but also from the unique procedural irregularities of the ERA's trajectory, including exceedingly late ratifications and rescissions.[288]

---

[282] *See Extending the Right of Suffrage to Women*, *supra* note 280, at 154–58 (reprinting Mary Beard & Florence Kelley, Why Women Demand a Federal Suffrage Amendment—Difficulties in Amending State Constitutions—A Study of the Constitutions of the Nonsuffrage States (1916) (pamphlet)).

[283] *See Equal Rights Amendment Extension House Hearings*, *supra* note 219, at 61 (statement of Thomas I. Emerson); *Equal Rights Amendment Extension Senate Hearings*, *supra* note 19, at 114 (statement of Thomas I. Emerson).

[284] *Equal Rights Amendment Extension House Hearings*, *supra* note 219, at 64.

[285] *See id.*

[286] *Equal Rights Amendment Extension Senate Hearings*, *supra* note 19, at 118.

[287] Ginsburg, *Ratification of the Equal Rights Amendment*, *supra* note 11.

[288] *See* Searching for Equality, *supra* note 13.

These are serious questions about the ERA that must be fought out in the political sphere.

The ground-zero "new beginning" for the ERA is a path for the ERA that would be consistent with Ginsburg's broader theory, which she developed as an academic rather than as a judge. But it is not the only path consistent with her approach. Justice Ginsburg's body of work as a scholar and a Supreme Court Justice put Congress rather than courts at the forefront of constitutional change. Congress can decide whether to pursue an absolute new beginning or to forge a new beginning by changing the deadline once again, retroactively. Justice Ginsburg's public statements wishing for "a new beginning" for the ERA did not opine on whether Congress could legitimately lift the ratification deadline. Whereas Justice Ginsburg's ideal procedural path for the ERA was to start over, that preference does not negate less ideal, more viable paths. The logic of her 1978 deadline extension testimony, synthesized with her scholarship and jurisprudence on sex equality, would allow Congress to save the ERA by changing the deadline again. However, because a retroactive deadline change a generation after it elapsed raises obvious doubts about procedural fairness, adding the ERA to the Constitution through this unprecedented path would require significant public debate to clarify the ERA's twenty-first-century purpose and public meaning, including its relationship to the Equal Protection Clause, to be accepted by the people as legitimate.

VII. The ERA's Viable Path Forward

In 2019, a subcommittee of the House Judiciary Committee held a hearing on the resolution lifting the ERA ratification deadline, which eventually led the resolution to be reported favorably[289] and embraced by a majority on the House floor.[290] Congressional hearings and floor debates are opportunities to create new legislative history for the ERA.[291] The text of the ERA includes

---

[289] H.R. Rep. No. 116-378, at 1 (2020); *see also Markup of H.R.J. Res. 79, Removing the Deadline for the Ratification of the Equal Rights Amendment, Before the H. Comm. on the Judiciary*, 116th Cong. 64 (2019) [hereinafter *House Markup of Removing the Ratification Deadline of the ERA*], https://docs.house.gov/meetings/JU/JU00/20191113/110212/HMKP-116-JU00-Transcript-20191113.pdf [https://perma.cc/YW82-R7AS].

[290] 166 Cong. Rec. H1142 (daily ed. Feb. 13, 2020).

[291] *See* Julie C. Suk, *Who Decides the Future of the Equal Rights Amendment?*, Take Care Blog (July 6, 2020), https://takecareblog.com/blog/who-decides-the-future-of-the-equal-rights-amendment [https://perma.cc/2WSW-3N4L].

words and phrases whose public meaning has changed since the 1970s when the ERA was adopted by Congress and ratified by most of the states. These evolving phrases include "equality of rights," "shall not be denied or abridged," and "on account of sex." The records of hearings and floor debates from 1970 to 1972 indicate that a primary (though not exhaustive) purpose of the ERA was to eradicate sex classifications in the law.[292] That is the purpose that became the focal point of the equal protection cases that were successfully litigated by Ginsburg in the 1970s. If the twenty-first-century ratifiers of the ERA want the Amendment to do more than the equal protection jurisprudence, that vision may not be apparent in the text or in the original legislative history. New legislative history is needed to update the meaning of the ERA. Without a legislative history providing guidance, these abstract words will be handed over to judges, inviting many plausible interpretations. Congress and state legislatures are best placed to determine what more needs to be done to achieve "equality of rights" beyond what the Supreme Court has achieved through the de facto ERA.

The process leading up to the House's vote to remove the deadline during the 116th Congress provides ample illustration. At the hearing before the House Judiciary Committee's Subcommittee on the Constitution, Civil Rights, and Civil Liberties on removing the deadline for the ERA's ratification, constitutional law expert Kathleen Sullivan testified that it was a "national embarrassment" that the United States remained one of the few constitutions that lacked a guarantee of sex equality.[293] In its report on the resolution, the House Judiciary Committee presented a twenty-first-century vision of the ERA, going beyond what was explicitly advanced by the ERA's 1970s proponents and framers.[294] The report suggested that the ERA, if added to the Constitution in the twenty-first century, could outlaw governmental practices that had a disparate impact on women, and it might also legitimize

[292] *See* SUK, *supra* note 7, at 57–82 (narrating the legislative debates about the ERA in 1971–1972).

[293] *See Equal Rights Amendment: Hearing Before the H. Subcomm. on the Constitution, Civil Rights, & Civil Liberties of the H. Comm. on the Judiciary*, 116th Cong. 18 (2019) (statement of Kathleen M. Sullivan, Partner, Quinn Emanuel Urquhart & Sullivan). *See generally* Julie C. Suk, *An Equal Rights Amendment for the Twenty-First Century: Bringing Global Constitutionalism Home*, 28 YALE J. L. & FEMINISM 381 (2017) (discussing countries that have gender-equality amendments and their development in addressing gender inequalities in cross-national comparison).

[294] *See* H.R. REP. NO. 116-378, at 6 (2020).

legislative efforts at the state and federal level to promote gender balance in decision-making positions.[295]

The House report illustrates how the legislature's serious consideration of these procedural considerations, like the time bar, has not only forged a procedural path forward for the ERA; it has created the forum for discussing the ERA's meaning today and expanding its meaning to make the ERA speak to disparate impact as well as to gender-equal power sharing. Indeed, at the House Judiciary Committee's markup hearing on the deadline removal bill, Representative Pramila Jayapal (D-WA) highlighted the persistence of pay gaps between women and men, which were more pronounced for women of color.[296] Representative Zoe Lofgren (D-CA) recounted the history of the ERA in Congress, pointing to the way men in the past wielded their power within the House Judiciary Committee to stop and delay the ERA procedurally.[297] "[W]e are fixing process," said Representative Sheila Jackson Lee, explaining why removing the deadline after all these years was justified.[298]

Women lawmakers embraced twenty-first-century commitments to eradicating pay inequity, overcoming disadvantages faced by working mothers and pregnant women, and addressing the needs of women of color, immigrant women, and low-wage workers in the House floor debates leading to a vote to remove the ERA's deadline. A wide array of congresswomen of diverse race and ethnic backgrounds, geographical districts, and ages devoted their short floor speeches to these themes. The bill's sponsor, Representative Jackie Speier (D-CA), said, "The ERA is about equality. The ERA is about sisterhood, motherhood, survival, dignity, and respect."[299] Congresswoman Sheila Jackson Lee noted the "nonexistent mandatory standards for workplace accommodations for pregnant women, post-natal mothers and persons with care responsibilities," and the disproportionate representation of women in poverty.[300] Speaker Nancy Pelosi highlighted that "[w]omen face discrimination as they raise families," citing the unfair treatment of

---

[295] *Id.*

[296] *House Markup of Removing the Ratification Deadline of the ERA*, *supra* note 289, at 35 (statement of Rep. Pramila Jayapal).

[297] *Id.* at 26 (statement of Rep. Zoe Lofgren) (recalling Judiciary Committee Chairman Emanuel Celler's opposition to the ERA in 1971, when she was an intern to Rep. Edwards).

[298] *Id.* at 28 (statement of Rep. Sheila Jackson Lee).

[299] 166 CONG. REC. H1130 (daily ed. Feb. 13, 2020) (statement of Rep. Jackie Speier).

[300] *Id.* at H1134 (statement of Rep. Sheila Jackson Lee).

pregnant women under the law.[301] Congresswoman Lucy McBath (D-GA) invoked Black suffragist Frances Ellen Watkins Harper and the long struggle of women "fighting tooth and nail for decades to be recognized as equal under the eyes of the law."[302]

Congresswoman Suzanne Bonamici (D-OR) pointed out that "[w]omen continue to face many barriers to true equality, including pregnancy and gender discrimination, unequal pay, and a lack of access to a full range of reproductive healthcare services."[303] Congresswoman Judy Chu (D-CA) said, "true equality is still a goal, not a reality" because of unequal pay and because "we still have men passing laws that dictate our choices about our bodies."[304] Congresswoman Barbara Lee (D-CA) pointed out "women have been relegated to the sidelines and left out of the Constitution, especially Black women and women of color."[305] Congresswoman Rashida Tlaib (D-MI) noted that she was proud to be the first Muslim woman in Congress and said that "this is about women of color, women with disabilities, transgender women, immigrant women. These women are affected by issues such as unequal pay, sexual violence, lack of access for healthcare, and poverty."[306]

The new meanings created by new legislative history can give guidance to the Supreme Court as it grapples with gender equality, both under the Equal Protection Clause and under the ERA, should it be legitimized through the process of lifting the deadline. If the Equal Protection Clause has become a de facto ERA, surely lawmakers' efforts to revive the ERA should inform how the sex equality jurisprudence under Equal Protection develops. And, should the ERA be added to the Constitution, the new legislative history indicates to courts what "equality of rights . . . not denied or abridged . . . on account of sex" means today. The ERA empowers Congress and state legislatures to implement a more robust vision of equality than that enforced by courts under Equal Protection.

---

[301] *Id.* at H1136 (statement of Speaker Nancy Pelosi).

[302] *Id.* (statement of Rep. Lucy McBath).

[303] *Id.* at H1137 (statement of Rep. Suzanne Bonamici).

[304] *Id.* at H1138 (statement of Rep. Judy Chu).

[305] *Id.* at H1138-39 (statement of Rep. Barbara Lee).

[306] *Id.* at H1140 (statement of Rep. Rashida Tlaib).

VIII. Conclusion

Justice Ginsburg did not live to show her granddaughter an ERA in her pocket constitution. Will we?

She often recounted the wisdom of her mother-in-law on the eve of her wedding. Handing her a pair of earplugs, Ginsburg's mother-in-law advised, "'In every good marriage,' . . . 'it helps sometimes to be a little deaf.'"[307]

In judging, too, earplugs are often essential. The rule of law requires judicial independence, and that often requires judges to filter out the noise of politics. Justice Ginsburg would hear nothing of the political pressure to retire in 2013 to ensure that a Democratic president would name her successor.[308] And her wish that the ERA process would "start over," free of the controversies about late ratifications and rescissions, was stated notwithstanding the recent political realities of partisan hardball, which make it tragically infeasible for two-thirds of both Houses of Congress to agree to anything, much less an ERA, if the process were to start over.

Justice Ginsburg's other "most fervent wish" on the eve of her death—that she not be replaced until after the winner of the 2020 presidential election was inaugurated[309]—also indicates the presence of political earplugs in her final moments. Senate Republicans, having insisted in 2016 that Justice Scalia not be replaced until a new president was inaugurated eight months later, moved quickly to confirm Justice Amy Coney Barrett to replace Justice Ginsburg days before the November election[310] and only five weeks after

---

[307] *See* Debra Cassens Weiss, *Marriage Advice from Justice Ginsburg's Mother-in-Law Has Helped her in the Workplace*, A.B.A. J. (Oct. 4, 2016, 7:50 AM), https://www.abajournal.com/news/article/marriage_advice_from_justice_ginsburgs_mother_in_law_has_helped_her_in [https://perma.cc/C57S-QWZW].

[308] *See* Joan Biskupic, *Exclusive: Supreme Court's Ginsburg Vows to Resist Pressure to Retire*, Reuters (July 4, 2013, 8:04 AM), https://www.reuters.com/article/us-usa-court-ginsburg/exclusive-supreme-courts-ginsburg-vows-to-resist-pressure-to-retire-idUSBRE9630C820130704 [https://perma.cc/52VM-JG4Q].

[309] *See* Matthew Choi & Josh Gerstein, *Ginsburg's Wish: 'I Will Not Be Replaced Until a New President Is Installed,'* Politico (Sept. 18, 2020, 11:26 PM), https://www.politico.com/news/2020/09/18/ginsburg-rbg-dying-wish-418108 [https://perma.cc/9KE8-BEZ5].

[310] Adam Liptak & Sheryl Gay Stolberg, *Shadow of Merrick Garland Hangs Over the Next Supreme Court Fight*, N.Y. Times (June 11, 2021), https://www.nytimes.com/2020/09/19/us/ginsburg-vacancy-garland.html.

Justice Ginsburg's death, 52–48,[311] without persuading a single Democratic colleague to support it.

With her death, let us respectfully remove the political earplugs that Justice Ginsburg wore as a living Justice. We can excavate and hear the voice of her scholarly, pragmatic account of Article V and human rights, which she developed as a law professor and advocate. We can listen to her account of Congress as the proper decisionmaker on the ERA's future, including its meaning. Under Article V, the consequences of ratifying an amendment past a congressionally created deadline are for Congress to determine, as is the effect of rescissions, as the historical precedent of the Fourteenth Amendment establishes. The process of making new legislative history in Congress's consideration of the deadline removal could unplug the ERA's path to constitutional legitimacy and reaffirm its most ambitious goals, updated for the twenty-first century.

Justice Ginsburg's vision for the ERA was as much about a healthy constitutional democracy as it was about women. She hoped for a dialogue and collaboration between courts and legislatures as well as more fulfilling relationships, unconfined by gender roles and expectations, between people at home and at work. While Justice Ginsburg's fans turned her into an icon and a diva, she took the spotlight off herself as a judge and shone it on the people and the representatives they elected in our nation's constitutional democracy. At the end of the day, she believed it was not lawyers or judges who most needed the ERA, but the people themselves, and the legislators they elected to make our constitutional values a lived reality. The ERA belonged in every modern constitution, including ours, to empower the people, including Justice Ginsburg's granddaughters, with the promise of women's fully equal stature in a legitimate constitutional democracy. Although Justice Ginsburg's legacy for the ERA might appear ambivalent, there is an unambiguous arc of wisdom to be gleaned from her passion and caution about it: how we strive for a "more perfect union" will shape how perfect it can be.

---

[311] 166 Cong. Rec. S6449-50 (daily ed. Oct. 25, 2020) (recording 51–48 cloture vote on Oct. 25); *id.* at S6588 (recording 52–48 confirmation vote the next day).

Afterword

On Ruth Bader Ginsburg's Equality Legacy in Light of *Dobbs v. Jackson Women's Health Organization*

—*Shannon Gilreath*

Ruth Bader Ginsburg's long career on the bench as both a circuit judge and as an associate justice ensured a wide-ranging judicial legacy. Parsing the breadth and depth of that legacy will be a project that could continue for decades. Indisputably, however, it is her sex equality work that made her a feminist icon in her lifetime and cemented her place as a significant figure in American history. As an appellate lawyer, she successfully argued landmark cases like *Reed v. Reed*,[1] and from her position on the Supreme Court, she authored important majority opinions, like *U.S. v. Virginia*,[2] and powerful dissenting opinions, in cases like *Ledbetter v. Goodyear Tire and Rubber Co.*[3] From all these vantage points, she used the constitutional promise of

[1] 404 U.S. 71 (1971).

[2] 518 U.S. 515 (1996).

[3] 550 U.S. 618 (2007).

equality to operationalize social equality through legal equality. The reality of American citizenship became more substantively equal as a result. Few individuals in American legal and political history have had this degree of influence on what it means substantively to be an American citizen. For this reason alone, our decision in asking the contributors to this book to focus specifically on aspects of Ginsburg's theory of "equal citizenship status" would have been appropriate and valuable.

However, the focus on Ruth Ginsburg's equality theory and practice appeared to us not only desirable but, in fact, *necessary* as the *Dobbs*[4] decision emerged as the unavoidable frame for thinking about her legacy. As she argued consistently over many decades, women do not and *cannot* have equal citizenship status if they do not have sexual and reproductive autonomy.[5] From her legal practice as an appellate lawyer to her last dissenting opinion issued in the July before her death in September 2020, Ginsburg always linked the regulation of contraception and abortion with the sex discrimination those regulations reflected, transmitted, and reproduced.[6] Contraception and abortion were for Ginsburg sex equality questions. She understood that because of the myriad ways that childbirth and motherhood mediate a woman's relationship to the rest of society,[7] profound sub-

---

[4] Dobbs v. Jackson Women's Health Organization, 597 U.S. 215 (2022).

[5] Ginsburg's equality practice, always intersectional, had an early and enduring focus on reproductive liberty. Ahead of her time, Ginsburg demonstrated sensitivity to how the lived realities of women's procreative capacity could vary along race and class lines. An early example is Ginsburg's work in Cox v. Stanton, 529 F.2d 47 (4th Cir. 1975), on behalf of Nial Cox, a black woman plaintiff challenging North Carolina's sterilization law, which joined equal protection, privacy, and cruel and unusual punishment claims in a legal challenge that ultimately led to the dismantling of North Carolina's sterilization scheme.

[6] In that opinion, *Little Sisters of the Poor Saints Peter and Paul Home v. Pennsylvania*, 140 S. Ct. 2367 (2020), Ginsburg chided the Court for a majority holding that she argued would make meaningful access to contraception much harder for poor women.

[7] Elise Gould, Jessica Schieder & Kathleen Geier, *What is the gender pay gap and is it real? The complete guide to how women are paid less than men and why it can't be explained away*, Economic Policy Institute (Oct. 20, 2016), https://www.epi.org/publication/what-is-the-gender-pay-gap-and-is-it-real/ ("After giving birth, women's pay lags behind pay of similarly educated and experienced men and of women without children. There is no corresponding 'fatherhood penalty' for men."); Leila Schochet, *The Child Care Crisis Is Keeping Women Out of the Workforce*, CAP 20 (Mar. 28, 2019), https://www.americanprogress.org/article/child-care-crisis-keeping-women-workforce/ ("Research supports that high child care costs and limited financial assistance are driving mothers out of the workforce. Over the past two decades, women's labor force participation in the United States has stalled while other major developed nations have seen continued growth. The high cost of child care is partly to blame: One study found that the rising cost of child care resulted in an estimated 13 percent decline

ordination results for women when reproductive agency is taken from them by the state. Doctrinally, this perspective led her to frame abortion as an issue of equal protection rather than as a question only of due process liberty–privacy, as both the *Roe* and *Dobbs* courts did.

There is no doubting that she would have dissented mightily from the reactionary judgment of the *Dobbs* majority and, in the process, would have exhorted us all to the barricades of equality. Therefore, in a book that honors Ruth Bader Ginsburg's contributions to what it means to be an American citizen, we must contend seriously with the danger that *Dobbs* and the constitutionalism it represents poses to her feminist legal project. *Dobbs*-style constitutionalism is the anathema of Justice Ginsburg's equality theory and practice, deployed over a lifetime of legal advocacy—on and off the bench. Ginsburg's constitutionalism celebrated the Constitution as meaningful and relevant to Americans still on our way to "a more perfect union" where "equal citizenship status" (to use a favorite Ginsburg phrasing) may be not only a constitutional promise but a lived reality.

Ginsburg understood in the 1970s what our present legal reality reaffirms: the persistence of sex inequality will require not only new applications of well-worn approaches, but, critically, it will also require thinking in new ways, always. Indeed, these attributes were the hallmarks of Ginsburg's legal approach and are indelible in her legal legacy. To that end, I will conclude this book by confronting directly the "originalist" theory of constitutional interpretation, which Ginsburg rejected as antithetic to the promise of the American Constitution. In painful contrast, the *Dobbs* majority embraced originalism to justify its decision to de-constitutionalize—for the first time in history—a fundamental right bearing directly on the physical liberty of American citizens and uniquely on the possibility of substantive equality for women. As this chapter develops, it is in fact Justice Ginsburg's more expansive interpretive approach to the liberty and equality espoused by our Constitution that is likely closer to the original understanding of the Framers than the historically stagnated, hidebound meaning of the Constitution resulting from so-called originalism. As an alternative to the due process

in the employment of mothers with children under age 5. What's more, the nation's failure to implement policies that support mothers to enter and remain in the workforce—such as child care and paid family leave—explains about one-third of the decrease in women's labor force participation when comparing the United States with 22 other Organization for Economic Cooperation and Development (OECD) countries.").

privacy rationale used to analyze the constitutionality of abortion by both the *Roe* and *Dobbs* courts, I will highlight Justice Ginsburg's alternative equality approach to abortion access, evident in both her legal practice and her scholarship. A complete outline of her argument about the meaning of constitutional equality and its relationship to constitutional liberty in the context of sexual and reproductive autonomy may be more critical today than at any point during her lifetime.

I. Polar Constitutionalism: *Roe*, Originalist Theory, and the Road to *Dobbs*

Ginsburg took the Framers seriously when they drafted the Constitution to point the way to "a more perfect union." Originalists, on the other hand, claim that the meaning of constitutional text and the scope of constitutional principle is limited to whatever the text was understood to mean at the time the disputed provision was drafted or ratified.[8] The alleged virtue of the originalist approach is that it restrains "judicial activism" whereby judges decide constitutional questions based only on their personal preferences as to the outcome of a legal dispute. However, critics of originalism, like Ginsburg, indict it as disingenuous—as a way for its adherents to accomplish their own reactionary social and legal preferences disguised as historical mandates and contrary to the progressive impulses driving our Constitution. Constitutional scholars Robert Post and Reva Siegel have gone so far as to label it as "living originalism,"[9] analogizing it to the so-called "living constitutionalism" for which originalism is claimed to be an antidote. Contrary to the claims of originalism's supporters that it is an objective and politically neutral interpretive method, originalism is thoroughly infused with political biases. Before it was taken up as a theory project by legal academics, originalism emerged first as a political product of the Ronald Reagan Department of Justice. As a tool for furthering Reagan's "family values" agenda, originalism was primarily aimed at undoing the legal and social progress

[8] At other times, originalism is stated in terms of what the Framers intended a provision to mean or to accomplish. Regardless, because originalism is so new and because it is the province of partisan politics, it is riven with internal disagreement as to what and how much is original enough to count. For a lucid overview, see generally Keith E. Whittington, *The New Originalism*, 2 GEO. J.L. & PUB. POL'Y 599 (2004).

[9] Robert Post & Reva Siegel, *Originalism as a Political Practice: The Right's Living Constitution* 75 FORDHAM L. REV. 545 (2006).

made by the feminist and gay-rights movements. It was also aligned with Reagan's stated objective to appoint justices whose rulings would reflect the conservative views of his administration.

Naked proof of the verity of this analysis is offered in the totality of the *Dobbs* opinion itself. While Ginsburg embraced the promise of the Constitution, Justice Samuel Alito's majority opinion is thoroughly backward looking. Purporting to look to history as his guide, he selects only that history that could produce his desired outcome. Indeed, he rejects without serious answer the *Roe* opinion's historical survey, which established a history of criminal sanction for abortion only after "quickening," that produced the clear-cut line of viability constitutionalized by the *Roe* majority.[10] Also, ignored—or, frankly, mocked—is half a century of stare decisis on the abortion right and decades of due process doctrine, wherein the Court consistently held that the meaning of due process liberty had to be divined through reference to legal tradition but also be informed by contemporary facts and understandings.[11] Instead, Justice Alito zeroes in on a brief moment in American history, focusing on a mid-nineteenth-century campaign to ban abortion, which he then pronounces as "sincere."[12] One might wonder who among those long-dead abortion opponents he had interviewed to gain the kind of subjective knowledge he must surely have in order to personally vouch for the sincerity of their anti-abortion beliefs in a judicial opinion issued over a century and a half later. Certainly, Justice Alito's historical narrative neglects the reality that the anti-abortion movement on which he focuses was a nativist, anti-Catholic movement centrally motivated by a worry that immigrants would soon overrun the nation if Anglo-Saxon birthrates dropped.[13]

Not very long ago, the "originalist" approach embraced by the Court in *Dobbs* was understood as a baseless fringe theory—dangerous to constitutional legitimacy—by conservatives and progressives alike. It was the bipartisan alarm over the anemic constitutionalism evident in Robert Bork's originalist ethic that led to the resounding defeat of Judge Bork's nomination

---

[10] Roe v. Wade, 410 U.S. 113 (1973).

[11] *See generally* Lawrence v. Texas 539 U.S. 558 (2003).

[12] *See id.* at 4.

[13] *See* Reva B. Siegel, *Memory Games:* Dobbs's *Originalism as Anti-Democratic Living Constitutionalism—and Some Pathways for Resistance*, 101 Texas L. Rev. 1127 (2023).

to the Supreme Court. To date, Bork's is the largest non-confirmation vote by the Senate in the history of the Supreme Court. Today, however, the same interpretive ethic embraced by Bork is no longer a liability; it is on the ascendant at the nation's highest court. And, in *Dobbs*, just as Judge Bork insisted that it should be, a pregnant woman's constitutional due process right to procure an abortion was nullified.

Originalism stands in stark contrast with Justice Ginsburg's purposive understanding of the Constitution, which she explained clearly in the majority opinion she authored in *U.S. v. Virginia:* "A prime part of the history of our Constitution . . . is the story of the extension of constitutional rights and protections to people once ignored or excluded . . . as our comprehension of 'We the People' expanded."[14] Unsurprisingly, Ginsburg's approach to constitutional interpretation and that of the originalists are at cross purposes with respect to a pregnant woman's right to terminate her pregnancy. Ginsburg's belief in a "We the People"[15] that is fully inclusive for women as well as men was the crucible of her understanding of the constitutional import of the abortion right.

While Ginsburg may have been surprised that the Court would revert to originalism to overturn *Roe v. Wade*, she always feared that *Roe's* privacy analysis would be too limiting to protect the rights at stake.[16] In *Roe v. Wade*, decided in 1973, the Supreme Court held that the challenged Texas abortion ban violated "Jane Roe's" Fourteenth Amendment due process right to privacy.[17] Consequently, Justice Blackmun concluded for the seven-justice majority, prior to the point of viability of the fetus, a state could not interfere with a pregnant woman's right to decide for herself whether to carry the pregnancy to term or to seek a medical abortion. Although the Court would later abandon the parameters set out in the *Roe* opinion to guide state legislators and abandon the strict judicial review of abortion regulations *Roe* had required, it preserved a (substantially more limited) right to abortion

---

[14] *See id.* at 2.

[15] In full, the Preamble to the U.S. Constitution reads:

> We the People of the United States, in Order to form a more perfect Union, establish Justice, insure domestic Tranquility, provide for the common defense, promote the general Welfare, and secure the Blessings of Liberty to ourselves and our Posterity, do ordain and establish this Constitution for the United States of America.

[16] 410 U.S. 113 (1973).

[17] 410 U.S. at 162–65.

grounded in due process privacy in *Planned Parenthood of Southeastern Pa. v. Casey*.[18] *Roe*'s result and reasoning were subject to immediate and unrelenting attack by critics claiming originalist fidelity. In the aftermath of his defeated nomination to the Court, Judge Bork, for example, writing in 1990 (and quoting Lenin, no less) claimed, "Whoever says A must say B. Whoever says *Roe* must say *Lochner*. . . ."[19] The comparison to *Lochner*,[20] the case in which the Court used an unenumerated right to contract to prevent state regulations of working conditions and other health and safety measures—a decision now regarded by most constitutional historians as a low point in the Court's credibility—is meant to underscore Bork's conclusion that *Roe* lacked any legitimate constitutional basis. Fast-forward roughly 30 years and Judge Bork's criticism of *Roe* resounds as the clarion call of the *Dobbs* majority.

From the outset, the *Dobbs* majority opinion by Justice Alito frames the interpretive stakes: "We begin by considering the critical question whether the Constitution, *properly understood*, confers a right to obtain an abortion."[21] What follows is a substantive due process analysis of the abortion right, as it was articulated in *Roe* and *Casey*, based on the selective use of history I have already outlined. In order to understand the operative differences in Justice Ginsburg's perspective on the constitutionality of abortion from that of the *Dobbs* court, it is not necessary to concede or to refute Justice Alito's due process conclusions. The critical point from Ginsburg's perspective is that the Court is working within the wrong frame of analysis.

II. Privacy versus Equality: Sexual and Reproductive Liberty from Ginsburg's Jurisprudential Perspective

The dominant social debate about abortion and the correlating privacy-based precedent by the U.S. Supreme Court have generally cast abortion in dichotomous terms: either a woman's or a fetus's interest should take constitutional precedence. The debate also asks whether the state or the woman

[18] 505 U.S. 833 (1992).

[19] Robert H. Bork, The Tempting of America: The Political Seduction of the Law (1990).

[20] Lochner v. New York, 198 U.S. 45 (1905).

[21] *See id.* at 4 (emphasis added).

herself should control her pregnant body. Ginsburg, however, conceived of the stakes in larger terms. The constitutional issue of abortion was the issue of "woman's autonomous charge of her full life's course . . . her ability to stand in relation to man, society, and the state as an independent, self-sustaining, equal citizen."[22] Ginsburg's principal disagreement with the reasoning in *Roe* was its emphasis on a medical autonomy model of abortion at the expense of any direct engagement with the larger sex equality question.

For Ginsburg, state control of women's reproductive liberty in all its facets—contraception, pregnancy, illegitimacy, and abortion—was inextricably "part of a pervasive design of sex-role allocation shored up by laws that impede social change."[23] By splitting abortion off from other questions of sex discrimination, according to Ginsburg, the Court failed to engage the equal protection injuries done to a woman's civic, economic, and sexual freedom when her reproductive liberty is curtailed. To Ginsburg, neither restraining a woman's body nor depriving her of the right to make informed medical decisions for herself was merely incidental to constitutional analysis. But the gravest issue of sex discrimination from Ginsburg's perspective was the imposition of gender-specific burdens attendant with motherhood that deprived women of civic and economic opportunities in ways that men simply did not face—an injury sharpened when anything resembling a choice in whether to assume these obligations and limitations was replaced with compulsion by the state.

Formulations of the principle that women must have "the opportunity to participate in full partnership with men in the nation's social, political, and economic life"[24] are foregrounded in her gender jurisprudence from the earliest cases of her appellate practice to *U.S. v. Virginia*. Interestingly, these formulations perhaps find fullest flowering in a set of Supreme Court opinions for which she does not claim named authorship: those involving the rights of gay and lesbian Americans. For example, *Lawrence v. Texas*, the 2003 decision that invalidated the nation's remaining anti-sodomy laws as violating the due process and equal protection rights of gay Americans, elaborated a concept of due process informed by the constitutional commitment

---

[22] Ruth Bader Ginsburg, *Sex Equality and the Constitution: The State of the Art*, 4 Women's Rts. L. Rep. 143, 143–44 (1978).

[23] Ruth Bader Ginsburg, *Gender in the Supreme Court: The 1976 Term*, *in* Constitutional Government in America, 217, 224 (Ronald K. L. Collins ed., 1980).

[24] Ginsburg, *supra* note 22, at 361 (quoting Professor Kenneth Karst, 1976).

to equality that had been articulated in nascent form in *Planned Parenthood v. Casey*. In *Casey*, the Court's liberty analysis had been cast in discernibly sex discrimination vocabulary. But it was in *Lawrence* that the Court held more explicitly that,

> Equality of treatment and the due process right to demand respect for conduct protected by the substantive guarantee of liberty are linked in important respects, and a decision on the latter point advances both interests. If protected conduct is made criminal and the law which does so remains unexamined for its substantive validity, its stigma might remain even if it were not enforceable as drawn for equal protection reasons. When homosexual conduct is made criminal by the law of the State, that declaration in and of itself is an invitation to subject homosexual persons to discrimination both in the public and in the private spheres.
>
> . . . The State cannot demean [petitioners] existence or control their destiny by making their private sexual conduct a crime. Their right to liberty under the Due Process Clause gives them the full right to engage in their conduct without intervention of the government.
>
> . . . Had those who drew and ratified the Due Process Clauses of the Fifth Amendment or the Fourteenth Amendment known the components of liberty in its manifold possibilities, they might have been more specific. They did not presume to have this insight. They knew times can blind us to certain truths and later generations can see that laws once thought necessary and proper in fact serve only to oppress. As the Constitution endures, persons in every generation can invoke its principles in their own search for greater freedom.[25]

Ginsburg's insistence that the Equal Protection Clause protected reproductive rights thus became part of the stare decisis of *Roe v. Wade*, which Justice Alito selectively ignored in *Dobbs*. He also elided this precedent in the short paragraph of dicta in which he attempted to wave away any equality import in the abortion right. Yet, in *Lawrence*, Justice Kennedy's opinion

---

[25] 539 U.S. 558 at 579 (2003). Justice Ginsburg joined the majority opinion as one of the six justices in favor of striking down the Texas law on both due process and equal protection grounds. Justice O'Connor concurred in the judgment on separate Equal Protection Clause reasoning.

for the Court acknowledged that criminal regulation of sodomy did much more than regulate specific conduct. The Court held that anti-sodomy laws demeaned the personhood of gay Americans and diminished their ability to enjoy full participation in society as equal citizens. In other words, the *Lawrence* Court recognized explicitly that a regulation purporting to regulate only conduct could in fact impact what Ginsburg called a citizen's "full life's course."

In similar ways, compulsory motherhood accomplished through state regulation of pregnancy and criminalization of abortion deprives women of their constitutional liberty because it relegates them to a subordinate form of citizenship through the imposition of sex differential burdens and the entrenchment of sex-role stereotypes. This is also true of conservative efforts to strip insurance coverage for pharmaceutical contraception on the basis of alleged conflicts with the religious scruples of employers. Contraception implicates the same sex equality concern for women's citizenship as abortion does, and the resurgent movement to limit access to contraception for women cannot plausibly be defended as based on alleged interests in protecting fetal life. Instead, what could only be—at best—indirect participation by unwilling employers in the "sin" of nonprocreative sex by virtue of an insurer's coverage of contraception is taken to outweigh the direct and profound effects that unplanned pregnancy can have on a woman's "full life's course." The dual efforts to ban abortion and restrict meaningful access to contraception for women, and the Court's most recent decisions on these issues, would appear to serve the same religious and political project that originalism was initially designed to advance: so-called family values conservatism. Ginsburg was thus prescient in her observation of nearly 50 years ago that reproductive liberty and gender equality are practically and theoretically inseparable.

III. "Created Equal" in "A More Perfect Union": The Jeffersonian Originalism of Ruth Ginsburg

In a way that would be too obvious to note in any other context, the question of American citizenship generally is inseparable from the question of women's citizenship specifically. Women constitute half of the American citizenry, after all. But neither the meaning of American constitutional citizenship nor

Justice Ginsburg's contributions to it can be accurately described in arithmetic terms alone. The existential character of citizenship makes equality considerations essential in any meaningful analysis. In the American historical context, equality is in fact a precondition of American citizenship. As the first of Thomas Jefferson's "self-evident" truths, equality is a—if not *the*—foundational principle of the American Revolution and our resulting nation. Is it possible to get more "original" than that? And yet for constitutional originalists, the Constitution's forward-looking optimism must be negated. Only when we look back—sometimes, a very long way back—can the societal structure that originalism strives to impose on modern Americans find anything resembling consensus support.

Surely, it escaped no one's notice that Justice Alito chose to freeze constitutional meaning with respect to reproductive liberty at a point in time when women could not vote, when they could not hold governmental office, and when, in law and in life, women were effectively the chattel property of their husbands to such absolute extent that it was impossible for a wife to refuse even the unwanted sexual advances of her husband. (Refusing sex was but one infraction in a range of potential misbehaviors that could be punished with corporeal discipline.) State laws from the historical era that Justice Alito chose as dispositive of the scope of women's reproductive liberty generally recognized the "right" of a husband to beat his wife[26] as he would a willful mare or, as he might have only a few years earlier, a slave.

And what of this? It seems fair to ask whether constitutional liberty provides any real safeguard against a state legislative determination that it is again lawful for a husband to correct an uppity wife by application of the rod. After all, this was the historically verifiable social reality of the time at which the *Dobbs* majority has now fixed the meaning of Fourteenth Amendment equal protection. This is not a rhetorical question. For years, when I have distributed in my constitutional law courses remarks made by Justice Scalia, concluding on originalist bases, that the Equal Protection Clause does not apply to women, these quotations have been met by a certain measure of laughter. Yes, as much as anything, this laughter was an intuitive response of students encountering for the first time the sheer absurdity of Scalia's position in a twenty-first-century context. Even with this

[26] *See, e.g.*, State v. Black, 60 N.C. (Win.) 262 (1864) upholding a husband's right of chastisement. Not until the twentieth century was spousal abuse a potential ground for criminal prosecution in the vast majority of the states.

understanding, I was always intrigued by the fact that among those laughing were consistently some women students. When I distributed the same material for the first time post-*Dobbs*, the comic overlay was still the effect for some students. But, significantly, one noticed that the women were no longer laughing. This trend has continued.

Paradoxical as it may seem in 2024, Americans attuned to issues of institutional legitimacy and constitutional integrity must decide between the alternative constitutional visions exemplified by the interpretive ethics of Justice Ginsburg and Justice Alito's opinion for the Court in *Dobbs*. In contrast to the majority in *Dobbs*, Justice Ginsburg understood the Constitution as purposively forward looking and oriented toward equality measured in terms of real-world (living, breathing) realities. Justice Alito's interpretation of the Constitution in *Dobbs*—purportedly rooted in textualist commitment—renders America's female citizens invisible at worst, superfluous at best, to the Constitution's equality norm, even though the relevant constitutional text includes no historical limitation or gendered qualifier. We must—each of us—if we are responsible citizens, examine for ourselves, then, exactly what this equality and this liberty really is and who is entitled to it. Our inquiry is both serious and of necessity, given that the Court made its decision in *Dobbs*, which entails serious and demeaning consequences for women. Extended to the extremes of its reactionary perspective, originalism interprets the promise of constitutional equality as simply inapplicable to even the most extreme cases of inequality for women, or for gay people, or because of gender or sexuality otherwise.[27] In the brief analysis that follows, I hazard an answer to the question of equality's meaning on originalism's terms, with Justice Ginsburg as my intellectual pole star.

Can constitutional principles have intended meanings that are not coterminous with social practices prevailing at the time of the ratification of the pertinent text? Justice Ginsburg's resounding "yes" finds support from generations of Americans much closer in time to the ratification of the

[27] *See* Dobbs, at __ (Thomas, J., concurring) (internal citations omitted) ("The Court today declines to disturb substantive due process jurisprudence generally or the doctrine's application in other, specific contexts. Cases like *Griswold* v. *Connecticut*, 381 U.S. 479 (1965) (right of married persons to obtain contraceptives)[1]*; *Lawrence* v. *Texas*, 539 U.S. 558 (2003) (right to engage in private, consensual sexual acts); and *Obergefell* v. *Hodges*, 576 U.S. 644 (2015) (right to same-sex marriage), are not at issue . . . . For that reason, in future cases, we should reconsider all of this Court's substantive due process precedents, including *Griswold*, *Lawrence*, and *Obergefell*. Because any substantive due process decision is 'demonstrably erroneous[.]'").

Fourteenth Amendment who certainly thought so. Having emerged on the other side of the deadliest conflict in American history, the Reconstruction congress purposefully reiterated the equality principle that had animated the revolutionary zeal that materialized this nation, as well as the painful civil war that preserved the nation. History is rather clear that powerful factions of the South's slave-holding elite believed that secession was necessary because they viewed "all men are created equal" to be, in fact, purposive rather than rhetorical; and, consequently, it was, for our constitutional governance by rule of law, a principle both systemically intrinsic and effectively negentropic. Yes, it is undeniable that slavery was the emergency of the moment, but the U.S. Constitution was never intended to speak only to a moment in time. It was never a flash-in-the-pan idea; the Preamble is quite clear on that point.

If this is the history behind the Fourteenth Amendment, it defies reason to insist that something like equal protection could have been a purposefully static concept. On the question of equality, and of constitutional liberty generally, any theory of constitutional interpretation that would make constitutional liberty into a historical dead letter in purported defense of something "original" to the Constitution is essentially a serpent eating its own tail. In contrast, Ginsburg's commitment was to the more perfect union at the root of our constitutional structure, as the foregoing chapters of this book lucidly demonstrate. That aspiration espoused in the Constitution's Preamble—the only pointed instruction as to the Framers' intentions that they provided—points to an equality that could, and probably must—be understood more fully in time as social and scientific facts evolve and as society gets on with the business of human becoming. To Justice Ginsburg, the idea that any of liberty's blessings might be secured "for posterity" by an interpretive ethic that affords only the meanest understanding of the revolution's ideals appeared ridiculous. As *Dobbs* illustrates, however, originalism's reactionary politics, masked as legal objectivity, results in real injustice in the real lives of real people. And as the Court's personnel changes resulted in a majority bloc of the Court that seemed more committed to originalism's reductionistic principles than any Court before, Justice Ginsburg's dissenting opinions became more emphatically urgent.

Justice Ginsburg intrinsically embraced the view that the Declaration of Independence spoke through the Constitution, where the ideals of the former were outcome-determinative for the latter. This view apparently persisted through the Civil War generation of Americans. Prominent leaders of the would-be Confederacy certainly understood the Constitution in this way. For example, Confederate Vice President Alexander Hamilton Stephens insisted that:

> Jefferson in his forecast, had anticipated [slavery], as the "rock upon which the old Union would split." He was right. What was conjecture with him, is now a realized fact. But whether he fully comprehended the great truth upon which that rock stood and stands, may be doubted. The prevailing ideas entertained by him and most of the leading statesmen at the time of the formation of the old constitution, were that the enslavement of the African was in violation of the laws of nature; that it was wrong in principle, socially, morally, and politically. It was an evil they knew not well how to deal with, but the general opinion of the men of that day was that, somehow or other in the order of Providence, the institution would be evanescent and pass away.[28]

In an interpretive context such as this, one arguably could read the Supreme Court's opinion in *Dred Scott v. Sandford*[29] as an intervention intended by the Court to short-circuit the system. In what Robert Bork once called the first "substantive due process" opinion by the Court, the *Dred Scott* opinion held that black slaves and their descendants were cognizable to the Constitution only in relation to the slaveholder's property right, which the Court divined as practically absolute. Slaves and their descendants, the Court said, could never be citizens of the United States within the meaning of the Constitution. Although the *Dred Scott* court was less than clear about its motivation, the Reconstruction congress that drafted the Fourteenth Amendment, mercifully, was not. A primary purpose of the Fourteenth Amendment, revealed to be clearly understood as such at the time by the totality of the legislative history of the amendment, was to repudiate *Dred Scott* and to undo the constitutional injury that it was widely recognized to be. From this perspective, the Aristotelian theory of equality

[28] Speech of Alexander Hamilton Stephens, March 21, 1861, Augusta, Georgia (quoted in Shannon Gilreath, *Cruel and Unusual Punishment and the Eighth Amendment as a Mandate for Human Dignity: Another Look at Original Intent*, 25 THOMAS JEFFERSON LAW REV. 559–92 (2003)).

[29] 60 U.S. 393 (1857).

that emerged in time as the controlling one employed by the Court is in fact a theory known to and discarded by the Framers of both the eighteenth and nineteenth centuries. Those who concede only the meanest understanding of constitutional citizenship with "originalism" as their ground seem to somehow miss this history of continuity, which is to miss quite a lot. The equality norm embedded in our Constitution is inseparable from Enlightenment—Jeffersonian understandings of equal citizenship—which is ultimately antihierarchical in character.

The project of originalist theorizing is to contextualize equality by limiting it to a century long past, which, in fact, decontextualizes it from the logical continuity that characterizes our constitutional structure. One critical constitutional question persists, however. What does "equal," constitutionally speaking, mean? The truth that we are all "created equal" is easy to read in our Declaration of Independence, but it is difficult to see in many respects in the founding generation or in our present generation. That the Framers were aware of this tension between truth and material reality in their own time is evident. And while it is useful to acknowledge and to criticize the abhorrently unequal concessions to expediency that the Constitution included, I think it is essential that we also see the Constitution as a radical act of hope, as Justice Ginsburg certainly did. As acknowledged by its drafters, with Madison, a disciple of Jefferson, at their helm, the Constitution was a means to a stated goal of perfecting our Union over future generations, essentially, a reiterated commitment to equality as propounded in the Declaration in literal terms. Forceful reassertion of this founding principle in the Fourteenth Amendment was a painfully necessary step on our way to becoming that "more perfect Union."[30]

A consensus comprehension of equality emerges across Enlightenment thought, from the much-vaunted Locke, to the frequently mischaracterized Smith, and to the historically lesser-known Petty (but no less a hero to Jefferson). The Enlightenment understanding is of a literal equality to which difference was, in most circumstances, immaterial because differences—intellectual, creative, and even moral—were primarily seen as artificially constructed and imposed rather than as natural and determinant. This view generally obtained even when natural or biological differences were cited as proxies for the political consequences affixed to observable traits.[31] Thus,

[30] U.S. Const. Pmbl.

[31] This is the view to which Justice Ginsburg led the Court in U.S. v. Virginia.

Jefferson's asserted "truth" of an unqualified equality—his intentional "all," which appears so at odds with what we know of that historical moment, and even with what we know of Jefferson himself—can be taken to mean exactly what the wording suggests. Jefferson's articulated aspiration, understood literally, could be *true* while at the same time not being real in a *material* way. As eminent American historian Garry Wills opined, "Jefferson believed in a literal equality more far-reaching than most educated people recognize today. For him, accidental differences of body or mind were dwarfed by an all-important equality in the governing faculty of man."[32] The Jeffersonian understanding of equality contrasts, therefore, with the Supreme Court's dominant approach to analyzing equal protection claims brought under the Fifth or Fourteenth Amendments to the Constitution, in which the Court focuses on assessing observable differences between discrete classes of American citizens.

It is too easy to say that the principles articulated in the Declaration of Independence are not part of the Constitution because it is a separate document. Our revolutionary ideals did not suddenly evaporate at Yorktown, and a substantial catalyst for the Constitutional Convention was the realization that the Articles of Confederation did not cohere a union of the states that could adequately defend those ideals from threats both internal and external. Jefferson's eloquently rendered touchstones of freedom for the individual citizen that did not upend the equality of all citizens with one another remained those blessings of liberty identified by the Constitution's Preamble. The Constitution and constitutional government provided a means of security and a framework through which those same animating principles might be more fully actualized in time.

This history underscores that Justice Ginsburg's optimism about the promise of a more perfect union animated the Founders. It also demonstrates the fallacy of originalism evident in *Dobbs*, which exposes its failure on its own purported terms. Of course, the process necessary to discern meaning from any written document starts with the text. But the drafters of the Constitution largely wrote in general rather than specific language. A "wholistic" view of the posture from which the Constitution is written arguably suggests that there was intentionality behind the Constitution's

---

[32] Garry Wills, Inventing Democracy: Jeferson's Declaration of Independence (2002) at 207.

ambiguity. In other words, even where the Framers easily could have used more-specific language to border obviously open-ended concepts or to indicate a fixed term of art rather than a sweeping principle, they very often did not do so. Inevitably, therefore, thematic, somewhat ineffable commitments collide with contemporary realities that were simply unimaginable to the Framers or that differ materially in form or substance from anything obtaining in centuries past. From the outset, Ruth Bader Ginsburg's legal work evinces an understanding that equal protection was an incipiently futuristic value. Her approach from the bench most often seemed to have one eye on the long-term integrity and systemic health of our democratic processes, which, as Suzanne Reynolds explains, was often cast in institutional terms. Judge Ginsburg seemed simultaneously focused on the duty of the judicial branch when the output of those processes failed to follow the constitutional mandate of equal protection—interpreted as an enduring commitment that could not be meaningfully fulfilled for successive generations of Americans unless adapted to respond to the realities of our own time.

Critics, like Justice Scalia, and even some feminist constitutional scholars, are quick to assert that the Fourteenth Amendment was not *intended* to apply to sex-based discrimination.[33] This claim is too much. Without a vehicle for time travel or a talent for necromancy, there is no certainty possible with respect to the scope of any constitutional principle. We do know that the Framers were specific in their intention not to create a civil code as this nation's highest law; two of the amendments comprising the Bill of Rights specifically rule out a text-as-exhaustive interpretive future. Where a right is inalienable in our tradition, it should not—must not—be conditional on the prejudices or superstitions of any moment in time. A judicial branch with life tenure and shelter from political pressures faced by the legislative and executive branches meant that the buck stopped, by design, with the courts. As the antebellum debate over slavery's longevity in constitutional context shows, the Framers were aware that constitutional aspirations could evolve in meaning and expand in scope beyond the exigencies that produced their rendering into text. This awareness of the ineffable character of liberty at any fixed point in time may have caused them to write in broadly descriptive terms that would allow the posterity they imagined the benefit of new

[33] *See* Jeffrey Rosen, *Editorial: If Scalia Had His Way*, N.Y. Times Week in Review (Jan. 8, 2011), https://www.nytimes.com/2011/01/09/weekinreview/09rosen.html.

knowledge that a future epoch may entail. The Framers of the Fourteenth Amendment surely understood this. Modeling the charter that they chose to perfect rather than to destroy, they spoke to future Americans in thematic rather than in specific language. Even Judge Bork acknowledged that equality was the "theme" of the Fourteenth Amendment.[34]

To put the question another way, one could ask whether those punishments prohibited to federal and state governments because they are "cruel and unusual" equate only and always to what would have been recognized as a cruel practice in the eighteenth century? Can it seriously be contended that the Framers did not expect—I dare say, intend—for something as culturally specific as the meaning of cruelty to change over time? Indeed, they were engaged in the process of conforming law with life themselves before, during, and after they were inventing the Constitution. They did not themselves want to live under laws that were hidebound to history's injustices, and it is nonsensical to think that they wanted the "blessings of liberty" secured for the "posterity" they addressed with such optimism to suffer such a fate.[35] There is no reason at all to accept the idea that equality, like "cruel and unusual" in the Eighth Amendment, was not foreseen as changing and changeable—expanding and evolving with the nation itself. This is the constitutional equality Ginsburg understood and for which she was an unequivocal advocate always: the Constitution must adapt and it must respond to the reality of a modern American life—to the hopes, anxieties, and, certainly, to the inequities—of a twenty-first-century republic, not an eighteenth-century one. For Ruth Ginsburg, it was the evolutionary momentum of the Constitution that was also its center of gravity. Unlike originalism's analytical and aspirational dead ends, Ginsburg took our Constitution's drafters at their word and committed herself to reading the Constitution's promises to posterity as promises that could, in fact, be kept.

IV. Conclusion

The organizing theme of this book, "on being American," was sparked by the rhetorical question Justice Ginsburg often posed in public lectures: "What is the difference between a bookkeeper in New York City's garment district [Ginsburg's mother] and an associate justice of the United States Supreme

[34] *See id.* at note 17.

[35] *See generally* Shannon Gilreath, *supra* note 28, at 559.

Court?" The answer was, of course, "a single generation." Indeed, this anecdote captures the optimism inhering in her vision for our constitutional democracy as one of ever-expanding inclusivity and equality of citizenship. An exemplar par excellence of Eleanor Roosevelt's admonition that our democracy depends, in the end, on the courage of the individual to live up to its values, Ginsburg was but-for causation personified in the feminist legal revolution of the women's movement's "second wave." When she started her work to eliminate overt gender-based stereotypes in law, the codes—civil and criminal—in each of our 50 jurisdictions were riven with such distinctions, which were usually as absurd as they were obvious. When she finished, the vast majority had been rendered unenforceable. That is amazing.

Ruth Ginsburg is gone now. No one can replace her pioneering role. Due in large measure to her innovative advocacy, we have moved toward a more equal society. Still, there is much work, both crucial and difficult, before us. Ginsburg made the speech that resonated with so many of us, accepting her appointment to the U.S. Supreme Court and taking the oath of that office, before most of my current law students were born. Her tone was hopeful and determined. In the aftermath of *Dobbs*, we are poised ever more sharply on the bleeding edge of the future to which she gestured—one in which "society values girls as much as boys." Her theory of constitutional equality, where the supreme law of this land is able to respond to subordination as it exists in the real world, here and now, and unblinkered by historical prejudices and superstitions, is needed now more than ever.

Lying at the heart of Ruth Bader Ginsburg's feminist legal theory and practice is an obvious optimism and an abiding belief that people can change—that even the law can change. Her own life in the law is proof-positive that one person, with a certain measure of seriousness about changing the world, can make a real and profound difference. The law can and *will* change. Why shouldn't you—any and every reader of this volume—be the one to change it. Keeping our constitutional promises of liberty and equality for each new generation is a civic responsibility that we all, as Americans, share. Living up to that responsibility requires courage and ability. It also requires a determined hope in the possibility of achieving our collective aspirations. As we confront the challenges before us now, it is crucial that we do not lose the hope that is essential always for the action of change—sometimes for *radical* change—that is both necessary and possible. May her memory be a revolution.

About the Editors

Shannon Gilreath is Professor of Law and Professor of Women's, Gender, and Sexuality Studies at Wake Forest University. He is nationally recognized as an expert on issues of equality, sexual minorities, and U.S. constitutional law and political theory. His many articles and books include *Sexual Politics: The Gay Person in America Today* (2006) and *The End of Straight Supremacy: Realizing Gay Liberation* (2011) (Cambridge University Press).

Suzanne Reynolds is Dean Emerita and Professor of Law Emerita at Wake Forest University School of Law. She is the author of *Reynolds on North Carolina Family Law* and numerous articles on family law topics. In North Carolina, she worked on the drafting committees that rewrote the law of adoption, alimony, domestic violence, and equitable distribution. Nationally, she served on the Uniform Laws Conference and was the reporter for a uniform law recognizing the domestic violence protective orders from other countries. For this and other work, she received public service awards from women's organizations, from Governor James B. Hunt, and from the North Carolina Bar Association.

About the Authors

Cary Franklin is Professor of Law at UCLA School of Law, where she writes and teaches in the areas of constitutional law, antidiscrimination law, and legal history. Her work focuses on the historical development of conceptions of equality in American law and how this history influences the shape of contemporary legal protections in the contexts of sex, sexual orientation, gender identity, and race. She is currently Faculty Director of the Williams Institute, a research institute at UCLA focused on sexual orientation and gender identity law and public policy, and Faculty Director of the Center on Reproductive Health, Law, and Policy. Her work has appeared in numerous publications including *Harvard Law Review*, *Michigan Law Review*, *NYU Law Review*, *Supreme Court Review*, *Virginia Law Review*, and *Yale Law Journal*.

Linda Greenhouse is a senior research scholar in law at Yale Law School, where she taught from 2009 to 2024. She covered the Supreme Court for *The New York Times* between 1978 and 2008 and continues to write regularly for the newspaper's Opinion pages. Greenhouse received several major journalism awards during her 40-year career at the *Times*, including the Pulitzer Prize (1998) and the Goldsmith Career Award for Excellence in Journalism from Harvard University's Kennedy School (2004). In 2002, the American Political Science Association gave her its Carey McWilliams Award for "a major journalistic contribution to our understanding of politics." Her books include a biography of Justice Harry A. Blackmun, *Becoming Justice Blackmun*; *Before* Roe v. Wade: *Voices That Shaped the Abortion Debate Before the Supreme Court's Ruling* (with Reva B. Siegel); *The U.S. Supreme*

Court, A Very Short Introduction, published by Oxford University Press in 2012; *The Burger Court and the Rise of the Judicial Right*, with Michael J. Graetz, published in 2016; and a memoir, *Just a Journalist: Reflections on the Press, Life, and the Spaces Between*, published by Harvard University Press in 2017. Her latest book is *Justice on the Brink: A Requiem for the Supreme Court* (Random House, 2021).

Reva Siegel is the Nicholas Katzenbach Professor of Law at Yale Law School. Professor Siegel's writing draws on legal history to explore questions of law and inequality and to analyze how courts interact with representative government and popular movements in interpreting the Constitution. Her books include *Processes of Constitutional Decisionmaking* (8th ed. 2022; with Sanford Levinson, Jack Balkin, Akhil Amar & Cristina Rodriguez); *Reproductive Rights and Justice Stories* (2019; co-edited with Melissa Murray & Kate Shaw), and *Before* Roe v. Wade*: Voices That Shaped the Abortion Debate Before the Supreme Court's Ruling* (2d ed. 2012; with Linda Greenhouse).

Julie Chi-hye Suk is Professor of Law at Fordham Law School. Professor Suk is an interdisciplinary and comparative legal scholar researching equality at the intersection of law, history, sociology, and politics in the United States and globally. She has authored dozens of articles and book chapters about comparative constitutional law; the procedural implementation of equality norms in the United States and Europe; gender quotas; and women, work, and family. Her 2020 book, *We the Women: The Unstoppable Mothers of the Equal Rights Amendment*, was the first book to chronicle and assess the twenty-first-century revival of the Equal Rights Amendment, culminating in Virginia's ratification in 2020. Her next book, *After Misogyny: How the Law Fails Women and What to Do about It*, on women's struggles toward inclusive constitutional democracy around the world, was published in 2023.

Alexander Tsesis is the D'Alemberte Chair in Constitutional Law at the Florida State University College of Law. He is also the general editor of the Cambridge Studies on Civil Rights and Civil Liberties and the Oxford Theoretical Foundations in Law. His most recent book is *Free Speech in the Balance* (Cambridge University Press 2020). His previous books include

Free Speech in the Balance (Cambridge University Press 2020), *Constitutional Ethos: Liberal Equality for the Common Good* (Oxford University Press 2017), *For Liberty and Equality: The Life and Times of the Declaration of Independence* (Oxford University Press 2012), *We Shall Overcome: A History of Civil Rights and the Law* (Yale University Press 2008), *The Thirteenth Amendment and American Freedom* (New York University Press 2004), and *Destructive Messages: How Hate Speech Paved the Way for Harmful Social Movements* (New York University Press 2002).

Index

F